HANNAH ARENDT

Hannah Arendt is volume 1 of *Female Genius: Life, Madness, Words—Hannah Arendt, Melanie Klein, Colette*, a trilogy by Julia Kristeva.

EUROPEAN PERSPECTIVES

For a complete list of books in the series, see pages 289–291

Hannah Arendt

by

Julia Kristeva

Translated by Ross Guberman

COLUMBIA UNIVERSITY PRESS NEW YORK

Columbia University Press wishes to express its appreciation
for assistance given by the government of France through the
Ministère de la Culture in the preparation of this translation.

COLUMBIA UNIVERSITY PRESS

Publishers Since 1893

New York   Chichester, West Sussex

Copyright © 2001 Columbia University Press

Le Génie féminin, Hannah Arendt © Librairie Arthème Fayard, 1999

Library of Congress Cataloging-in-Publication Data

Kristeva, Julia, 1941–

[Hannah Arendt, English]

Hannah Arendt / by Julia Kristeva ; translated by Ross Guberman

p. cm. — (European perspectives)

Translation of : Le genie feminin, t. 1, Hannah Arendt.

ISBN 0–231–12102–4 (alk. paper)

1. Arendt, Hannah. 2. Political scientists—Biography.

I. Title. II. Series.

JC251.A74 K7513   2001

320 .5'092—dc21   2001017262

∞

Casebound editions of Columbia University Press books
are printed on permanent and durable acid-free paper.

Printed in the United States of America

Designed by Audrey Smith

c 10 9 8 7 6 5 4 3 2 1

TRANSLATOR'S ACKNOWLEDGMENT

I thank Julia Boss, a doctoral candidate at Yale University, for her invaluable research assistance. As always, I also thank Julia Kristeva, a magnificent thinker and a good friend. Finally I would like to dedicate this translation to my wife, Heidi.

CONTENTS

FEMALE GENIUS: GENERAL INTRODUCTION

*One of the most fervent passions
is the genius's love of truth.*
Laplace

"What a genius!" Our recent claims of discovering "genius" within ourselves—whether in the form of a talent, a natural gift, or a prolonged search for truth—have put an end to the ancient deification of personality. At first, the divine spirit charged with watching over the birth of the future hero was transformed into a viable means of innovation.[1] As Voltaire put it, "this invention in particular appeared to be a gift from the gods; this *ingenium quasi ingenitum* was a sort of divine inspiration." Whether by simple metonymy or by analogy, "a genius" later became someone who "displayed genius," if not someone who simply happened to influence someone else.[2]

Hannah Arendt, one of the protagonists of this three-part work, made light of "the genius," whom she considered to be a product of the Renaissance. Tired of being reduced to the fruits of their labors, the men of the Renaissance became increasingly munificent, and as they lost touch with God, they grafted His transcendence onto the very best among their ranks. Since that time, the *divine*, disguised as a genius, has made up for this loss by producing a mystery play that has transformed the creator into something unique. Does this mean that the absolute has descended upon us? Or that we should consider this loss to be a challenge to humanity? Is it a demand from a superman? Or is it a refusal to lower ourselves to the level of "products" or "appearances" in a society plagued by "consumption" and the "spectacle"? Suffice it to say that "genius" is a therapeutic invention that keeps us from dying from equality in a world without a hereafter.

Even so, do we dare speak about "genius" without ignoring the "evil genius" who devoted all his resources to deluding Descartes himself? In our day, it would appear, the word "genius" stands for paradoxical occurrences, unique experiences, and remarkable excesses that manage to pierce through an increasingly automated world. The troubling, even formidable, emergence of such phenomena helps us understand the meaning of human existence. Does this mean that genius helps substantiate the meaning of life? The protagonists of this work believe that it does not: as we shall see, my geniuses consider life to be substantiated through more modest means indeed. They do suggest, however, that our existence can be perpetually revived by that which is extraordinary. Significantly, however, this brand of extraordinariness is not achieved by gaining entry into the hallowed halls that record the rigorous ordeals of history. Like the ancient Greek heroes, my geniuses displayed qualities that, while no doubt exceptional, can be found in most of us. And they (the geniuses, which in this case are three *female* geniuses) did not hesitate to make mistakes and to let us know their limitations. What distinguishes these geniuses from us is simply that they have left us to judge a body of work rooted in the biography of their experience. The work of a genius culminates in the birth of a subject.

Each of us leads some sort of existence, and many of us have lived through adventures, often interesting ones, that can provide fodder for family legend and sometimes for the local newspaper or even the nightly news. Yet such experiences are not the stuff of a noteworthy biography. Let us agree here to use the term "genius" to describe those who force us to discuss their story because it is so closely bound up with their creations, in the innovations that support the development of thought and beings, and in the onslaught of questions, discoveries, and pleasures that their creations have inspired. In fact, these contributions touch us so intimately that we have no choice but to moor them in the lives of their authors.

Some works of art have an impact that is greater than the sum of their parts. The way these works affect us depends ultimately on the historical disturbances they bring about and on the way they influence other people and their followers—in sum, their effect depends on the way *we* respond to them. When someone finds himself at this juncture and capitalizes upon it, he becomes a genius—even if all he ever did was be born into the world, work, and then die. We endow him with a biography that fails to explain the excess, the indulgences, or the invasiveness of his life. Still, the reason we afford such a biography to geniuses, and not to just anyone, is to sound an alarm: regardless of whatever creation, work of art, or deed has come about, someone has lived. Are we someone? Are you someone? Try to be someone!

A Mozart concerto, a funny Charlie Chaplin scene, and Madame Curie's discovery of radium were all events as unusual as they were inevitable, and as unforeseen as they were indispensable. Since "it" took place, we cannot imagine a world without "it," as if "it" has always been with us. The temporary shock caused by such acts and works makes us want to explain "it" away by conjuring up the superhuman and by contemplating the destiny or the genetics that preside over the birth of individuals. That is, when we do not make "it" into an everyday occurrence by proclaiming, as did Buffon, that "genius is endless patience" or, for the more romantic among us, by repeating Valery's words: "Genius! O endless impatience!" At the same time, when geniuses demand that we endow them with a life that amounts to less than their "genius" itself, they play another trick on us: they make us look at ourselves in a way that is just as ingenious as the way they locate their extraordinary character between their own pleas and the unpredictable opinion of the human beings who respond to them and who ordain them. At heart, they are geniuses for us—and for eternity, so much so that we become geniuses ourselves, the sort of geniuses that accompany "our own" geniuses.

And what role do women play in all this? Is it true, as La Bruyère and others have written, that women have "talent and genius . . . only for handiwork"? Of course, it has long been asserted that women's only genius is the genius of their patience, whereas style is the exclusive province of men.

The twentieth century has put an end to the notion that women are the birthing half of a species of mammals. The growth of industry, which demanded a female workforce, and then the growth of science, which has slowly increased our knowledge of procreation, have effectively freed women from the constraints of the life cycle. Although these trends have been underway for thousands of years, only privileged minorities and a few exceptional personalities have been able to take advantage of them thus far. The twentieth century has made this emancipation accessible to the majority of women, particularly in the industrialized world, and we have every reason to believe that women in Asia, Africa, and Latin America are prepared to follow a similar path. For better or for worse, the next century will be a female one—and female genius, as described in this work, gives us hope that it might be for the better.

The feminist movement is the third stage in the progress of women (the first being the suffragist movement in the late nineteenth century and the second being the militant struggle for equal rights in all aspects of life, as described in Simone de Beauvoir's manifesto *The Second Sex*). The feminist movement, beginning with the unrest in the late 1960s, focused with a heartfelt violence on this newfound freedom and on the unforeseen differences that such freedom laid bare: the existence of another sexuality, another language, and another politics. But this rejection of tradition did not avoid falling prey to excess, the most troubling example of which was to see motherhood as the ultimate proof that women have been exploited by every imaginable form of patriarchy since time immemorial. In the manner of libertarian "movements," the feminists have assembled "all women" into an emancipating force, or even a revolutionary force, as is the case with the majority of proletariat groups and developing countries. These downward drifts, far from being a thing of the past, have become tainted with a reactionary conformity that manages to discredit any notion of feminine specificity or freedom that is not based on seduction—which means not based on reproduction and consumption. Putting that aside, and putting aside the balancing act that characterizes all manner of social mores, much evidence points to a revival of women's emancipation.

One example may be found in the prominent (and growing) role that women play in the political life of democracies. We can safely assume that this display of political and economic competence will only become broader and more widely accepted, not only in the Western world but also in developing countries.

Motherhood, which has benefitted from scientific progress and which was demeaned at one time in certain quarters, has since emerged as the most essential of the female vocations. In the future, motherhood will be desired, accepted, and carried out with the greatest blessings for the mother, the father, and the child. Will mothers become our only safeguard against the wholesale automation of human beings?

In the end, the particular accomplishments of each woman and her personality, which cannot be reduced to the common denominator of a group or a sexual entity, have become not only possible but also proclaimed with great pride. It is because I am myself, and specifically myself, that I am able to introduce the contributions of women to a large segment of the world.

This particularity is where we shall find the sparkle of female genius. Recognizing the substantial contribution made by a few extraordinary women whose life and work have left their mark on the history of the twentieth century is one way to call attention to the singularity of every woman. Is it not true that going beyond your own limits presents a more appealing antidote to the various forms of "groupthink," whether they be generously libertarian or sensibly conformist?

We still must acknowledge that, no matter how far science may progress, women will continue to be the mothers of humanity. Through their love of men, too, women will continue to give birth to children. That fate, though tempered by various techniques and by a sense of solidarity, will remain an all-consuming and irreplaceable vocation. Everyone knows that women, through an osmosis with the species that makes them radically different from men, inherit substantial obstacles to realizing their genius and to contributing another specific, if not ingenious, talent to the culture of humanity that they shelter in their wombs. Many people have thumbed their noses at these insurmountable natural conditions that appear to banish female geniuses for good—and such caricaturists have not always been wretched misogynists. Think of the marvelous Mlle de Merteuil, who thought that certain women, such as the Présidente de Tourvel, would never amount to "more than a type of species." Joyce, that unsurpassed wordsmith who knew his Molly from personal experience, believed he was in the right when he accorded time to men while reserving space and the species for women: "Father's time, mother's species."

And Baudelaire, the most disdainful of them all, scoffed at "the childish side of motherhood."

These views are not wrong, but they fail to tell the whole story. Mothers can be geniuses, not only of love, tact, self-denial, suffering, and even evil spells and witchcraft but also of a certain approach to living the life of the mind. That approach to being a mother and a woman, at times warmly accepted and at times outright refused or wrought with conflict, bestows upon mothers a genius all their own. Women, greater in number and in confidence than ever before, have proved this beyond cavil: though curled up like children in space and in the species, women are also able to work toward unique, innovative creations and to remake the human condition.

The three women who are the subject of this work are by no means the only women to have left their mark on the increasingly diverse pursuits of our time. My personal affinities are what led me to read, enjoy, and choose Hannah Arendt (1906–1975), Melanie Klein (1882–1960), and Colette (1873–1954). I hope that by the end of this work, the reader will be persuaded that my personal choices are worthy of a more objective selection.

The twentieth century was one in which the accelerated progress of technology revealed, more forcefully than before, both the excellence of humankind and the risks of self-destruction that lurk within it. The Holocaust alone proves this to be the case, and it is hardly necessary to add the atomic bomb and the dangers of globalization to the list.

With value systems fallen by the wayside, we now deem life to be the ultimate good. It is both a threatened life and a desirable life—but in the end, what sort of life is it? Hannah Arendt was consumed with such thoughts when she responded to the death camps of two totalitarian regimes by setting her hopes on a respectable political activity that would lay bare the "miracle of natality."

But Arendt did not wish to believe that language could turn

mad and that the "good sense" of humanity could conceal the threat of lunacy. It would be up to Melanie Klein to investigate these chasms of the human psyche and to devote herself to studying the death drive that gives life to the speaking being from the onset, although melancholia and paranoid schizophrenia question the primacy of that operation.

The sensualists and seductresses who become intoxicated with the flesh of an apricot, with the arum of their lover's member, or with a schoolteacher's lilac-scented breasts have not, for all that, abandoned the atomic age. If the twentieth century turns out to be more than just a terrible memory, it will be in part because of the pleasure and immodesty of the liberated women that Colette described with the impertinent grace of the insurgent that she was. A zest for words, when grafted onto the robots that we have become, may be the most wonderful gift that female writing can offer the mother tongue.

I include here two German-speaking Jewish women who explored, in the English language and in London and New York, the weightiness of politics and the limits of human nature. I also include a French countrywoman who rekindled the fire of the materialists and a sophisticated debauchery. The genius of these three women has restored, with a complexity that complements the truths they tell, the many faces of modern Time.

These three women lived, thought, loved, and worked with men—with their men, sometimes by tolerating the authority of a master or by depending on his love, and sometimes by running the risks inherent in rebellious acts that are tinged with an unimpeachable innocence. In each case, however, these women were able to maintain more or less respectable independence.

It may come as a surprise that this book discusses, among Arendt's other writings, the political works on anti-Semitism and totalitarianism that made her famous. Tracing the development of her work seemed to be the most fruitful avenue, tracing the portrait of the woman-thinker whose substantial contributions to political thought have been either praised or criticized by others before me. I also consider how Arendt gave voice to Heidegger's concept of *Dasein* [Being] and yet replaced the solitude of the "being-thrown-in-the-world" with the virtuosity of the "appearance." Heidegger's concept of errancy, when cast against the anonymity of the "they," becomes suddenly unrecognizable once Arendt focuses on the miraculous "birth of each person" into the "frailty of human affairs," that is, into political life. Though she always remained attentive to the great philosopher's work, Arendt, that lover of pure thought, was able to move beyond it and to become a political theorist in a class by herself—one who has been discussed at length and yet who remains just as topical today. Not only was Arendt the first person to link the two totalitarian regimes because they both destroyed human life but also she made it known that the "appearance" is a condition intrinsic to humanity: she reveals the irreducible singularity of each person, provided that he finds the courage to partake in the common sense of those around him. After all, the media frenzy that has shaken up the world since Arendt's death amounts perhaps to more than just a curse, particularly if we examine it through the lens of the genius of this woman who revalued political meaning as a "taste" for showing, observing, remembering, and recounting.

Freud had just discovered the unconscious as well as the relationship between mental illness and sexuality. He was surveying the pitfalls of pleasure while settling scores with the social conformists who did not want—and who still do not want—to admit that the human body is a being of desire. To this concern for Eros and Thanatos, the founder of psychoanalysis added far more strident battles with his disciples that were primarily Oedipal in nature. It was at that time that Melanie Klein devoted herself to studying decompensation. Caring for children had taught her that in the beginning is the urge to destroy, an urge that eventually is transformed into madness but that always remains a conduit of desire. Freud had already said as much, but it was Klein who fully developed the notion. A more radical pioneer of child psychoanalysis than was Anna Freud, Klein created the real possibility of a psychoanalysis of psychosis, one that could circumvent the spiritualism of Jung that had wandered, against Freud's teachings, into that very domain.

Despite the dogmatism of the ferocious explorer that she is accused of being, Klein's work lends itself to a popular readership. Her work has been carried forward by original and fruitful developments that proved her right all along: W. R. Bion and David W. Winnicott were not her disciples but her followers. Without them, and without the modern psychoanalysis of psychosis and autism that dominates her work, we still would not understand the distinguishing mark of modern culture that is the ever-present risk of madness and the wide range of treatments we can use to stave it off.

The idea that pleasure is not only organic but also emerges in words, as long as those words become sensory, has never been articulated more effectively than by the French geniuses after Rabelais, particularly by the eighteenth-century sensualists and libertines. And yet it is Colette who can claim the privilege of saturating the French language with the pagan tastes that make up the charm of our civilization, all the while telling us how this sort of sensuality is rooted in the sexual antics of the well-bred or in the poignant pleasures of the common folk. To realize her genius, Colette, unlike Arendt and Klein, did not first have to overcome a master: she saw her husbands, Willy and then Jouvenel, as primarily a source of assistance and protection, and in the end, an annoyance. Rather, Colette had to face the authority of the mother tongue, which forced her to confront both reason and femininity, to love both of them equally, and to transmute one into the other. Colette's only real rival would prove to be Proust, whose narrative search has a social and metaphysical complexity that goes well beyond the adventures of Claudine and her counterparts. And yet Colette far surpasses Proust in the art of capturing pleasures that have never been lost.

These three experiences, these three truth-telling works were produced at both the heart of the twentieth century and at its margins. Though Arendt, Klein, and Colette were not truly excluded or marginalized, they nevertheless lay outside the norm. These women manifested their freedom to explore without heeding the dominant trends, institutions, parties, or schools of thought. Arendt's work is interdisciplinary (is it philosophy? political science? sociology?), and it delves into religions and into ethnic and political groupings; her work avoids the mainstream views of the "Right" as well as the "Left." Klein, for her part, challenged the conformity of the Freudians, and without fearing the consequences of being disloyal to the prevailing psychoanalytic orthodoxy of the day, she broke entirely new ground in the study of the Oedipus complex, fantasy, language, and prelanguage. At first provincial and outrageous, and then worldly while remaining a woman of the people, Colette was never fully part of the literary establishment until she developed her insight into social mores and her sensual rebellion.

Though innovative in its refusal to conform, the genius of these women came at a price: rebels glean their stimulation from their genius, and they pay for it by being ostracized, misunderstood, and disdained. That fate is common to all geniuses. Is it also common to women in general?

Life, madness, and *words*: the three women relied on them to become lucid and passionate investigators while drawing on their existence as much as on their thinking and while sharing their unique perspective on the most important issues of our time. I attempt to study these women without limiting myself to the well-known themes always linked to their names. Hannah Arendt is more than just "the banality of evil" and the Eichmann trial, and more than just the linking of Nazism and

Stalinism. Melanie Klein went further than the "precocious paranoid projection," the "want and gratitude" commanded by the "part object" that is the mother's breast and the "multiple splitting" that culminates in endogenous psychosis. And the provocation of the little urchin who acted outrageously in order to prevail at the Académie Goncourt does not fully account for the magic of Colette. These themes are no more than a few trees obscuring forests that are far more appealing but that are also dangerously more complex.

Of course, the zeal of the experts has already put to rest these commonplace associations: our three protagonists, often misunderstood or even persecuted during their lives, have since acquired their own set of commentators and fanatic adherents. I do not devote a great deal of time here to the work of the many specialists who have already spent much energy, with scrupulous attention to detail, on reconstructing various controversies and on clearing up the inevitable misunderstandings that shaped the paths of these three women.

Instead, I limit myself to studying these three women carefully and faithfully so as to reconstruct their individuality while putting each in her proper perspective—not to liken what cannot be likened, but to portray, amid the resonance that will sound among these three compositions, the complexity of twentieth-century culture as well as the major role played by women in its most vulnerable arenas: life, madness, and words.

Do we owe these uncommon forms of genius and these unforgettable innovations to these women's femininity, so unusual in itself? It is a question worth asking, and the title of this work implies that we do. At this early stage, however, I would rather not respond to the question. I began this study with the hypothesis that I knew nothing, that "woman" is an unknown, or at least that I preferred not to "define" what a woman is so that an answer might emerge out of a careful accumulation of examples. So perhaps, after accompanying each woman into her own genius, we will strike a chord that appears to bring them all together. We may hear some music composed of singularities, dissonant keys, and counterpoints that go beyond the fundamental tonalities. Perhaps that is what female genius is—that is, if female genius even exists. For now, I suggest that we reserve judgment until the end of our journey.

Life

Hannah Arendt
or action as birth and estrangement

LIFE AS A NARRATIVE

"It seems as if certain people are so exposed in their own lives (and only in their lives, not as persons!) that they become, as it were, junction points and concrete objectifications of 'life.'"[1] Hannah Arendt (1906–75) wrote these words, which foreshadowed her own fate, when she was only twenty-four years old. By that point she had already met and loved Heidegger, who remained an intriguing presence throughout her life, and she had already defended her doctoral dissertation in Heidelberg. Her thesis, translated into English as *Love and Saint Augustine*, was written under the direction of the same Karl Jaspers in whom she confided her deepest thoughts. From the start, she found herself so exposed that she crystallized herself into the "junction points and concrete objectifications of life."

After considering a life devoted to theology, and then turn-

4 / LIFE AS A NARRATIVE

ing to the study and "dismantling" of metaphysics, the young philosopher focused much of her thinking on *life*. In the beginning it was life for its own sake: in the name of self-preservation, Arendt was forced to flee Germany in a 1933 exile that helped her escape the Holocaust. At first she stayed in Paris, and then, in 1941, she landed in New York, where she became an American citizen ten years later. As a political theorist in New York, she completed a major study of the history of anti-Semitism and the origins of totalitarianism before returning to some fundamental reflections on the life of the mind.

Gripped from the start by that unique passion in which life and thought are one, Arendt's journey, so turbulent and yet so profoundly coherent, consistently put life—both life itself and life as a concept to be analyzed—at the center of her work. Far from being a "professional thinker," Arendt placed her thought at the very core of her life. It is tempting to see this specifically Arendtian trait as a particularly female characteristic, all the more because the "repression" considered so "problematic" in women is what kept Arendt from withdrawing into the obsessive edifices of pure thought and anchored her instead in corporeal experience and in bonds with other people.[2]

Even more important, the theme of life guides her thinking throughout all her writings, growing in purity and structure as it intersperses political history with metaphysical history. It underlies her thought process as she establishes with great intellectual fortitude—in a move that would prove eminently controversial—that Nazism and Stalinism are two sides of the same horror, totalitarianism, because they both partake in the same denial of human life. With the upsurge of technological progress since World War One, this destructive contempt for life, already apparent in other civilizations, has attained unparalleled heights. The totalitarian regimes, which found themselves on the same trajectory because they shared, however distinctly, the same denial of life, were united through the phenomenon of the concentration camps. To that end, Arendt

FIGURE 1 Hannah Arendt, 1927
(©AKG)

FIGURE 2 Hannah Arendt, 1933

(©Leo Baeck Institute)

wrote that "the mass man's typical feeling of superfluous-ness—an entirely new phenomenon in Europe, the concomi-tant of mass unemployment and the population growth of the last 150 years—has been prevalent for centuries in the con-tempt for the *value of human life*." She went on to add, "the old adage that the poor and oppressed have nothing to lose but their chains no longer applied to the mass men, for they lost much more than the chains of misery when they lost interest in their own well-being: the source of all the worries and cares which make human life troublesome and anguished was gone. Compared with their immaterialism, a Christian monk looks like a man absorbed in worldly affairs."[3]

Arendt's somber tone, one of anger tinged with irony, presaged the sometimes apocalyptic concern that surrounded her deter-mination that "radical evil" resides in the "perverted ill will," in Kant's sense, to make "men superfluous." Put another way, the adherent of totalitarianism destroys human life after obliterating the meaning of all life, including his own. Even worse, this "superfluousness" of human life, whose origins Arendt ascribes to the rise of imperialism, reemerges in those modern democracies that are consumed with automation: "Radical evil has emerged in connection with a system in which all men have become equally superfluous. The manipulators of this system believe in their own superfluousness as much as in that of all others, and the totalitarian murderers are all the more dangerous because they do not care if they themselves are alive or dead, if they ever lived or never were born. The danger of the corpse factories and holes of oblivion is that today, with populations and homelessness every-where on the increase, masses of people are continuously ren-dered superfluous if we continue to think of our world in utili-tarian terms. Political, social, and economic events everywhere are in a silent conspiracy with totalitarian instruments devised for making men superfluous."[4]

In the face of this threat, Arendt crafted a passionate defense of life in *The Human Condition*. On the opposite extreme from the sort of life that is numbingly reproduced by the vitalist relentlessness of the consumer culture and of the modern technology allotted to the "life process," Arendt sings an ode to the uniqueness of every birth and praises its capacity to inaugurate what she does not hesitate to call the "miracle of life": "The miracle that saves the world, the realm of human affairs, from its normal, 'natural' ruin is ultimately the fact of natality, in which the faculty of action is ontologically rooted. Only the full experience of this capacity can bestow upon human affairs faith and hope, those two essential characteristics of human existence which Greek antiquity ignored altogether. . . . It is this faith in and hope for the world that found perhaps its most glorious and most succinct expression in the few words with which the Gospels announced their 'glad tidings': 'A child has been born unto us.'"[5]

Today we find it hard to accept that life, a sacred value in both Christian and post-Christian democracies, is the recent product of a historical evolution, just as we find it hard to imagine that at one point this value may have been endangered. It is precisely the questioning of this fundamental value—its formation in Christian eschatology as well as the dangers that it faces in the modern world—that quietly unifies Arendt's entire work, from her dissertation on Saint Augustine to her unfinished manuscript on judging.

A BIOGRAPHY "SO EXPOSED"

Before turning to the major phases in my exploration of Arendt's concept of life, I lay out a few key moments in her life, as relayed to us by her biographers.[6]

As Arendt wrote Jaspers in 1930, it was an "exposed" existence that appears to have conditioned her to become, with her life and work intertwined, an "objectification" or a "juncture

point" of "*life*."(I shall return to the meaning of this "condition" as it is defined in *The Human Condition*.[7])

Born near Hanover, Germany, in a town called Linden,
Hannah was the daughter of Paul Arendt and Martha Cohn.
The Arendts were an "old Königsberg family," as the philosopher described them in a 1964 television interview with Gün-
ter Gauss.[8] The family, Reform Jews who admired Hermann
Vogelstein, one of the most prominent leaders of liberal German Jewry, was critical of the Zionists. At the same time, however, they often invited Kurt Blumenfeld, the future president
of the German Zionist Organization, to their home. Blumenfeld played with little Hannah at the home of her grandfather
Max, and he supervised the affirmation of her Jewish identity.

Hannah's maternal grandfather, Jacob Cohn, who was born
in what is now Lithuania, turned the family business into the
most important Russian tea importing company in Königsberg, which until that point had imported only English teas.
The Cohns relied a great deal on such "generous and sensitive"
widows as Fanny Spiero-Cohn, Arendt's grandmother and
Jacob's second wife, who was fond of Russian peasant costumes
and who spoke German with a thick Russian accent.

Trained as an engineer at Königsberg's university, the
Albertina, Paul Arendt worked for an electrical engineering
firm. Martha, for her part, studied French and music for three
years in Paris. Both parents sympathized with the German
socialists and subscribed to the Goethean ideas of the German
cultural elite [*Bildungselite*]. The family naturally affirmed its
Jewish identity, although Christianity also insinuated itself
through the presence of Ana, the family maid who watched
over Hannah. From the moment their daughter was born, the
Arendts kept a notebook, *Unser Kind*, to track Hannah's development. The notebook stands out for Martha's insightful
remarks; she was an attentive mother who didn't miss a trick.
At one year of age, Hannah "loves to be surrounded by turbu-
lence"; at a year and a half "she mostly speaks her own lan-

guage, which she enunciates very fluently. She understands everything." When Hannah was two years old, her musician mother faced her first disappointment: "[Hannah] is now singing—off key, unfortunately!" At three, however, Hannah was able to say "just about anything . . . even though it may not always be intelligible to someone who is not close to her" [are these the early signs of a philosopher?]. Described as "extremely lively, always in a rush, very friendly even with strangers," at six years of age "she learns easily, is apparently gifted, mathematics in particular is her forte."

This joyous time was short-lived, however, and it turned dark and somber once Paul Arendt's health declined due to syphilis. This condition, which Paul had contracted as a young man but which had remained stable for a long while, worsened two years after the birth of his daughter. His syphilis reached tragic proportions in 1911, afflicting him with lesions, ataxia (a form of paralysis), and paresis (a form of insanity). Paul was forced to quit his job, and the family moved to Königsberg, where he was institutionalized.

Grandfather Max helped pass the time by displaying his storytelling talents during the walks he took with his granddaughter. And when the philosopher later pays tribute to the life story, *bios*/biography, which she contrasted with biological life, *zōē*, we will be reminded of this other father's storytelling magic, which kept Hannah in contact with life while Paul Arendt was suffering through his horrible demise.

Max died in March 1913, and Paul died later that year in October. Martha recorded in *Unser Kind* that Hannah did not seem fazed by these losses. "She tells me that we should not think of sad things too much, that there is no point in being saddened by them. That is typical of her great zest for life. . . . She sees his death as something sad for me. She herself remains untouched by it. She attended the funeral and wept, as she told me, 'because of the beautiful singing.'"

Did Hannah's reaction merely reflect the innocence of a

seven-year-old girl? Or was it the first signs of a life that unfurls in thought and that appears to know that we can control the object of our thoughts—whether it be something sad (to be avoided) or music (much better)? Is it not the case that when I am deep in thought, I long for nothing? We might assume as much after reading the reflections of Hannah's mother: "She has recently started thinking about her grandpa again, and she speaks about him with love and affection, but does she really miss him? I don't think so." Is thinking the only way to live with the dead, to keep from losing them and to deal with grief? We will find a trace of this precocious circumvention of death in a thought that longed for nothing: in the implicit debate that Hannah Arendt would later conduct with Heidegger's "being-toward-death." Without shying away from her heart-breaking distress, Hannah created new ways of thinking about the common ground of the appearance: bonds with other people, sharing, and action.

That respite lasted only a year, however, and with World War One and with the young girl's sexual development, troubles soon began. Hannah was no longer happy, *Unser Kind* informs us: her teeth were crooked, which required braces that she found unpleasant; her written work was not up to her abilities; and she was even less adept at her oral performance—which says it all! An exceptionally sensitive girl with a wry sense of humor, Hannah was prone to fits of anger. To these traits were added a series of recurring minor illnesses: fevers, nosebleeds, sore throats, and headaches. Puberty was clearly on its way, and Hannah had still not decided to be as robust as her father. As Martha said, "like her father." That will come!

An innocuous remark made by this eight-year-old girl (we are now in 1914) points to her developing identification with men: "If a child were born to us now, it wouldn't know its father," Hannah said to her mother. Strange words indeed! Beneath the desire to know where children come from and to recognize one's parents in the same way one is recognized by them, these words reveal the proximity between the two women as well as the desire they shared for the absent man—a desire to have this man, to be this man. Hannah's words also evince her concerns about her place between the two of them: if we had a child, who would be the father? Since Paul and Max are dead, where is the man? Who is the man? You? Me? A stranger? Does he exist? Who might know him and who will ever know for sure? Who could provide us (me) with a child? You? Me? Nobody? If a child came to us now, he wouldn't know his father. Who is the father? An intense rapport that "included" a man was developing between the two women, so much so that in 1927, the mother-daughter "couple" celebrated the twenty-fifth anniversary of Martha and Paul. At that time, Hannah was twenty years old and a doctoral candidate at Heidelberg.

In 1920, Martha got remarried to Martin Beerwald, a businessman, a widower, and a father of two daughters, Clara and Eva. From all accounts, Hannah's relationship with her stepfamily, and with her stepfather in particular, was stormy. She shielded herself by embarking on "spontaneous outings," perhaps creating an adolescent version of a life in which desire was intertwined with friendship. She became a close friend of Anne Mendelssohn's (a descendant of the composer Felix Mendelssohn, who was the grandson of Moses Mendelssohn, the leader of the social and cultural emancipation of Jews during the Enlightenment), who herself was the girlfriend of Ernst Grumbach. Five years older than she, Grumbach was enrolled in Heidegger's course, and he relayed to Hannah his enthusiasm for the brilliant professor from Marburg. It was Anna who, a few years later, presented her friend Hannah with a rare edition of the works of Rahel Varnhagen, whose "life" Arendt would subsequently write.

In the meantime, Hannah's intellectual virtuosity and erudition amazed her many friends. She quarreled with one of her secondary school teachers, however, and then got herself expelled. As always, her mother protected her; the unruly student would have to sit for her final examination, the *Abitur,* as an unenrolled candidate. She passed with flying colors in 1924 (one year before the rest of her class) and was awarded a gold medal bearing the effigy of Duke Albert I of Prussia. After Anne left for Allenstein, Hannah became the girlfriend of Ernst Grumbach, which became a news event in the community and which—in another tribute to life—made her seem more desirable and fulfilled. Under the approving eye of her mother, whom Hannah Arendt declared in her interview with Gauss to be a person who personified a "specifically Jewish humanity," was capable of "standing outside of all social connections," and displayed a "complete absence of prejudice."[9] I shall return to the Arendtian notion of the "worldlessness" of the Jewish people, who were deprived of any territory or political concepts and who compensated for this lack with "an unusual warmth" that nevertheless threatened to disappear after the founding of the State of Israel.[10]

In Berlin, the theology student, an ardent follower of Kierkegaard, threw herself breathlessly onto an aporia: "I had some misgivings only as to how one deals with this [theology] if one is Jewish . . . how one proceeds. I had no idea, you know."[11] At that point she decided to lend her ear to everything interesting about philosophy that was being said in the nation's universities, which is how she wound up in Marburg with Heidegger. "The rumor about Heidegger put it quite simply: Thinking has come to life again; the cultural treasures of the past, believed to be dead, are being made to speak, in the course of which it turns out that they propose things altogether different from the familiar, worn-out trivialities they had been presumed to say. There exists a teacher; one can perhaps learn to think. . . . The idea of a *passionate* thinking, in which thinking and aliveness become one, takes us somewhat aback. . . . This passionate thinking, which rises out of the simple fact of being-born-in-the-world . . . can no more have a final goal . . . than can life itself."[12]

Enthusiastic and full of life, Hannah, nicknamed "the green woman" after the pretty green dresses she often wore, fell in love with the professor who, for his part, was passionately attracted by her beauty and by the depth of her thinking. Their clandestine romance began in February 1924; Hannah was eighteen years old and Heidegger thirty-five. The recently published correspondence between Arendt and Heidegger complements Elzbieta Ettinger's controversial book on their relationship and allows us to reconstruct the strength of their bond, which was surpassed only by its inherent impossibility. Heidegger, who was the father of two sons and who was married to Elfriede, a dynamic woman with Nazi convictions as well as some "feminist" ones, had no intention of getting a divorce. Still, the professor was taken by an intense passion, as shown in the following excerpt from a May 13, 1925, letter he wrote to Arendt:

> This time I am at a loss for words. All I can do is cry, and I find it hard to stop. I cannot tell you why—and while waiting hopelessly to understand, the reason for my tears disappears in the expression of your gratitude and your faith.
>
> And I think of your victory when you act like a saint, when you open yourself to me completely. Your face hardens from the inner force of an expiation (*Sühne*) that your existence has endured.
>
> My love, how do you do it? And how do you maintain so much respect and dignity?
>
> Life is drawn to respect (*Ehrfurcht*) and lends it its grandeur.[13]

With the ceremonial codes of their clandestine meetings, and with Hannah's distancing herself by going to Heidelberg, where, for obvious social and non-ontological reasons, she wrote her dissertation under the direction of Karl Jaspers, a friend and correspondent of Heidegger's, she became overwhelmed by the complexity of their relationship. Wounded but ever proud, the young scholar defended herself as best she could, shielding herself behind a slew of friends and lovers: Hans Jonas, a Zionist; Erwin Loewenson, an essayist and an expressionist writer; Benno von Wiese, who would become a National-Socialist and, after the war, an esteemed professor of German literature at the University of Bonn; and Günther Stern, whom she would marry in 1929. Himself a student of Heidegger's, Stern was preparing a doctoral dissertation on the philosophy of music that would earn him the disapproval of Theodor Adorno before the rise of National-Socialism proved fatal to his academic career.

Heidegger pretended not to understand that this defensive strategy was a plaintive plea for his undivided love, a love he was in no position to indulge. The budding philosopher began to revel in the melancholia that she had already expressed in poems like "Dream," "Weariness," and "Adieu" that reflected her relationship with Ernst Grumbach. In 1925 Hannah sent Heidegger a self-portrait, *Die Schatten* [The shadows], which was followed with more poems the next year. Written in the third person and employing the Heideggerian lexicon, Hannah's verse was intended to assuage her anguish and her feelings of being alienated and foreign to the world [*Fremdheit*], as well as her bitter awareness of her own uniqueness [*Absonderlichkeit*]. Hannah's anguish was fierce and her fears relentless: the "fear of reality overcame the defenseless creature—this senseless, groundless empty fear before whose blind gaze everything becomes like nothing, which means madness, joylessness, disaster, annihilation. . . . An almost matter-of-fact expectancy of some brutality. . . . Unless she tried in docile devotion to cling to it, pale and colorless and with the hidden uncanniness [*Unheimlichkeit*] of passing shadows." That uncanniness was scarcely abated by the coquettishness of a lover who feared that her love story would make others think that she had become "uglier and more common, even to the point of being dull and licentious."[14]

The project of writing Rahel Varnhagen's life came at just the right moment. By projecting herself onto this biography and by recounting the life of another disappointed lover, an assimilated Jewess who wound up as a "conscious pariah" who eventually returned to her roots, Hannah Arendt appears to have accomplished a cathartic, even auto-analytic, act. At the same time, Arendt, under the influence of Kurt Blumenfeld and her other Zionist friends, became aware of the gravity of the situation in Germany, and she eventually joined the side of the resistance. She participated in underground railroad rescue operations in Berlin, provided assistance to the Communists in the spring of 1933, accepted a mission from the German Zionist Association, got arrested by the police and then miraculously escaped, and then finally left Germany with her mother in August 1933 to take refuge in France.

Heidegger took over the rectorship of Freiburg University in the spring of 1933, after his Social Democratic predecessor was dismissed for refusing to post a notice forbidding Jews from teaching at the university. Heidegger believed he was saving the culture by transferring to the National-Socialist project and the cult of the people this "rescuing of Being" that was the initial thrust of his philosophical meditation.

Hannah had married in 1929, and her relationship with Martin ended in 1930.[15] "I think I understand that you will not be coming to see me," she wrote him in 1928. "The path you have shown me has proved to be longer and more difficult than I expected. It would require *an entire life, a long life.*" Hannah declared herself ready to set forth on this solitary path because it appeared to her to be "the only way *to live.*" For Arendt, living meant loving Heidegger: "I would have lost my right to *love* had I lost the love I have for you." Without signing the letter with her usual *Deine Hannah,* she wrote: "And God willing, I shall love you even more upon my death."[16]

Hannah Arendt kept her promise, the meaning of which would change with the passing of time. She first went down a path of combat and political reflection that had nothing in common with Heidegger's philosophical work. Later, toward the end of her life, she returned to his fundamental meditations with an intimacy that was vigilant, perhaps ironic, and no doubt divergent, an intimacy that led her to posit a veritable deconstruction of Being. One might ask whether a certain feminine dependency, in the sense of a sublimated passivity, did not quietly accompany this trajectory. After the war, Arendt got as far away as she could from Heidegger,[17] whom she blamed for Husserl's being fired from Freiburg University—a misperception that Jaspers would later correct in a letter to her.[18] It was important for Arendt to let Jaspers know that she completely disavowed Heidegger's personality and that Heidegger showed no interest in her work as a woman: "[Heidegger] should have resigned. However foolish he may have been, he was capable of understanding that. . . . I can't but regard Heidegger as a potential murderer. . . . Nothing but inane lies with what I think is a clearly pathological streak."[19] "All my life I've pulled the wool over his eyes, so to speak, always acted as if none of that existed and as if I couldn't count to three, unless it was in the interpretation of his own works. Then he was always very pleased when it turned out that I could count to three and sometimes even to four. Then I suddenly felt this deception was becoming just too boring, and so I got a rap on the nose. I was very angry for a moment, but I'm not any longer. I feel instead that I somehow deserved what I got, that is, both for having deceived him and for suddenly having put an end to it."[20]

Even so, Arendt went to visit Heidegger in 1950 and again in 1952. They started up a correspondence, and, from 1967 until her death in 1975, Arendt went to Germany each year to meet with him. The letters from Heidegger that have been preserved show him to be moved and oddly seduced by the relationship he encouraged between Hannah Arendt and Elfriede Heidegger, his wife. After recalling the role his wife Elfriede played in the construction of his work space [*Hütte*] and referring to the recent presumed/desired harmony between the two women, Heidegger wrote Arendt on February 8, 1950, "I hope that in future, the harmony we have achieved will adopt the warm hues of the wooden walls of this room. I am pleased to know that your thoughts will be making their way to this workshop as well as to the mountains and pastures around it."[21]

One month later, on March 19, 1950, Heidegger reminisced about his first visit with Hannah after the war: "I knew it when I found myself in your presence on February 6, and I used the informal 'you' with you. I knew that it was the beginning of a new era for us and that we were pressuring ourselves to cloak everything about our love in the strictest confidence. Were I to tell you that the love that I have for my wife has only recently found its way, it would be only because of your loyalty, your faith in our relationship, and your love."[22]

Heidegger went on to urge Hannah to try to get closer to his wife: "I need her love, which has lasted all these years but which has continued to grow. I need your love, which remains mysteriously rooted in its beginnings. And I would also like my heart to foster a secret friendship with your husband, who has become your partner during these difficult years." To this ménage à quatre were added some clichés about the German countryside: "Hannah, when your city tears you away from me too forcefully, think of the immense pine trees that grace the tops of the snow-covered mountains we can see basking in the crisp midday air."[23]

From that point on, the green dress would become a brown one. On April 12, 1950, the lover who sought to remain faithful focused uncannily on the symbolism of this brown color as well as of its earthy overtones by associating their reunions in Freiburg with the first time they met, twenty-five years earlier, in Marburg: "When we saw each other again for the first time and you approached me wearing your prettiest dress, I had the impression that you had traveled the twenty-five years. Hannah, have you noticed the brownish color of a freshly ploughed field bathing in the moonlight? Everything has been completed and anything can happen. I want your brown dress to remain a symbol for me of the moment we saw each other again. I want this symbol to become ever more meaningful for us."[24]

In 1969 Arendt wrote "Martin Heidegger at Eighty," an article that glorifies "the wind that blows through Heidegger's thinking" as well as the dangers it entails, but whose praise barely conceals the compromises that such thinkers as Plato and Heidegger make with tyrants and dictators.[25] As the years went by, Arendt strove to defend Heidegger and to make his work known in the United States, repelled the attacks directed against him, and crafted her own work in conjunction with the work of her master. "It is a work that owes almost everything to you," she wrote him on the subject of *The Human Condition,* and she wrote the following on a separate sheet of paper that she never sent: "*De vita active* / This book is dedicated to no one. / How could I dedicate it to you, / you who are so dear to me / and to whom I remain faithful / and unfaithful, / without ever stopping loving you?"[26] And without ever ceasing to wonder about the "fox's . . . trap."[27]

"Faithful and unfaithful." That is precisely how we find Hannah all throughout our reading of her intellectual experience. Belying the solitude of *Dasein,* Arendt's writings offer a way of thinking about life-and-action that might appear modest as compared with the glory of developing Being. The Arendtian adventure remains no less ambitious, however, in light of the impasses that faced the "professional thinker" and her "work" when they sought to confront the plurality of the world.

But for the moment we are back in 1933. The life of the young philosopher was intertwined with the history of her people and of the peoples of the twentieth century, though not to the point where Hannah had stopped leading the existence of a desirous woman who articulated her passions. Subtly confessed through the passions of Rahel and propelled by an extraordinary mix of denial and sublimation, Arendt's passions would later inform her meditation on what she termed "the human condition."[28] Arendt's experience as an intellectual proves, quite simply, to be an examined life—a life uprooted from biology through *labor, work,* and, in particular, *action.* Yet it was also a life that harbored the superior form of human existence that is varied and incomplete thinking, provided such thinking is shared with a diverse and contradictory world. As she would write in *The Life of the Mind,* "The worldliness of living things means that there is no subject that is not also an object and appears as such to somebody else, who guarantees its 'objective' reality. . . . Plurality is the law of the earth."[29]

Arendt met Heinrich Blücher (1899–1970) in Paris in early spring 1936. We can imagine what she thought of him by reading her sketch of Rosa Luxembourg's partner, Leo Jogisches: "He was definitely *masculini generis,* which was of considerable importance to [Rosa Luxembourg]. . . . In marriage, it is not always easy to tell the partners' thoughts apart."[30] Difficult to pigeonhole, Blücher was at various points a Communist, a Spartacist, a would-be revolutionary, a friend of Kurt Blumenfeld's, and a believer in Zionism even though he wasn't Jewish. In any event, his biographers have all agreed to call him an *anarchist.* Married two times before he married Hannah, a self-taught man deeply educated in the prevailing political and artistic culture of the day, this *Drahtzieher* [string-puller, puppeteer]—which is how he liked to describe his profession on his German identity papers—would later become a philosophy professor in the United States. Though Blücher—"*masculini generis*"—was able to finesse Hannah's political education by persuading her to read Marx and Lenin, his most important contribution, as evidenced by the correspondence between the two lovers and soon-to-be spouses, was to give her emotional stability and to help her devote all her efforts to thinking while still remaining in contact with the outside world.[31] Was the bohemian puppeteer able to strike a chord with the exuberant little girl as she was *before* her father passed away? *Unser Kind* recounts that Hannah was given a marionette theater for her sixth birthday. The little girl invented a drama that was so complicated and emotional that she could no longer go on and burst into tears.

Among the many tricks he had up his sleeve, Heinrich Blücher (hadn't Blücher once been an assistant to Fritz Frankel, the Adlerian psychoanalyst?) prided himself on his ability to cure a depressed hysterical woman without recourse to any sort of psychoanalytic interpretation. The woman was unable to leave her bed, so Blücher simply doused it with kerosene and set it on fire. Just as effectively, Blücher successfully cured Hannah's notorious early morning melancholic moods, which had a way of upsetting her mother. He paid no attention to Hannah's bouts of depression and would go right back to bed, slipping easily into a peaceful sleep. Hannah was using illness as a way to blackmail her mother, and Blücher was not duped. Of course, as we know, Arendt had nothing but scorn for psychoanalysis.

Interned at the camp of Gurs among "foreigners of German origin," Arendt managed to escape five weeks later, and then went on to marry Blücher, her second husband, in 1940. The figure of the absent man, whose "shadow" had tainted Hannah's childhood and adolescence with so much sadness, had finally returned. Strange and foreign, a non-Jew, a German, and a proletarian: was Blücher's identity not a perfect way for him to avoid stifling her and instead to nurture her own virility and true femininity?

"Ever since I was a little girl, I have always known that love was the only thing that could give the feeling of truly existing. And I was always so afraid that it would overwhelm me. When I met you, I finally stopped being afraid. . . . It still seems impossible for me to experience 'true love' without losing my identity. . . . But in truth, I have only had an identity since I found love. I finally realized what it means to be happy." This love and trust dispelled the archaic fear that had tormented Hannah since the death of her father, a fear that her affair with Heidegger, far from assuaging, had only intensified: "When I met you, I could finally get rid of my childhood fear that was still haunting me as an adult."[32] In a mixture of modesty and candor, Hannah Arendt revealed her sensual and personal awakening, to which her lover responded, "Have I really shown you what happiness is? Do I really make you happy in the same way you make me happy? For you are my one true happiness, so perhaps I have simply shown you something of yourself? Are you becoming who you really are? I am too. So, my love, have I made the young girl you once were into a woman? How sweet it is—I do not know how I did it, for it was through you that I finally became a man." A year before, Blücher made an affectionate display of his regard for her: "Yes, of course you can ask me what you ask of yourself, and you must treat me the same way you treat yourself—except that you must treat yourself even better; that is my goal at least: to treat you better than you treat yourself. . . . I know what I have been given and I know what sort of woman you are and are becoming and will be; let me be the judge of you, for how could you ever know yourself?" In response, she said, "When certain people have professed their love to me but have found me cold, I have always thought, 'Do you have any idea about the danger your love poses for me and would pose for me?'" And Blücher, in response, drew on the two sides of his wife: "And thus I see both sides. As a person you are as free and independent as I could imagine and as a wife you are as dependant as I could ever wish."[33] Despite her mother's disapproval (or was it precisely because of that disapproval?), Hannah was satisfied: the capricious Blücher successfully became the lover, the friend, the husband, the brother, and the father. Upon his death, Hannah wanted Blücher, who was not Jewish, to have a funeral service complete with the Hebrew Kaddish.

Independent and free, Blücher and Arendt enjoyed a relationship based on a sexual and intellectual independence as well as on the powerful rapport that they shared. They both were able to overlook whatever dangers and difficulties their relationship entailed. Still, Blücher's affairs with other women wounded Hannah's fidelity, although in the end she managed to overcome her feelings and to remember what really mattered. Blücher wrote, "My love, what a gift from the gods it is to experience a feeling that seems so likely to last forever in its present form, that is, if it does not grow even stronger with time." And he added, "Another fundamental reason why I love you is that we have always shared the same opinions on the most weighty questions of life. There is no difference between us. That is how it is and that is how it shall always be."[34]

The exile made their rapport even stronger, and it justified Hannah's need to protect herself within the "four walls" of their relationship. "Stups, for the love of God, you are my four walls." She later told him, "Believe me, my love, women must live inside a couple."[35] And then Blücher, who disliked writing, crafted this lovely definition of the couple, a definition that is tentative and ironic but that nevertheless rings true: "Like a magic formula, here is my definition of the couple: the couple multiples everything by two. This is a truly living formula, for it, like life, is as serious as it is ironic. Who would ever want to live a single life if he could live a life multiplied by two, and who would ever believe that he could risk what such a life would entail? . . . One thing is certain. Once people decide to live together, separation breaks them in half. You have no idea, and nor did I, about how much I miss you. This time I take no joy in being alone. . . . The sort of solitude that we have promised to share and the sort of solitude in which we would like to be joined against the world—those are the kinds of solitude that are founded implicitly on what is between two people."[36]

It took Blücher a long time to discover the affair between Hannah and the sage from Todtnauberg, no doubt at some point after World War Two when Heidegger was accused of Nazism. Blücher appears to have underestimated its intensity, unless he saw in this assignment the strategy the "puppeteer" needed for his couple to prosper, and for Hannah to resolve the conflict with Heidegger's thinking that she described as follows: "I have clearly joined the ranks of those who for some time now have been attempting to dismantle metaphysics."[37]

And yet her way of "joining" had nothing "joined" about it. No conformist, Hannah relied on a series of diverse actions to assert herself by imposing her difference of thought and judgment, particularly with respect to Heidegger. Arendt considered this quest for uniqueness to be the apogee of human life (she traced it back to Duns Scotus, whom she was careful to laud in her own writings) without going so far as to shape it into a clarion call for female difference.[38]

Arendt's encounter with Blücher ignited a passion for politics and a taste for appearance, the cheerier side of Arendt's personality since birth. Faced with the solitude of the philosophical sage who lost his way in history (Heidegger) and the impetuousness of the bit actor who lost his way in politics while charging ahead with the authenticity of a rebellious life (Blücher), Hannah had to choose one or the other or, at the very least, to blend them both together. These companions in body and spirit were also her creations, at least to the extent of their being-for-her. Heinrich, the political science "professor," learned a great deal from his wife's philosophical depth and precision, and their correspondence testifies to this mutually beneficial dialogue. In contrast, Heidegger's scant enthusiasm for reading Arendt's work—if not his outright resistance to it—suggests that the "professional thinker" got nothing out of his young student's work. Their published correspondence does, however, describe several political and intellectual exchanges that occurred toward the end of their lives: Is it not true that the sage of Todtnauberg cynically appropriated, before the war, his mistress's social position in the face of

Nazism? Is it not true that Arendt needed to be close to Heidegger's thought so she could moor her own thinking in a fundamental tradition, to immerse herself in it and then to emerge from it? In any event, as in a Greek agora or as in one of those theatrical scenes in which the spectator watches a play but also improvises and participates in it while re-creating it, Hannah Arendt developed her original thought "between the two of them"—at once as a protection against withdrawal and an engagement in action.

Many of Arendt's contemporaries spoke to her womanly seductiveness; those from the New York salons mused about the "Weimar flapper," while others reacted as did Hans Jonas, who admired that his friend could "enjoy the attentions that men reserve for women" while remaining "one of the greatest minds of the century."[39] In Jonas's eyes, Hannah was neither a "thinker" (which would be tantamount to the relationship between the part and the whole) nor a "person" (an asexual term), but a "woman."[40] And yet Arendt would not opine on the female condition unless she had to. Was she, as was often said, more feminine than feminist? She did not believe it was wise to support the "cause" of women.[41] When Arendt was reminded that philosophy as a profession was practiced mainly by men, she simply responded, "it is entirely possible that a woman will one day be a philosopher," though she made sure to clarify that she was not speaking about herself: the philosophers did not see her as one of them, and she defined herself as a "political theorist" or even a "political journalist." "It just doesn't look good when a woman gives orders. She should try not to get into such a situation if she wants to remain feminine. . . . The problem itself played no role for me personally," she told those who persisted in their wish to hear her opine on the struggle for women's emancipation.[42]

That said, Hannah was no more inclined to *give* orders than to *take* them. Indeed, this passive docility, which some people would deem a "feminine" trait, was manifested during Eichmann's trial in Jerusalem through his absence of thinking, also known as the "banality of evil." Is this the vault of pseudofemininity that Arendt detected in the Nazi when she observed that Eichmann, though not completely lacking in intelligence, was banally and shockingly devoid of thought? And when she noted that he did not give the abject orders himself, but was happy simply to jot them down and communicate them? Was Eichmann a sort of nonman, a sort of fake woman, a clown?: "I read the transcript of his police investigation, thirty-six hundred pages, read it, and read it very carefully, and I do not know how many times I laughed—laughed out loud! . . . Three minutes before certain death, I probably still would laugh."[43]

If that is the case, however, how can we define a woman, if she does not give orders, execute them, influence them, or obey them? "What is important for me is to understand. For me, writing is a matter of seeking this understanding, part of the process of understanding. . . . And if others understand—in the same sense that I have understood—that gives me a sense of satisfaction, like feeling at home."[44] The simplicity of this "comprehending" posture conceals a rich assortment of hidden meanings. The *com*-prehender waits, accepts, and welcomes; an open space, she allows herself to be used, she sets forth, she is *with (cum-, com-),* a matrix of studied casualness (what Heidegger calls *Gelassenheit*) that allows itself to be fertilized. At the same time, the comprehender apprehends: she selects, tears down, molds, and transforms the elements; she appropriates and re-creates them. Alongside others but accompanied by her own selection, the comprehender is one who gives birth to a meaning that harbors, in altered form, the meaning of other people. It then falls upon us to unravel the process that turns thought into action, that constructs and deconstructs.

Would it be appropriate to speak of a body of work here? Of course it would be. In academic and publishing circles, Hannah Arendt is universally acknowledged to be the author of one of this century's most important bodies of work (though for now we should bracket the question of whether her work is political, philosophical, or feminine). Her biting style, economy, and fluency, and the enormous (though never exhaustive) erudition displayed in her writings have all been given their due. The repetitions and heterogeneity of her work, moreover, have provided fodder for various experts of all persuasions. But in the end, it is the way these qualities are anchored in personal experience and in the world around her that makes her writings appear to be less a body of work than an action. On that front, Arendt's undeniable uniqueness comes to the fore: it is neither meticulous nor complete, and it does not place her discourse above the fray. The "comprehender" seizes the opportunity, questions the obvious, converses with "authors," whether known or unknown, all the while interacting with other people and, in the first instance, with herself. Trapped in this labyrinth of arguments, thinking may forgo sophisticated refinement, but only to resonate more effectively with memories of different pasts and to delve into the current state of the world.

A photograph taken in the 1950s offers, in my view, the most unsettling image of "the comprehender" (fig. 4). The mounting tension (what Heidegger calls *durchschauen, Durchsichtigkeit*) and the penetrating eyes lend her face a masculine air and an ironic voracity. Her smile and her valiant expression, on the other hand, are lit up by a furtively pleasant demeanor that reveals as much confidence as understanding. And yet her maturity and her intellectual exploits have pushed away the sweet young girl with the long locks who, at eighteen years of age, seduced her Plato of Marburg (figs. 1 and 2). The smoking urchin herself, whose intense visage is seen addressing the audience of a 1944 New York City conference, had settled down with a vengeance (fig. 3).

Hannah Arendt hated celebrity, but she never stopped celebrating appearance and spectacle. She would have had no objection to our lingering over the traces of her appearances that she left us. Returning to the earlier photograph (fig. 4), we

FIGURE 3 Hannah Arendt, New York, 1944

FIGURE 4 Hannah Arendt about 1950

(© Studio Fred Stein)

come back to the eternal question: "What is a woman?" Is she merely a "girl-phallus," the erection of a female model that whets men's phallic appetite—that the psychoanalysts make out to be part of the seductive appeal of the "pretty girl" of 1927 (fig. 1) and 1933 (fig. 2)? This scenario seems all the more likely because a seductress, particularly when she is thinking, is only rarely devoid of androgynous ambiguities.[45] Or is she the buxom mother of our dreams, a form of magic that abates our predominantly oral frustrations? Even if we manage to see a bit of Hannah in this first cliché, she certainly seems to have avoided the second. Or, in the end, is she the "comprehender" whose image scares away the women's magazines that track "your beauty" (fig. 4)? Her face is practically a caricature of the very battle scars that had allowed her to comprehend. Without a tenacious commitment of this sort, the mind remains unrealized and invisible, but when it emerges, femininity—like being?—beats a retreat and, of the two sexes, only the male one overcomes the spectacle with imprudence. By working through her psychic bisexuality, the image of Hannah Arendt at the end of the 1950s shows the signs of a peak in virility. There, we find not a mask of deception aimed at integrating a woman with a man's world, nor do we encounter simply the unconscious truth of a repressed homosexual. Rather, we find the necessary path toward this thought-into-acts, toward this contemplated action that, for Arendt, is tantamount to life.

LOVE ACCORDING TO SAINT AUGUSTINE

Hannah Arendt defended her doctoral dissertation, "Love and Saint Augustine," on November 28, 1928.[46] The cool evaluation written by her thesis director, Karl Jaspers, concluded that his student "has the ability to spot the essentials. She has not simply gathered together everything that Augustine says about love. . . . In the quotations some errors appear. . . . The method does some violence to the text. . . . Through philosophical work with ideas the author wants to justify her freedom from Christian possibilities, which also attract her. . . . Can unfortunately not be given the highest grade."[47] It is true that Arendt tended to prefer Augustine the philosopher to Augustine the theologian. The three parts of her dissertation ("Love as Craving," "Creator and Creature," and "Social Life") are structured according to Jaspers's notions: Arendt searches for a systematic paradigm in Augustine's work, even if such a paradigm is far removed from Augustine's religious intentions. She does not wish to force his work into a system per se, but Heideggerian terminology is already quite present. The theologians are disappointed and taken aback.

Years later, Arendt wrote Jaspers that she was surprised to find traces of herself in this remote work.[48] Indeed, her first piece of abstract, purely philosophical writing seeks to question—at the heart of the transcendental bond of Christian love—the diverse bond that unites people in the world. The aims of her later work begin to take shape here: the theme of life, presented through the theme of love, structures this inaugural text and allows us to reread Augustine in the light of Arendt's subsequent body of thought.

Arendt uses several terms to denote the concept of love in Saint Augustine's work: *love, desire* (with its two variations, *craving* and *libido*), *charity,* and *covetousness* all form, in her view, a true "constellation of love" that asserts that the conduit of this nomenclature is desire: "Desire has the function of procuring the 'good' from which happiness will result. The trouble with the wrong desire, the love of the world, is not so much that man does not love God as that he does not stay in himself but [by virtue of having dismissed God] has gone out of himself as well." The various forms of love are distinguished only by their divergent objects, though love is always coextensive with life: it is the "postulated and claimed reality of a human life."[49] But what is life? Arendt will direct all her efforts, by way of the variants of love according to Augustine, toward answering that question.

For Augustine the Christian, life, the "supreme good," is a "life that cannot be lost"—an everlasting life without death and without an end. The *beate vivere,* the absolute "good," then, is nothing less than the "eternity" that lies beyond our existence. Love is attracted to this outside existence (echoing what Heidegger taught us: to this Being), this blessed, everlasting totality of the supreme good [*summum bene*] that is the everlasting Life in God. And although this supreme Good is situated outside humankind, it challenges what exists per se because existence is always already familiar with what exists through retrospective recollection. (On this score, Arendt the philosopher emphasizes the way Plato is reworked into the heart of Augustine's thought.) This tension, unique to the life of the being, divides the good into two parts, finiteness and eternity, with love being the sign of the division as well as its potential for unity. Love targets a good found outside these designs. But because what remains of the exterior side of life is desired only by the love of life, life is what we should strive for.[50]

This thought process suggests a splitting, if not a dialectic, of life: an absolute exteriority of eternal Being, on the one hand, and the introduction of that exteriority into the interiority of he who loves, on the other. A life of love, then, is a Life. God, who is Love, thus becomes He who identifies living with eternal Being. Accordingly, we can reach God only if we live with love. But how?

The identification between living and Being in God stands in contrast to the present life that is so easy to neglect: only covetousness would grant exclusive importance to such a life. Just as the lover loses himself in the face of his beloved—Arendt would later say that the lovers' bond, like Christian "goodness," is "otherworldly"—present life is forgotten in the face of life.[51] And yet the subject (the believer) rejoices in life (in God: in *summum esse*) by loving it, and this rejoicing is possible only to the extent that the subject places his beatitude in an outside world where God *is*.

Temporally speaking, the outside world is nothing less than the indissoluble future of the past. The happy life is always already in the past, such that it is brought into the present only through the recollection. Accordingly, the role of remembering is central because it restores our access to beatitude. Arendt likes to point out that Saint Augustine uses memory and rejoicing to unite the blessed life, the present life, and remembering. The happy life is a life that is projected beyond and toward the future (that is, toward eternity) solely because of the "retrospective articulation of desire" that discovers it in the past (by remembering). The attempt to reach the origin of earthly life is at the foundation of every human aspiration.[52] In other words, life is what saves being from a fate of rejection from Being, and life is what links being, through recollection or confession [*ricordari*], with eternity as long as life is identified with love.

Although life does not abandon memory, it is a not a pure remembering of the past. Rather, life, like desire, makes itself known as an aspiration toward the happy life. Though dependent on nature and even more so on "the One who 'made me,' " a life in love thus harbors a sort of independence: it projects, surpasses, raises, and even *desires* memory. "Hence, transcending the faculties of perception, which we have in common with the animals, and rising gradually 'to Him who made me,' I arrive at 'the camps and vast palaces of memory,' " wrote Augustine in a passage from *Confessions* 10:12 that Arendt discusses.[53]

Thus, through this return to Being that is the life of love, being is faced with a permanent everlasting, and it acquires a permanent everlasting for itself: the human life cannot change because its being is immutable.[54] This very space shapes the difference between the Christian view of life as a way to reconcile with the everlasting, on the one hand, and the contemporary view of the rebellious man, on the other. This rebellious return, this desire for rupture, renewal, or renaissance that informs modern man and that is manifested by the revolutions that Arendt would subject to a trenchant reflection in *On Revolution* does not tone down a stabilizing "brush with God." The aspiration toward eternal Being has been replaced with the ideal of modification and of perpetual displacement. In Arendt's reading, however, Augustine's thought paved the way for a conception of life as mobility, alterity, and alteration. For Augustine, the creature contributes something quite specific to the homeostasis of immutability sought by the happy life. To the simultaneous and eternal universe, the subject adds what Arendt calls Augustine's "deflecting the Christian conceptual context."[55] By being born into a lasting simultaneity, man puts into motion a temporal succession.

Another aspect of life is introduced here: a life that is not the eternal life, but one that comes to pass in and through birth. Bearer of life and borne by life, "birth" (which will be a recurring theme in Arendt's writings), the life span between birth and death [*cite*], in the eternity of being, a world [*mundum*] in which life is revealed to be the product of our will: "Rather, it is from the divine fabric [*fabrica Dei*], from the pre-existing creation, that man makes the world and makes himself part of the world."[56]

This new definition of life is worthy of our attention: life constitutes the world. To the fact that the man born in Being lives in it and loves it is added another dimension: the dimension of *beginning* and *doing*. Beginning with the divine *principium*, human *initium* involves births and actions. As such, life transforms "creation" into the "world"—the creature befriends the world, of course, but even more important, he establishes it; he finds it already there [*invenire*], but at the same time, he makes it what it is [*facere*]. This inventive split is what gives rise to the possibility that the man-being can question his own being.

The end result, as Arendt infers from Augustine, is a new richness of life. As a beginning, birth gestures toward what has come before (ante) and, going beyond its end in death, the loving living being announces the duration of time to come (in Being, in the everlasting). In other words, the birth of man engenders time as well as a separation from Being, both of which generate questions: "Human life is viewed again as enclosed by the world rather than simultaneous with it. For continued life after death corresponds to birth 'after the world.'"[57]

This new sense of life represents an important shift. No longer eternal happiness or a recollection of Being of God in the beatitude of the lover, life has become a process of *questioning*. Flanked by the "not-yet" and the "already-more," life given to birth goes beyond the world by questioning itself. *Quaestio mihi factus sum*—"I have become a question to myself."[58] The Augustinian formula that Arendt explores even in *The Life of the Mind* depends on the experience of love that is born at the same time as are the will and the inner life of man.[59] This experience verges on Being [*tendere esse*] and, as an outgrowth of this tension, the creature is constituted "one more time" after being created by the Creator. By going from Being to Being and from eternity to eternity, life does away with the significance of finitude.[60]

We see here that Arendt, in reading Augustine, wished to get beyond the dichotomy between the objective and the subjective and to moor human freedom not in an internal psychic disposition but in the very nature of human existence in the world. The *initium* and the subsequent *principium* denote the presubjective determination that human freedom "begins spontaneously," as Kant puts it. It is because there is a beginning that we can begin, and by beginning with birth, we are destined for renewable births tantamount to acts of freedom. Heidegger's writings on the "worldhood" of *Dasein* foreshadow Arendt's reading of Augustine, as does his work on the "initial."[61] Although Arendt is inspired by Heidegger's notions, she approaches both beginning and birth with a perspective more akin to the perspective of Augustine's loving Christianity, and she diverges dramatically from the western European patriotism that Heidegger professed in his later work.[62]

Yet as innovative as it may have been as compared with ancient thought, Augustine's introduction of the birth-death sequence remains in some respects within the confines of an unequivocal endorsement of eternal Life, to the detriment of the present life. Day-to-day life is of no real consequence in the face of a reconciliation with the eternity of Being in beatitude. Leaving behind what she calls "the pre-Christian sphere of Augustine's thought," and indebted to Neoplatonism as well as to Greek autarky, the philosopher seeks to show that a new form of Augustinian reasoning is under way, one that generates a new logical train of thought that provides a place for the Creator.

No longer a cosmic being, but an Other of the creature even though He behaves like a human, the Creator God chooses through love, though He also *demands* and *forbids*. Accordingly, the law places itself at the heart of man, like an authority that poses questions and that thus returns to the questioning we have faced, so much so that the life that does not ask itself questions, the routine life, is what appears in biblical thought to be the "real sin" more than does ordinary desire. Furthermore, if the law forbids the world ("Thou shalt not covet"), God stands against life in the world, and concomitantly, the creature in the world stands against God. The authority of God is ever-present in this opposition: God is "the ever-present authority that man keeps confronting on his way through life."[63]

Arendt enjoys pointing out that life is a conflict under the biblical view of a Creator God. I would add that this idea of opposition and revolt increasingly applies to modern man, who draws from it not only the need to benefit from the goods offered by this world (which will culminate in the secularization that Arendt often disdains in her later writings) but also the faculties to develop his ability to pose questions. This psychic realm of questioning transmits rejoicing and guarantees the survival of the living being through its ability to represent, provided that the subject can oppose authority or at least oppose the boundaries of the Other. It is a rejoicing about love, of course, but a love that is conflicted: in all its fullness, a love of support and rejection, of pain and joy.

Freud's work gave voice to this conflict by revolutionizing our relationship with meaning. In fact, in direct contrast to the reconciliation of man in his isolation in the face of God [*coram Deo esse*] that we find in Augustinian recollection, psychoanalytic anamnesis reveals that permanent conflict is a precursor of psychic life. Saint Augustine had already developed this perspective by grafting his biblical reading onto Greek autarky. Unaware of Augustine's work in this regard, Freud, who also alluded to the Bible but who relied explicitly on the Oedipal tragedy, would later lend his ear to a dramatic, irreconcilable being. But Christian eschatology resuscitated this contentiousness only to ease it through the love of Life in life. This easing was successful, thanks to a subtle arrangement between a Life-*mimesis,* or a similitude with Being, and a Life-*questioning* from the standpoint of the interval between birth and death. When Arendt examines this success, on the other hand, she comes back to an eminently modern question: the question of the conflict and revolt endemic to the human condition, framed as a psychic life and an absolute Life. At the same time, she traces the origins of that question to the core of Augustine's thought. Without delving into the psychoanalytic repercussions of Augustine's discovery, Arendt explored, toward the end of her life, what Saint Augustine considered to be the primary faculty for human interiority focalized in this way—willing—and she also contemplated how it could be deconstructed.[64]

Finally, after birth and the conflict, it is the immediate that, for Augustine, provides the basis for the concept of "life" that

Arendt will "dismantle" throughout her entire work. And yet how can there be an immediate, an "other," if the world is forbidden? In the first instance, the immediate is represented by our "forebears" with whom I am linked by birth [*cognatio*], that is, with the large family made up of Adam's descendants. We encounter here the theme of the concrete, historical life, and we delve into the *socius* by way of our filiation with Adam. Yet what interests the Augustinian man about the intrinsic split in his life between eternal Life and present life is not the singularity of Adam, but simply what unites us all: our common sin and our common salvation in the life of Christ the Redeemer. I am indifferent to the unique life of my neighbor because, in this life, what matters to me is something else entirely: "the self-oblivion of craving would let man see his neighbor as well as himself only from an absolute distance." "For you love in him not what he is, but what you wish that he may be."[65] Augustine affirms, "*volo us sis*" [I wish that you were], the wish addressed to the other implicating a concern not for individual moral growth but for a rapture toward God [*rapere ad Deum*]. Arendt's writings include several iterations of the Augustinian formula *volo ut sis,* which Heidegger employed in a letter he wrote Hannah in May 1925 as well as in (he was not worried about repeating himself to the various women he loved) a letter to another lover, Elizabeth Blochmann, in 1927.[66]

Augustine's "innovations," particularly the way he adorns life with historical possibilities that are interspersed with the essence of beatitude, inspire Arendt's approval as well as her uneasiness. Thus the passage of humans through birth [*generatione*] evokes equality, plurality, descent, sinfulness, and death—in a word, the totality of the "human race"—and it shatters the autarky of the Greeks. In addition, the notion of a "neighbor" spawned from this human species acquires a new meaning that had not been apparent before Saint Augustine: the sinful equality of birth becomes a *"freely chosen . . . coexistence of people in their community,"* which for each of us is both freely chosen and newly restrictive.[67] By way of the Bible, Adam, and the Creator, Augustine proposes, in Arendt's view, a way of living in the world that is not merely the life of someone "created" in foreignness. Arendt engages in an implicit conversation with Heidegger on this front, a conversation that will become more pronounced in her later writings. The idea is one of a familiar life that, through its origins in the *generatione,* poses the question of the Other as a "new life," thereby commemorating the furthest reaches of the past, death, and the otherworldly. Will the link between the "former society" [*societas*] and this Other be possible? Impossible? Expressed not in the anonymity of "one," but in the mutual love [*diligere invicem*] that dissolves reciprocal dependence?

For centuries, Catholic theology would follow the path laid out by Augustine, a path that Arendt would later describe and develop in a way all her own. Though a stranger to the world, man continues to live in it; familiar and equal to the other, man can join the world only if he does away with the old life in the name of a new Life in Christ. The "new society" of life becomes a possibility, but only in suffering (by exaggerating our belonging to the Body of Christ) and in isolation (the other merely performs the function of a "passage" to our direct and solitary relationship with God). Lived in this way, life permanently changes man and is a cause for concern, in part because life itself and its progeny are endangered, but also because people can nevertheless be saved by grace, by the intermediary of a common concern for the immediate in a life of love: *volo ut sis.* This life-alteration, this life-split, as renewed by our reading of Arendt, proves vulnerable to promises and to historical occurrences as long as it does not neglect important concerns. By emphasizing the "nexus" formed by the human life's belonging both to the "human race" and to a "new being-together" in the life of love, the young student paved the way for her subsequent political thought. In all her work, Arendt would borrow notions from Christian philosophy but unknown to antiquity such as the "promise" and "forgiveness" that she would use as a reference and a political hypothesis.

It is thus tempting to see this youthful book and the way it reveals Augustine's concept of life not only as an elaboration of the "loves" Arendt experienced during those years (and whose suffering she gave voice to in her 1925 "Shadows") but also as a foundation for her later reflections. In fact, although the disastrous reality of Nazism and Stalinism drove Arendt to think about the sociohistorical causes of totalitarianism,[68] she would come back to the logical processes of life, termed the "human condition," to put forth a hierarchy of ways to articulate human experiences: *vita activa* on the one hand, *vita speculativa* on the other, and within *vita activa,* three types of activity: labor, work, and action.

By focusing on the life of thinking while taking issue with the metaphysical tradition that elevates the reflective life over the active one, Arendt shines a light on the active life, arguing that action itself ensures life. At the same time, *The Human Condition* wholly denounces the notion of "life" as the ultimate nihilistic value. Arendt violently denounces the vitalist activism that triumphs over *homo faber* but that ultimately entraps him in an automated way of knowing that "calculates" without "thinking." Arendt, then, in response to the reflections on life that Saint Augustine deems to be "insignificant" when it is not caught up in the love of the *beate vivere* or the *summum esse,* rails against the consumerism that overtakes human life when it forgets what is lasting and durable. She denounces the cult of the "individual life" and, in particular, the cult of the "life of the species" that is held out to be the ultimate modern good but that can no longer lay claim to even the most humdrum aspirations toward immortality. The life "process" replaces immorality, and it is presented as a fundamentally nihilistic value. Throughout this gradual paradigm shift, one that is ushered along by science and technology, Arendt points directly to Marx, who rendered men natural by stipulating that "the thought process itself is a natural process."[69] At the same time, Arendt does not neglect the relentlessness of scientists who ensure the triumph of *animal laborans* under the guise of a life sacred unto itself that contains no reference to the Other.

Arendt contrasts these wayward trends with a "specifically human" life. That expression stands for the "interval between birth and death," provided that such a space can be represented by a narrative and can be shared with other people. Such turns of phrase exquisitely refine her youthful reading of Augustine, a reading finessed by her subsequent political experiences as a female philosopher: "The chief characteristic of this specifically human life, whose appearance and disappearance constitute worldly events, is that it is itself always full of events which ultimately can be told as a story, establish a biography; it is of this life, *bios* as distinguished from mere *zōē* that Aristotle said that it 'somehow is a kind of praxis.'"[70] Thus the possibility that we can envision birth and death, that we can contemplate them within time and that we can speak about them with the Other by sharing with other people—in a word, the possibility that we can tell a story—is at the heart of the specific, nonanimalistic, and nonphysiological nature of human life. By implicitly referring to Nietzsche, who saw in the "will-to-power" a desire for life, and to Heidegger, who guided the biologism of Nietzsche, who he considered to be the "last metaphysician," toward the "serenity" of the poetic word, Arendt gave new life to the praxis of narrative. Challenging this quiet withdrawal from the poetic work, the young political thinker believed that action as narration and narration as action are the only things that can partake in the most "specifically human" aspects of life. This conception, which has Aristotelian origins, forges together the destinies of life, the narrative, and politics. The narrative governs the everlasting essence of the work of art, but as a historical narrative, it also accompanies the life of the polis and transforms it into a political life in the noble (and, since the Greeks, "threatened") sense of the word.

Hannah Arendt's reflection then moved toward a third and final stage. The meditation of the *vita activa,* though not abandoned, moved to the background and straight to the heart of the reflection on the "life of the mind" that she illuminated by "dismantling" it into its three components: thinking, willing, and judging. This process was already begun, however, in *The Human Condition.* If it is true that we can disturb only with impunity the hierarchy of human activities (labor, work, action; *vita activa/vita contemplativa*), and that such disturbances threaten both thinking and life by destroying either one, it becomes essential to preserve life by returning to the permanent exploration of its split and alteration, and of the complex figures that ensue. A product of the intertwining of life and thought that characterizes Christian eschatology and philosophy, Arendt drew a link between history and the deconstruction of the mind to show that life is not a "value" unto itself, as humanist ideologies would have it, but something that is realized only if it constantly *questions* meaning as well as action: "the revelatory character of action as well as the ability to produce stories and become historical, which together form the very source from which meaningfulness springs into and illuminates human existence."[71]

Hannah Arendt's many pronounced concerns about life-and-meaning authorize us to make some digressions whose timeliness is far removed from the preoccupations of our author but whose significance is implicit in her line of questioning.

Action, even as Arendt understands the term,[72] cannot by itself guarantee a free and creative life. The resumption of the "life of the mind," on the other hand, is capable of providing such a guarantee, as Arendt proved in her later writings. Despite her hostility toward psychoanalysis (which she viewed as an excessively scientific reduction of the "life of the mind" to mere generalities[73]), she considered the psychic realm to be open to the realm of other people, and she saw the world as a place in which the life of the mind could link the demands of praxis to the demands of a meaning poised for endless questioning—two demands that Arendt held dear. No one would deny today that labor turns the employees of the society of the spectacle into robots. The work of art itself has disintegrated into the baseness and minimalism of non-sense and nonmeaning. And political action, far from being a path toward what Arendt calls "disclosure," has been reduced to the mockery and emptiness of marketing gurus susceptible to influence and corruption. In other respects, scientific, philosophical, and psychoanalytic inquiries—the multidisciplinary approach that Arendt adopted with little fanfare and in her own style, though without laying claims to "pure philosophy" but rather "political theory" or even "political journalism"—have shaped the "life of the mind" as a diverse complexity of logical processes that produce multifaceted representations. These processes affect more than merely thinking, willing, and judging, which they do attempt to explore as carefully as they can. The plurality in question allows these logical categories or capacities to give rise to the untapped reserves of what can be sensed and represented.

The narrative, the ability to put a biography into words, thus becomes as necessary as it is problematic and as dangerous as it is heterogeneous. With the exception of her article on Kafka's metaphysical conflicts and an essay on Natalie Sarraute, Arendt the philosopher did not delve into the style of modern literature with its crises, conflicts, and discoveries. The classic narrative, which was Arendt's implicit point of reference, has now been damaged. Through such a narrative, a writing in search of rejoicing and demystification seeks to record the human condition. Like an expansion of Arendt's "narrative," when it is not an explosion of such, such writing explores and renews the psychic realm and, while using the recollection as a basis for examining the retrospective bond between man and meaning, between the creature and the eternal, and between the subject and Being, it exposes and puts into practice an incessant tendency toward conflict: a revolt. Life as a revolt is actualized in the nonthought of writing.[74] It also seeks to grow within the permanent questioning of recollections, pleasures, certainties, and identities, a questioning that underlies the psychoanalytic experience despite its worldly trappings.

Are we capable of envisioning other strains of discourse and action that would be the modern figures of mutability, of this perpetual outburst of meaning and the senses that Arendt sought?

With the exception of Arendt in her reading of Saint Augustine, no one else, in modern times, has reflected upon birth as a constant succession of new beginnings for a unique story, an unusual narrative, or a biography.[75] In the realm in which Nietzsche spoke of the "Eternal Return" that is not monotonous repetition but "the highest possible form of affirmation," Arendt, in line with biblical, evangelical, and Augustinian tradition, maintains a scansion: each birth is the "miracle" of this reviving, threatening, and promising "Eternal Return."[76] One could subject this cyclical incantation that accompanies the theme of birth in Arendt's writings to her own remarks on the idea of the Nietzschean "Eternal Return": "What makes [the 'thought of Eternal Return'] modern is the pathetic tone in which it is expressed, indicating the amount of willful intensity needed by modern man to regain the simple admiring and affirming wonder [*thaumazein*], which once, for Plato, was the beginning of philosophy."[77]

And yet, with humanity poised to program births and to alter genotypes, thereby shifting the dangers of innovation to an automatism, the question is transformed into something else: is it still possible to leave room for the flash of a surprise or for the grace of a beginning? Is it still possible to love the "specifically human" life outside the vitalist race for progress and success? Can we still parse this headlong rush by our shock or concern, by the potential and promise of this "miracle of birth" that sometimes runs the risk of being a humdrum or ill-fated event (an illness, a handicap, or stupidity) but that, through its status as an "event," serves as the ultimate, if not the only, way to revive our questioning the meaning of *every* life? Or has life as an event and a source of questioning become outmoded because it has been secured, standardized, and trivialized by technology?

Precisely because there are births—the fruits of men's and women's freedom to love one another, to think, and to judge before they become products of genetic engineering—we are able to enjoy the possibilities of will and freedom. Our freedom is not (or at least not solely) a psychic construction, but the result of our own existence, of being born: *initium,* or what Heidegger calls a "thrown-Being-in-the-world." Arendt retorts that our freedom results from starting something entirely new within the confines of the "frailty of human affairs": "The very capacity for beginning is rooted in natality, and by no means in creativity, not in a gift but in the fact that human beings, new men, again and again appear in the world by virtue of birth. I am quite aware that the argument even in the Augustinian version is somehow opaque, that it seems to tell us no more than that we are doomed to be free by virtue of being born." But Arendt is not content simply to detach the will from all psychological decision making by ensuring that the will depends on birth, which is itself distanced from any attempt at planning because it emerges within the tension of love. When Arendt returns to a later work of Heidegger's, she inscribes will with death, not as the future of life, but as the internal and intimate dimension of its occurrence, "sheltered" and "concealed" in the experience of the biography understood to be a "realm."[78] She also quotes a few lines from Goethe: "The Eternal works and stirs in all / For all must into Nothing fall / If it will persist in Being."[79]

Thus the intersection between this borrowing and revising gives rise to Arendt's conception of life and birth, which she sees not as biological experimentation but as the ultimate experience of renewable meaning. A woman who bore no children, Arendt bequeathed to us a modern version of the Judeo-Christian affection for the love of life through her constant drumbeat of the "miracle of birth" that combines the risks of beginning and the freedom of men to love one another, to think, and to judge.

Arendt left us with this thought so we might share it, and we can count on its being so shared, particularly by other women, regardless of whether or not they are "philosophers" or "political theorists." Indeed, the relative freedom of women today allows them to contemplate their motherhood more easily than ever before. The ordeal of motherhood in the very presence of the newborn to whom a woman bequeaths her being, far from fulfilling her, leaves her vulnerable and weakened. This ordeal links the mother to her child through an extraordinary bond that has no other analog in human existence, a bond that results not from a desire for an object (or a subject) but from a love for the Other. Maternal love could be seen as the dawning of the bond with the Other, a bond that the lover and the mystic will come to rediscover and that will be explored primarily by the mother as long as she resists using her sexual partner to settle scores with her own mother. This Other is not chosen, moreover, but is "ordinary."[80] It is in no way superior, but simply new, beginning dramatically and often tragically and sharing our encounter with death. That ordeal, if it is susceptible to the contemplation that Arendt invites us to undertake, could transform the women of the future into the guardians of the very possibility of life.

We should try, then, to understand the word "life" as Arendt did. It is not a "survival of the species" (which we have learned is possible with women as well as without them, in light of scientific achievements that multiply ruses and other forms of cloning). Rather, life is like a love for the ordinary person or for the neighbor, a love that is just as fragile as I am in the face of death and that, through my love as a woman-mother, constantly reinvents the infinite meaning of the diverse lives that such love gives me in return.

Thanks to contraception and abortion as well as to the techniques of artificial insemination, women today are protected from a fate of fertility or sterility. Women can also realize their personal goals as full participants in a modern age in which the human condition is dominated by science and shielded from transcendental laws. And yet this immersion in a scientific era does not preclude—indeed, it fosters—the *desire* to procreate and to be a mother. Even if this acute, even agonizing, desire to be a mother often resembles a will to possess, it is susceptible to analysis and is capable of embodying, in the context of what are now desanctified human affairs, the concern for the Other that lurks in the love for the other—a love that begins anew with each birth and that, through the father, rediscovers in maternal anguish its sense of perpetual questioning. This questioning does not bear on an eternity or on a transcendental *summum esse* but on the infinite meaning of what remains well within our grasp, my all-other, my all-the-same, the ordinary one. Within these psychic folds of maternal love shines the ultimate brilliance of the sacred that *homo religiosus* succeeds in transmitting to *homo laborans,* which devours him in turn. To transform the nascent being into a speaking and thinking being, the maternal psyche takes the form of a passageway between *zōē* and *bios,* between physiology and biography, and between nature and spirit. In this way, the legacy bequeathed by the Judeo-Christian tradition can be preserved, brought to light, and modernized—that is, if women manage to live it and to think it through.

To the extent that psychoanalysis questions a diverse subject—drive *and* meaning, unconscious *and* conscious, somatic *and* symbolic—it finds itself along the same frontier and it helps keep open, both parallel to the maternal journey and apart from it, the question of life as meaning and meaning as life. It is by unearthing the psychic functioning of each individual in the face of birth and death, by analyzing the structures and the dramas of the family triangle, and by knowing the way in which that triangle affects the psychic sexuality and unique thought processes of each subject that analysts can preserve our destiny of making sense in perpetuating the human species.

Maternal love for the ordinary life—and not the progress of vitalist technology that can engulf this love or, on the contrary, the backward-looking rejection of this progress on the part of conservative religions that are vociferously probirth—is in a position to guarantee our human condition as beings concerned with the meaning of being there. From this perspective, and taking into account the threats faced by this life (a life that some people venture to reproduce through technology in "total freedom" and that others mandate through religion and thus grant no freedom), we could predict that life, as Arendt understood the term, is either a feminine life or nothing at all. Of course, psychic bisexuality, which psychoanalysis sees in everyone, allows us to posit that a man could assume femininity of that sort, or even experience maternity defined as a tension present in the love between *zōē* and *bios*. And this situation will endure until technology has eliminated the threat of death—but will that ever be possible?

In the shadows of the Holocaust, it is worth noting that it was a woman, a Jewish woman, Hannah Arendt, who took the initiative in reopening the question of birth by breathing new meaning into the freedom of being. And therein lies the brilliance of her genius, whose very core touches on the crisis of modern culture along with its ultimate fate of life or death.

THE MEANING OF AN EXAMPLE:
RAHEL VARNHAGEN

Though a great fan of the "recounted life" and of the *bios-graphy*, Hannah Arendt wrote neither an autobiography nor a novel.

Only a single text from her early days, *Rahel Varnhagen: The Life of a Jewess,* comes close to the sort of narration to which the philosopher–political thinker accorded, like Aristotle, the privilege of fulfilling "life" in its dignity of "action." With the exception of the final two chapters, which she added in 1938, Arendt completed this work in 1933, that is, after she completed her dissertation on Saint Augustine but before she left Berlin later that year. Her book would not be published until 1958, with a dedication, "To Anne, since 1921," and a preface that clarified the author's intentions without truly revealing their full meaning:[81] "What interested me solely was to narrate the story of Rahel's life as she herself might have told it."[82] This telling declaration introduces a work that is dense, out of the ordinary, and peppered with many details that Rahel had revealed in her letters and diaries and that the author often repeats without citing them as such, intermixing them with philosophical reflections on the emotional life of a woman, on the difficulty of being a Jew (and, in particular, a Jewess), on spiritual life, and on social and political choices and constraints. Far from empathizing with her heroine, Arendt appears to be settling scores with Rahel, a being held dear, an alter ego that Hannah herself could never be although it threatened her, an alter ego that she dislodged of any compassionate depth with a relentless severity that was as ruthless as it was insightful.

The kaleidoscope of this writing could not be called a confession or a "romantic autobiography," even given the broadly diverse forms of this protean genre today. Rather, Arendt's book is an enacted example: the "special case" of Rahel is maneuvered, even manipulated, by the author in the name of a staging or screenplay that lets us see the marriage as well as the breakups that takes place between the heroine and the playwright.

Arendt's example, in the Kantian sense of the word, is one she will return to in her later writings: not a "case study" that illuminates an abstract point, but an individual or an event that stimulates the imagination. "The example is the particular that contains in itself, or is supposed to contain, a concept or a general rule [hence, Saint Francis, Jesus of Nazareth, or Napoleon]. The validity of this example [i.e., Napoleon] will be restricted to those who possess the particular experience of Napoleon, either as his contemporaries or as the heirs to this particular historical tradition. Most concepts in the historical and political sciences are of this restricted nature; they have their origin in some particular historical incident, and we then proceed to make it 'exemplary,' to see in the particular what is valid for more than one case."[83] Rahel's life, which becomes, in these terms, an "example," is transformed into a veritable laboratory of Arendt's political thought that shapes her future concepts in the face of this "particularity" whose "historical tradition" she shares.

The laboratory is also a spectacle in which Arendt the puppeteer pulls the wires, although this time she does not get as flustered as she did when she was a six-year-old girl. Arendt, an exceptionally talented actress, reminded her contemporaries of the famous actress Sarah Bernhardt and of Proust's Berma: "a magnificent stage diva," "a chthonic goddess, or a fiery one, rather than the airy kind," even in her lectures she made the drama of the mind and the dynamics of thought appear visible to the eye: "Watching her talk to an audience was like seeing the motions of the mind made visible in action and gesture."[84] For Hannah, then, the spectacle was important, but for her heroine, it was all-consuming, focused as she was on social visibility and recognition: "She carried about with her the outrageous conviction of being herself the 'battlefield'; that being herself nothing but the scene of action, she in reality provided the essential connection between disparate events. . . . She did not herself want to become entangled again; she wanted to be the immutable soil which absorbs everything into itself."[85]

In addition to her innate predisposition, Arendt had intellectual reasons to love the stage. She saw the "appearance" not only as the supreme manifestation of action but also as the most hospitable realm for those who decline to participate in action and who are happy to stand back and observe so that they might offer a candid judgment of their own. In that sense, Arendt had something in common with Kant, who admired the French spectators of revolutionaries more than the revolutionaries themselves, and whose insightful sympathies turned the French Revolution into "a phenomenon *not to be forgotten,* or, in other words, that made it a public event of world-historical significance. Hence: What constituted the appropriate public realm for this particular event were not the actors but the acclaiming spectators."[86]

This alchemy between making something visible and participating in it from a distance is precisely what frames the judgment of Arendt the biographer. Psychological exploration, though real and persistent, is subordinated at every turn to the political essay. The author denies any identification with a protagonist who clearly exerts an influence on her, and she discredits the introspective genre (which she attributes, with or without citation, to Rahel alone). In its place, she employs the interpretative style of a psychologist turned sociologist.

In sum, this *Life* is of a strange genre indeed, one to which she will never return, but one that, from the beginning, shows Arendt to be a theoretician outside the norm. In contrast to the ideal thinker of which Heidegger, at the beginning of one of his courses on Aristotle, said, "He was born, he worked, and he died," thereby suggesting that philosophers must minimize themselves for the sake of philosophy, Arendt, in this "example" taken from Rahel and an abreaction of her own personal judgment, presents a theater of thought that is invisible in her later writings but that is shown by *The Life of a Jewess* to enjoy a fertile logical process that will underlie Arendt's subsequent work. And we should keep in mind that Arendt, in *The Human Condition,* wrote the following about her favorite genre: "The theater is the political art *par excellence;* only there is the political sphere of human life transposed into art. By the same token, it is the only art whose sole subject is man in his relationship to others."[87]

But why did Arendt choose Rahel? A daughter of a jeweler and the product of a Jewish social niche that was well off without being truly affluent, Rahel Levin (1771–1833) was blessed with neither beauty nor grace. She lived comfortably, benefitting from the philo-Semitism of Frederic II of Prussia, but she was eventually confronted with the hostility of the bourgeoisie and the nobility. Indeed, ever since the new regime came into power in 1810, the ideas of the Enlightenment, which professed at least some sort of aspiration to equality as a complement to its nationalism, rekindled a latent anti-Semitism. Passionate about literature and philosophy although she herself was not a writer, Rahel managed to sustain, in her garret on the Jäger-strasse in Berlin between 1790 and 1806, one of the most scin-tillating romantic salons, a salon frequented by the Humboldt brothers, Friedrich Schlegel, Friedrich Gentz, Pastor Scleier-macher, Prince Louis-Ferdinand of Russia and his mistress Pauline Wiesel, the classicist Friedrich-August Wolf, Jean Paul Brentano, Ludwig and Friedrich Tieck, Chamisso, Fouqué, and others. Rahel even received Goethe there, having suc-ceeded in getting the great poet to write her a letter accepting her invitation to pay her a visit. In addition to her salon, Rahel was well known for her letters and diaries, some of which her husband published in 1834 in a three-volume set entitled *Ein Buch des Andenkens fur ihre Freunde* (The book of memories).

At once fascinating and irritating, Rahel Levin devoted her-self at first to a passion for life that she experienced as a sort of secular mystic would. Shifting between an emotional sensibil-ity and the loss of the self in a lover's abandon, she glorified pain, and sometimes nature, along with patriotic pursuits. Toward the end of her existence, she would return to her Jew-ish origins that she had previously disparaged: "Her whole effort was to expose herself to life so that it could strike her 'like a storm without an umbrella.' ('What am I doing? Nothing. I am letting life rain upon me.') . . . All that remained for her to do was to become a 'mouthpiece' for experience, to verbalize whatever happened. This could be accomplished by introspection, by relating one's own story again and again. . . . 'But to me life itself was the assignment.' To live life as if it were a work of art."[88]

That could have served as Rahel's credo, eager as she was to embody the cult of the exceptional, complete, and androgynous romantic personality—a goal that Arendt judged to be the "great error that Rahel shared with her contemporaries." Although Arendt describes her book as a contribution to the history of Jews in Germany from the perspective of the destruction of Jewishness that preceded Hitler's rise to power, she retains traces of the plea for a directed life that emerges from her dissertation on Saint Augustine's conception of love. Arendt contrasts Rahel with the need to take "her own person" more seriously, rather than the "life and history it imposes on the individual." Arendt tries to secure "a personal destiny" between "an individual's life" and "intellectual and social life." "If this book is considered as a contribution to the history of the German Jews, it must be remembered that in it only one aspect of the complex problem of assimilation is treated: namely, the manner in which assimilation to the intellectual and social life of the environment works out concretely in the history of an individual's life, thus shaping a personal destiny."[89]

Although she enjoys revealing the psychological details that punctuated her heroine's various passions, Arendt never discusses the pathology of this emotional woman whom she finds so appealing and yet so repulsive. Not once, in fact, does Arendt mention hysteria, depression, or paranoia. When Arendt recounts Rahel's oft-repeated complaint about her "infamous birth," she interprets Rahel's fate, intertwined in her eyes with Romanticism and German history, from the perspective of a failed assimilation.[90]

On that score, Arendt adopts the notions of pariah and parvenu, as well as conscious pariah and unconscious pariah, which
she learned from Kurt Blumenfeld but which originate with
Bernard Lazare (1865–1903).[91] Lazare, a legal adviser to the Dreyfus family, a friend of Péguy, and the author of *Anti-Semitism: Its
History and Its Causes,* attributed the rebirth of French anti-
Semitism to "the triumph of the secular state over the Christian
state. The Church held the Jews and the heretics responsible for
its defeat . . . and it began by attacking Israel. . . . Democracy has
allowed anti-Semitism to grow without protest."[92]

Later, in an important study entitled "Herzl and Lazare,"
Arendt endorsed Lazare's point of view.[93] What Lazare calls the
conscious pariah, "the carrier of a hidden tradition that is nur-
tured by the pride and grandeur of the persecuted," must abandon the prerogatives of the schlemiel who takes refuge in nature
and art, must reject the "parvenu" as a "filth" that "poisons," and
must rely on revolt to defend an oppressed people and its
nation.[94] Bolstered by this insight, Arendt pushes psychology
aside and, though she still does not avoid the traps of denials,
projections, and predominantly involuntary or unconscious
confessions, sets out by way of Rahel to surpass her own psychic
upheaval and to develop a political body of thought that is
rooted in experience. When all is said and done, then, Arendt's
book provides a veritable *history* of her political thinking in the
etymological sense of the word, a word whose root, as Arendt
likes to point out, is in the Greek *istor:* he who judges even as he
latches on, like a sensitive spectator, to exemplary events.

The evolution of her work explains why Arendt, even long
after the war, was relentless in her efforts to convince the German courts that *The Life of a Jewess* was a dissertation that she
wrote so she would be qualified to teach at the university. She
brought an action for damages against the West German government, alleging that she had almost finished her dissertation
before she left Germany in 1933, but that she had been unable
to defend it because of the hostility on the part of the academic

community of the day toward women, particularly Jewish ones. Although her petition was backed by Jaspers (who had earlier written her a letter that judged the book harshly and that even discouraged her from publishing it in German[95]), as well as by Benno von Wiese, and although she claimed that her text had been praised by Heidegger and Dibelius, Arendt's efforts at first led nowhere. In the end, though, she got a favorable verdict from the court in November 1971. Deemed qualified to teach as of July 1, 1933, she was awarded restitution for the salary she would have earned since that time. These machinations only call attention to the symptomatic aspects of her work, all the while rooting it even more passionately in her biography.

The recent English edition of the book shows that Arendt touched up her protagonist a bit. Although she corrected the errors of August Varnhagen, who cut out whole sentences and who hid the Jewish names of his wife's correspondents to make her writings more "respectable," Arendt herself adopted a sort of "husband's role" by making edits of her own.[96] In particular, she overlooked the fact that Rahel remained loyal to her newfound Christian faith even though she came to terms with her Jewish roots shortly before her death. Hannah Arendt, for her part, would not really question her initial interest in Christian theology, which she had pushed aside during the war, until she wrote the penetrating pages of "Willing," the second part of *The Life of the Mind.*[97] With Rahel, Hannah felt pressed to denounce assimilation from the perspective of two temptations: Catholicism and Enlightenment universalism. How can she conduct herself as a citizen without betraying Judaism? Does being a woman and a Jew mean that you do not lose yourself but that you also do not lose your own people? But must you detach yourself from Enlightenment culture, from romantically inspired philosophy, from your interest in Germany, and from yourself? Hannah Arendt achieved this renaissance by lovingly cutting into the flesh of another woman.

At the same time, it is as if Rahel and Hannah set forth, in the first nine chapters of the book, to highlight the experience of life—the individual life of a woman in love. Rahel's birth as a Jew as well as the rejection that it incited take a backseat to the trials and tribulations of love. She wallows in those tribulations, so much so that the reader wonders if her social status is the only determinant of the borderline states they entail. Rahel's biographer does not fail to notice this and remarks, "Rahel's struggle against the facts, above all against the fact of having been born a Jew, very rapidly became a struggle against herself." Despite her "faulty relationship [with other] people," a personality split between "treatment and judgment, 'before and after,' the decision taken behind the back of the person concerned," a tendency toward presumptuous interference when it is not the likes of suicide, Rahel is appealing because of her lucidity and because of the exceptional vivaciousness of her mind.[98] Wasn't she the first to judge herself even more harshly than did her detractors, naively and without any trace of insincerity?

And yet Rahel's lack of sangfroid and self-control irritated her biographer, who did not hold back in making some serious digs at her heroine's expense. Similarly, when Arendt states that Rahel lived "without ties," that her "freedom from ties was expressed in a senseless, objectless talent," and that she lacked any "fixation upon a particular historically conditioned world," she is internalizing the pejorative image of Jews that depicts them as awkward and adaptable, parvenus or mendicants (*schnorrer*) who know "neither models nor tradition." Rahel's "lack of style, disorder, and wanton delight in paradox" irritated Arendt, even though her "originality is genuine" and her "mania" remarkable. What a shame, though, that she "needs a whole life to form every opinion."[99]

Far from being wholly negative, the characteristics of the conscious pariah, who is deprived of any consolation, proves to be a formidable source of inspiration for the culture of truth and individuation that Rahel was more familiar with than were the Romantics, who came to her salon to learn about it. "Rahel had no home in the world to which she could retreat from fate; she had nothing to oppose to her destiny; hence there remained nothing for her but to 'tell the truth,' to bear witness, to gather in 'the splendid harvest of despair.'" The Jewish salon, and Rahel's salon in particular, is shaped as an external social realm far removed from convention; it plays to the artist's desire to be outside the world and outside tradition. That illusion enraptures Rahel, who believes that her guests authenticate her even though in truth they are utterly indifferent to her. "[She] shielded herself against [death] by [remaining in] contact with many people."[100]

By fleeing to Paris after her breakup with Finckenstein, Rahel was able to describe what a surprising pleasure it was to feel foreign by virtue of depersonalization: "Foreignness is good." Yet it is Hannah who adds the following, without citing Rahel: "to submerge, to be no one, to have no name, nothing that serves as a reminder; and thus to experiment, to try out, to see what things can still give pleasure." Arendt goes on to add the following unusual remark (applicable to both women?) about children: "The company of children also has the advantage of having almost nothing human about it." Such relations are a rapture rooted in relentless suffering, a rapture in which "people did not matter, but only what happened to them, their suffering, their living and dying. To know about this living and dying of theirs was enough for her; for herself she wanted nothing more, neither suffering nor joy. [That is what she had resolved.]"[101] Although the notion of resolution recalls Heidegger's "decision" or "resolution" [*Entscheidung, Entschlossenheit*], the psychological context surrounding Arendt's "example" of Rahel suggests psychoanalytic reasoning more than ontology. Rahel's biographer made a penetrating analysis of dissociation in the hysterical personality, one that may be likened to what woman analysts of the era were beginning to discuss: what

Joan Riviere called "the masquerade" and what Helene Deutsch called "as-if personalities."[102] Imperceptibly tinged with the already distant memories of Arendt's "shadows," Rahel's many passions and failures in love wove through her turbulent past: the Swede Karl Gustav von Brickman; Wilhelm von Burgsdorff and David Veit; Count von Finckenstein (her fiancé from 1795 until 1800); Friedrich Gentz; then the handsome Spanish secretary of legation Don Raphael d'Urquijo (also her fiancé, from 1801 to 1802); Alexander von Marwitz; and finally Varnhagen, the "beggar by the wayside," as he called himself, whom she would marry in 1814.

The aristocratic Finckenstein proved a sorry figure in Rahel Levin's salon. In the end, he realized this himself and withdrew, though it was his mistress who first thought he should step aside. But how painful it must have been to be a woman who depended on a man, on men, and on the "theater of 'life' in general." Indeed, "since Finckenstein's love had made her a specific person without a specific world and without specific patterns, outlined only by love . . . she was thrown back into the despair and hopelessness out of which she had come."[103]

On Rahel's relationship with Gentz, Arendt had the following to say: "He had only the alternative of officially loving her or officially denying her. . . . It contained, after all, another chance for reality, . . . a chance to have everything anyhow, in the world's despite. He would have been able to oppose to reality a second reality so strange, so unique, so complete within itself, that the true world could scarcely have surpassed it."[104] But he didn't do it, any more than Heidegger did.

And yet Gentz was not oblivious to the extraordinary bond they shared: "What we two together know, no mortal soul can even guess. I reproach myself bitterly now for not having, that time, insisted upon enjoying what you called 'that trifle.' Something so new, so extraordinary, as a physical relationship between people whose inner selves are reversed in each other, cannot possibly have existed yet."[105]

Gentz's remarks, which Arendt copied directly into her book, resonate with some letters from Heidegger to Hannah, as described by Elzbieta Ettinger: "The letters he wrote her that overflowed with lyricism, letters whose turns of phrase, approaching kitsch, contained awkward descriptions of a vibrant passion, must have left Hannah suspicious and confused about the desire he had for her. Heidegger's language betrays the discomfort he experienced when his reason gave way to passion. His first letters were measured and sophisticated, each word chosen with great care. His subsequent letters, on the other hand, are noteworthy for their conventional sentimentality, if not questionable taste. They speak in the unbridled language of emotion." Doesn't Hannah appear oddly close to Rahel, considering her extraordinary dependence on her lover after she decided to leave him in order to love him even more strongly: "I would have lost the right to live had I lost the love I feel for you" (April 22, 1928)?[106]

Although Arendt's correspondence with Blücher as well as her own notes show that between 1950 and 1953 she caught on to Heidegger's attempts to manipulate her, calling him a "fox" and a "liar,"[107] and although Blücher himself called Heidegger a *Hosenmatzdeutscher* [little-boy-in-first-pants German], Hannah's dependence on her professor-lover persevered in the form of an intellectual passion. Did she not write that *The Human Condition* was a book that "owed almost everything to him, in every way"?[108] And yet it was in the context of this loyalty that Arendt affirmed her difference—a difference with regard to thinking. She did so, however, without being able to avoid emotional actings-out, such as when she took a sample of Heidegger's handwriting to ask a handwriting analyst whether he was married (in other words, how could he be with another woman?) and whether Heidegger was "homosexual."[109] In the 1930s, through the example of Rahel, Hannah insisted that he was, though she was speaking of Gentz: "Not for a moment did he want her and her only; what he wanted was a situation, a connection, a 'relationship whose like there have perhaps not been many in the world.'" "He" wanted her "understanding," and would have "given up everything for her"—but that would have meant "giving up his place in the world," and he couldn't. In the Rahel-Gentz couple, on the other hand, we see another aspect of the Hannah-Heidegger couple: although "he" is a "party" to the real and to a clear-headedness that is more than just mere empathy, "she" cannot keep herself from always wanting to change the world: she is what Gentz called "anarchic."[110]

With Urquijo, the foreigner who provided Rahel with a "human shelter," Rahel was exposed to a cult of nudity and beauty that would become the ultimate manifestation of her passion. But that world was intended only to help her abandon the "life that made her a *schlemiel*" and to try to get her in touch with her soul, which is all he could do. A woman who loves more than a man could only have humiliated the diplomat in front of his circle of friends, all the more because Rahel, in her excess, seemed to be less interested in the "man" than in the "event." Humboldt and Gentz mocked the way she was so oblivious of individual differences; in their view Rahel was no more than a passionate person who "imitates" to excess and foolishness. She is at once "paradoxical [and] inexplicable." Much later, in Arendt's letters with Jaspers, during the time he was her thesis director, Arendt ironically remarks upon her own tendency to "exaggerate": "It's the nature of thought to exaggerate. . . . Besides, reality has taken things to such great extremes in our century that we can say without hesitation that reality is 'exaggerated.'"[111] In the end, who is exaggerating, Hannah or Rahel?

One last flame fired her up: Alexander von Marwitz. A distinguished *Junker*, disappointed with society, well established in his social class but concerned about having to belong to the real world, von Marwitz is able neither to live nor to commit suicide. Of course, Rahel projected her own thoughts onto him, "as concerned for him as for herself." Rahel's biographer points out her androgynous identification and nobiliary fantasy, deemed to be widespread in "assimilated" Jews but resisted by Marwitz. Marwitz is radically different from her and feels no need to justify himself; he displays his "contempt" and "disgust." Arendt hones in on this "disgust." In *What is Metaphysics?* (1929), Heidegger identifies Being with repulsion. Although Rahel, on the other hand, is rebellious, she lays claim to her own role and to "equal human rights." The amused reader cannot help gloating as Arendt pokes fun at the two lovers. She really digs into Marwitz, who strives to live a life that is "more muted, milder, less personal, . . . with constant awareness of the greatest perceptions of the spirit" and who refers his mistress to God! Indeed, Marwitz is none too worried about a woman so sublime. Let her revel in her extraordinary solitude. Let her take up her concerns with God. "I who [know] the God to whom you refer me. . . . Shall I be exiled without being dead?" moans a despondent Rahel under the caustic eye of her biographer.[112]

Arendt prefers a different Rahel, one who is "full of rebellion and full of fear" and one who is predisposed to such bald pretensions as the following: "I am as unique as the greatest phenomenon on this earth." And yet that Rahel is also capable, with the wisdom of age, of sharply criticizing her life "experiences," which, she acknowledges, amounted to trickery. Or do they mask a false personality? "I lied. The loveliest lie, the lie of a truly great passion." Rahel distances herself from her life and her being, consumed with anxious, "ghostly" fantasies: "She saw her life from outside as a mere game, like something she had never lived. . . . Her life became a narrative to her." Arendt's heroine manages to metabolize the tragedies of her life by relying on a sort of self-analysis stimulated by the narrative lucidity that she held dear and that would be facilitated by her own circumstances, such as her correspondence with Rebecca Friedlander and Pauline Wiesel, as well as by political developments.[113]

Karl August Varnhagen, born in 1785 and fourteen years Rahel's junior, played a decisive role not only in her assimilation but also in the evolution that incited her rebellion. This "beggar by the wayside" professed to her his boundless enthusiasm, and he discovered the meaning of his life by witnessing the life of his wife. An Enlightenment figure like Gentz (but without his high standing), and a humble man like Finckenstein (but without his nobility), Varnhagen aspired only to "serve [her] as if [she] were a Greek classic." Arendt scoffs at "the preposterousness of making himself the prophet of a woman," and she does not hide her scorn for a husband whose "priestly fidelity" made him "chained to his wife like a priest to his idol." Varnhagen made Rahel into "the anecdote on which he fed all his life" and "saw her only as a tremendous curiosity, . . . the third glory of the Jewish nation" after Christ and Spinoza. It is just too much, for the biographer prefers a man who is a man and who fulfills his role as such. And yet Arendt also lays bare the manipulations of the generous husband, a threat that Rahel should have pushed away and left behind. Although Rahel never truly loves him, she convinces herself that Varnhagen is "her only reliable friend" and that he "understands" her. It is enough to snatch away from her biographer these sumptuous lines on the human force of understanding that, beyond its effect on individual people, opens the doors to the marvelous palaces of "language" and "friendship." "If the appeal fails, if the other refuses to listen to reason, there remains nothing human, only the eternal differentness and incomprehensible otherness of inorganic substances. We can love alienness with the complex tenderness that lovely forms extort from us. We can turn away from the alien with that utter indifference or total disgust we reserve for abortive products of nature. But that cannot prevent the abortive appeal from reacting back upon ourselves, from transforming ourselves into a product of nature and debasing rationality to a mere quality. . . . Thanks to . . . the human communication provided by language, [differences] could be included in the development of a friendship."[114] Having dispelled her "shadows," a new Arendt emerges, a wizard of friendship who, despite her "fits of anger" and "tendency to exaggerate," was considered to be a great friend by all those who knew her.

Varnhagen made some headway into diplomatic circles, working at the embassy as a secretary-journalist in an era in which everyone was stricken with a patriotic and assimilationist fervor. Beginning in 1810 Rahel changed both her first name and her last name and became Friederike Robert, like her brother who had had himself baptized, and then had herself baptized in 1814 and married Varnhagen. At that point she became Antoinette Friederike Varnhagen von Ense. And thus the pariah, sometimes conscious and sometimes not, became a true parvenu. "The Jew must be extirpated from us, that is the sacred truth, and it must be done even if life were uprooted in the process."[115] By reading Fichte's *Addresses to the German Nation,* Rahel found some valid reasons for adhering to such a truth, and she abandoned the arrogance of the pariah who lays claim to extraordinary experiences. But she also realized that, to the extent that the Jews became emancipated, they became isolated. What could she do about it?

She first decided to save herself by what her biographer called "finding an individual way out." She would let herself "be carried along by someone who was still below, but on his way up." Through her social and patriotic actions that nevertheless failed to integrate her completely with the German nation, Rahel was able to set aside for a time her melancholia and to take on the likes of "a personality" without shying away from the fact that "her rejection was really final."[116]

The superficial parvenu knew she was an inveterate pariah, which did not spare her from being the brunt of Arendt's sarcasm, particularly when she dreams of a world peace initiated by the female sex: "I have *such* a plan in my heart to call upon all European women to refuse ever to go along with war."[117]

We remain perplexed in the face of the biographer's mocking harshness; she feels not the least bit of sympathy for this feminist pioneer. After all, is Rahel's feminist and pacifist naïveté really so appalling? But that is not the path that interests Arendt, and even if she pokes fun at the precocious European, she still awaits impatiently the parvenu's rebellion against Judaism.

Rahel owed her rebellion to two precious confidants: Rebecca Friedlander and Pauline Wiesel. Between 1805 and 1810, the mediocre novelist Rebecca Friedlander received 150 letters from Rahel, who was pleased finally to have someone to confide in and to share her "curiosity" with someone who knew how to "eavesdrop" on her: "Is it not worthwhile, if only out of curiosity, to live one's life through and to eavesdrop on sorrow and joy?" Along the way, as Rahel came to take refuge in writing, she discovered the force of Goethe's poetry and genius. Goethe's own Judaism is never mentioned, even though it was through a woman of his people that Rahel experienced for herself the force of his words, before she rediscovered in Goethe's verbal magic the veritable assimilation of poetry and life—so she could appropriate it for herself without any hesitation: "That is exactly as my [sic] life seems to me. . . . His words freed her from the mute spell of mere happening. And her ability to speak provided her with an asylum in the world." Is "she" Rahel or Hannah? Rahel thus devoured Goethe's *Wilhelm Meister* and interpreted it to be an important source of stimulation for getting rid of her originality to become "a human among humans," tantamount to being German, or rather a parvenu. Arendt suggests on this score that Goethe's role in the history of the Jewish people was to facilitate the Jews' entry into German culture under the guise of the cultivated Jew. It will be pointed out later that "the cult of Goethe initiated by Rahel . . . produced a sort of mythology of the parvenu . . . the illusion . . . that one can escape his Jewish destiny be becoming famous, as Goethe did."[118]

Although Rahel's feelings of being excluded were exacerbated by the growing hostility of the ruling class and other groups, she eventually came back to her origins. Her change of heart is particularly apparent in her correspondence with Pauline Wiesel, the mistress of Louis-Ferdinand, who frequented her salon on the Jägerstrasse. A woman of easy virtue, Pauline tried to seduce Varnhagen herself. Rahel took no offense, but was rather amused by Pauline's freshness, which she deemed proof of her nonconformist leanings. Arendt interpreted this display of female attachment as Rahel's desire to remain a pariah while accepting that she was a parvenu. Increasingly panicked by her assimilation, Mme Antoinette Friederike Varnhagen von Ense asked herself, "Can one get entirely away from what one truly is? . . . After all, the much-praised freedom of the outcast as against society was rarely more than complete freedom to feel despair over being nothing . . . not a sister, not a sweetheart, not a wife, not even a citizen."[119]

In this psychosociological portrait, Arendt overplays her hand as a well-meaning confidante. She does not deprive herself of the pleasure of psychoanalyzing her heroine by decoding Rahel's dreams in a strange chapter entitled "Day and Night." How odd to include such an intimate section in a thesis aimed at "qualification." All the protagonist's dreams represent thinly veiled acts of sexualized exclusion and humiliation. Arendt interprets the dreams to be a refuge in a nocturnal universe. They protect Rahel from exclusion but, more important, reveal the conflicts that she pretends to have smoothed over in her day-to-day existence, which is made up of deceptions and compromises. "Thus the continuity of the day was constantly challenged by the night."[120]

Remarking upon a dream about a white animal, half-sheep and half-goat, Arendt makes an effort to transplant the words Rahel emits as she "called this loving darling my pet," a pet who, in reality, was Finckenstein. These words bear an uncanny resemblance to some poems from Hannah's own youth, "Lost in Self-Contemplation" and "The Shadows."[121]

Behind the symbol of duplicity (half-sheep, half-goat), the lover's bestial appearance suggests that lovers are in fact excluded from humanity—another theme dear to Arendt the Augustinian, who places love outside the world. And the painful repetitions of this dream express an intolerable tension, as we learn from our improvisatory analyst's insightful diagnosis.[122]

Another dream stages a new rejection scenario: Rahel sees herself pushed from the top of a rampart by all the citizens of Athens.[123] Aren't the Athenians the model citizenry for Arendt, and for the idol of the post-Romantics in whose eyes the Greeks announced the essence of their Germanism? It would be hard to conceive of a dream more foreign to the Jews. And in another dream, Rahel is sleeping between Bettina Brentano and Mary, the mother of God. Is Rahel finally accepted by the mother of all Christians? Indifferent to the sexual (or, in this case, homosexual) meaning of dreams, Arendt sees only the relentless presence of an attractive yet threatening universe of goyim to which the dreamer so painfully aspires, though to no avail.

By "becoming ultimately incapable of grasping generalities, recognizing relationships, or taking an interest in anything but [her] own person," Rahel the parvenu nevertheless preserves too many of the pariah's faults—as well as too many of his good qualities—such as an awareness of the falsity of her situation, which spares her from becoming a simple parvenu who finds herself completely taken in. Once Rahel acknowledges the "bankruptcy of life," she learns to compensate for the prevarication of the parvenu through a "view of the whole."[124] Is an autobiographical narrative in the form of a "view of the whole" the only available cure for the masquerade that she constantly stages and manipulates?

Arendt believes as much, with the caveat that we not forget Rahel's birth. Taking refuge in assimilation "had been a desperate attempt at rebirth" even though "it was not possible to be born a second time."[125] Arendt returns here to the Augustinian theme of birth, but for the first time she casts it as a definition of the Jewish being. As she later put it, Arendt considered herself a Jew not by virtue of her belonging to a religion, but "by birth": "I have always regarded my Jewishness as one of the indisputable factual data of my life, and I have never had the wish to change or disclaim facts of this kind. There is such a thing as a basic gratitude for everything that is as it is; . . . for things that are *physei* and not *nomo*."[126] And yet, following Arendt's work on Saint Augustine, the term "birth," which Arendt uses here to indicate Rahel's Jewishness, is incapable of being limited to a piece of biological data, even one that is recognized and that deserves such recognition. The same reading will reveal a prepolitical attitude that the philosopher adopts, although at the same time she considers it to be a setback and a merely temporary solution. Nor is birth a pure given of Being; rather, it exposes newness at the heart of a plurality to be forever rediscovered and reconsidered. We realize here that Arendt uses the theme of birth as manifested in Rahel to recast fundamental notions of ontology into both political sociology and a poetics of narration, with psychology (or psychoanalysis) lurking in the shameful "shadow" of this intellectual adjustment.

Arendt's approach to birth becomes more explicit toward the end of her biography of Rahel. Indeed, once life became one with Rahel's enemies, "it was transformed into an unending succession of insults." Arendt flushes out of every assimilation the trap of assimilating anti-Semitism. In her view, Enlightenment universalism can cause the Jew to abandon "the historical actuality of [his] entire people" and "the aid of other Jews" and to fade away into the "sphere indicated for me by nature" before realizing that he has "tumbled from these sublime heights into the hands of enemies who rejoiced in having for once caught a wholly isolated Jew, a Jew as such, as it were, an abstract Jew without social or historical relationships. They could treat this Jew as the very essence of Jewishness." Arendt then goes on to emphasize the "equivocation" of the assimilated person (male or female) through an analysis that foreshadows *The Origins of Totalitarianism*: "To negate Jewishness fully and without ambiguity would have had the same effect as an unequivocal affirmation. Being a Jew could develop from a politico-social circumstance into a personal, individual problem only for persons who for whatever reason equivocally wanted 'to be Jews and at the same time to not be Jews' (as the contemporary liberal theologian H. E. G. Paulus once brilliantly phrased it). *As a personal problem the Jewish question was insoluble.*"[127]

What was she to do? Arendt approves of—and exaggerates—Rahel's return to her origins, and she praises Rahel for acknowledging to Pauline Wiesel her overwhelming insubordination: "[You should not] be ashamed of your Jewish birth and of the nation whose misfortunes and defects you know all the better because of it; you must not abandon them for fear of people's saying that you still have some Jewishness about you!" Embracing a Saint Simonian vision of a Europe founded not on conquests but on equality—a vision that Arendt's later writings would elaborate upon in much greater detail—Rahel began to write her brother in Hebrew. She welcomed the young Heine with open arms, seeing in him someone extremely "enthusiastic" about "the cause of the Jews and their attainment of equality before the law." Arendt prefers to forget about Rahel's Christianity, her dedication to the cult of the Enlightenment and the cult of German patriotism, and her German friendships; instead, she concludes with Rahel's letter to Heine in which she communicates with assurance "the history of a bankruptcy and a rebellious spirit." In a 1952 letter to Jaspers, who criticized the "distortions" and "errors" Arendt made with respect to her heroine, Arendt explains that her book "was written from the perspective of a Zionist critique of assimilation."[128]

In the final analysis, and in conjunction with the political lens that forms the undeniable backdrop of her book, Arendt, as she accompanies Rahel, is working through the hysteria of a woman—not to dispose of it or even to analyze it but to transform it into a way of "living well" in the sense of the Aristotelian ideal that she so enjoys evoking. We can safely call this alchemy a sublimation, particularly because Arendt turned her Rahel into a "qualification" and a "thesis." A narrative that is dramatized and shared with other people served as an essential mediator for this metamorphosis. Thanks to this appropriation of the life of a Jewess at the peak of the Romantic era, another life of a woman and a theoretician could be experienced and described, though this time within the context of political reflection. Perhaps Hannah was a Berma who could have played the role of Rahel. Following this self-analysis in the company of Rahel, Arendt became the Berma of the concept. Say goodbye to the "professional thinkers"!

ARENDT AND ARISTOTLE:
A DEFENSE OF NARRATION

The missing link between Arendt's early work and her celebrated writings on totalitarianism may be found in her conception of human life as a political action that is revealed to us through the language of a story and of history. Before we begin interpreting her later political texts, we would be well served by turning our attention to the apparent defense of narration that infuses all her writings. Pausing here for a moment will make us better able to appreciate the ethical and philosophical ambition of those later texts, which in turn may help clear up the many problems and ambiguities that her commentators have been so quick to point out.

We must tell the story of our life, then, before we can ascribe meaning to it. Arendt praises Rahel's ability to spin a tale, which is what enables her heroine to avoid both the "pure continuance of life" and "oblivion," and "to fit herself [instead] into history, to save her own little portion of history." Is the philosopher defending the work of art here? Not exactly. After lauding the art of narration, Arendt ignores it, not only because Rahel's narrative accounts—"pitiful trivialities"—are the result of a "despairing game" but also, and more fundamentally in light of Arendt's later thinking on the subject, because the narrative alone, however brilliant it may be, is incapable of saving a life. *Action* is what Arendt advocates, thereby giving a taste of what was to come in *The Human Condition*: "From such impoverishment, too, only solidarity with certain others afforded salvation. . . . It did not suffice to be an example; it was necessary to have been an example for the sake of someone else."[129] Narration matters, but action is what ultimately prevails, provided that it is a narrated action. Harkening back to Aristotle's position in *Nichomachean Ethics* and the *Poetics,* Arendt discusses Heidegger's Platonism.

Arendt's critics are quick to contrast her Aristotelianism and Kantism with Heidegger's Platonism, that is, when those same critics are not attributing her alleged political irrationality to the influence of Heidegger's political thought. Both of these disparate and schematic readings have been disputed.[130] In truth, Arendt subscribes to the Heideggerian strategy of deconstruction [*Abbau*] and repetition of metaphysics, to the Heideggerian themes of disclosure [*Erschlossenheit*], unveiling [*Unverborgenheit*], and publicness [*Offentlichkeit*], and to his emphasis on finitude, contingency, and the otherworldly as structures inherent in human freedom. At the same time, she takes these concepts out of their existential context and transposes them into a political one. All the while, Arendt's rereading of Aristotle and Kant, which complements her familiarity with Nietzsche and Heidegger, was the very motor behind her project of appropriation and transposition.

Arendt's reading of Aristotle's *Nichomachean Ethics* in *The Human Condition* causes her to distinguish *poiesis,* the activity of production, from praxis, the activity of action. Arendt downplays the limitations inherent in the production of works of art: "works" or "products" "reify" the fluidity of human experience into "objects" that are "used" as a means to an "end." Reification and utilitarianism already play a role in a *poiesis* understood as such. On the other hand, the heart of the polis, in the sense of a "space of appearance" or a "public space," sees an action (praxis) that is not a fabrication but the "greatest achievement of which human beings are capable." Rooted in the Aristotelian notion of *energeia* [actuality], the term "praxis" applies to all activities that do not pursue an end [*ateleis*] and that leave no work behind [*par' autas erga*] but that "exhaust their full meaning in the performance itself."[131]

The polis, which is modeled in Arendt's view after Homer, Herodotus, and Thucydides, is the ideal space for action as she understands the term. This polis is not an actual location, as was the Roman city-state with its legal underpinnings, but an "organization of the people as it arises out of acting and speaking together" that can emerge "almost any time and anywhere" as long as "I appear to others as others appear to me." The polis is thus the locus of the in-between, a political model that is founded on nothing less than "action and speech," though never one without the other.[132] What sort of speech is it?

Loyal to Heidegger's teachings, Arendt insists that poetry, whose material is language, is perhaps "the most human . . . of the arts. . . . Condensed" and transformed into "memory," poetry actualizes the essence of language. And yet poetry is also the "least worldly" of the arts; it stands apart from the in-between.[133] How is this poetic speech able to emerge in the polis so that it might describe the virtuosity of its heroes?

Phronēsis, which means practical wisdom, prudence, or judging insight—as distinguished from *sophia,* which means theoretical wisdom—is what inserts speech into the "web of relationships."[134] But we must first find a discourse, a lexis, that can respond to the question, Who are you? a question implicitly addressed to each newcomer that forces him to consider his actions as well as his words.[135] Such a discourse will be the province of the narrative, an invented story that accompanies a true one. In interpreting Aristotle, Arendt articulates the space between these two types of stories with an originality that distinguishes her theory from formalist narrative theories as well as from the narrative theory of Paul Ricoeur.[136]

Arendt implicitly acknowledges the disconnect between a true story and an invented one, and the theoretician highlights the particularity of this endeavor as it emerged in the Greek model of the city-state. The Homeric *hērōs,* though no half-god, connoted his own distinctiveness, but it was "no other than [that of which] every free man was capable." The space of appearance in the polis invites each person to display an "original courage" that is nothing less than the "willingness to act and speak," to leave behind a private sanctuary, to expose himself to other people, and, in their presence, to "risk the disclosure."[137] Therein lies the first political condition for the "disclosure": to manifest *who* I am, not *what* am. Then, in the agonistic ordeal of competition, the "*who* [I am]" is pitted against other people and uses that very rivalry to prove its stature. Just as this stature is not measured based on the motivations or results of action, it resides not in victory, but in "greatness" [*megethos*].[138] In the end, it is a uniquely political question because the heart of the web of human relationships is where we shall define what is uncommon, what is extraordinary, and "what is great and radiant—*ta megala kai lampra,* in the words of Democritus."[139]

We must acknowledge that the actor himself, no matter how heroic his exploits themselves may be, cannot constitute wonderful action. Action is wonderful only if it is memorable. And where should we search for memory? The spectators are the ones who "accomplish" history, thanks to a thought that follows the act. This accomplishment takes place through recollection, without which there is simply nothing to recount. It is not the actors but the spectators (provided that they are capable of thinking and recollecting) who make the polis a productive place to organize memory and/or history and stories.

This brings us right to the heart of Arendt's notion: for a true story to become a recounted story, two related events must occur. First, there needs to be an in-between that leads the way to memory and testimony. Second, the type of narrative must be determined by an in-between that provides the logic of memorization as a means of detachment from lived experience ex post facto. Only when both conditions occur can the "happening" be turned into "shared thought" through the articulation of a "plot."

Arendt returns to this "dimension of the depth of human existence" that is memory when she stigmatizes the crisis of modern culture as being the "risk of forgetting": "The tragedy began . . . when it turned out that there was no mind to inherit and to question, to think about and to remember. The point of the matter is that the 'completion,' which indeed every enacted event must have in the minds of those who then are to tell the story and to convey its meaning, eluded them; and without this thinking completion after the act, without the articulation accomplished by remembrance, there simply was no story left that could be told."[140]

Having thus acknowledged the disconnect between the enacted story and the narrated story, Arendt does not believe that the essential feature of narration can be found in the fabrication of a coherence within the narrative or in the art of spinning a tale. She is not unaware of this "formal" or "formalist" aspect of Aristotle's theory: what is beautiful does in fact demand greatness [*megethos*] as well as the uniting of the disparate parts [*taxis*].[141] But she spends little time on the technical structure of the narrative, focusing her attention instead on *Nichomachean Ethics*. In Arendt's view, the most important thing in the narrative-testimony is to recognize the "moment of accomplishment" and to "identify the agent" of the story.[142] The art of the narrative resides in the power to condense the action into an exemplary space, in removing it from the general flow of events, and in drawing attention to a "who." We can turn to Achilles, whose exploits were short lived, for an example of great narration. The shortness of the narration itself favors disclosure because the "who" emerges, as Heraclitus put it, in an oracular manner: the oracles "neither reveal nor hide in words, but give manifest signs."[143] The sign is condensed, incomplete, and atomized: it gives rise to the infinite action of interpretation.

That still leaves the dangers intrinsic to speech, which "hardens" or "reifies" the fluidity of signs and which at any moment can root the *energeia* of this action and its narrative [*muthos*] in the finitude of a character, when it is not in the notion that is "produced" by such and such an "author." In truth, history owes its very existence to humans, but it is not "made" by them, according to Arendt and Plato.[144] If we get too wrapped up in the coherence of a plot, we forget that the main goal of plot is to disclose.[145] Disclosure has two important characteristics: the beginning as it is ordered by each action, and speech to the extent that it generates a biography ex post facto.

A narrative of this sort, one that is formulated in the web of human relationships and that is fated to the political in-between, is fundamentally bound up with action. It can manifest that essential logical process only if it becomes action itself. In other words, such a narrative must expose itself and act as if it were "drama" or "theater" and as if it were "playing a role." Only then can *muthos* remain *energeia*. If narrative is to become a means of disclosure and not simply remain stuck in reification, it must be acted out. Opposing the static mimesis, Arendt reclaims the gestural theater as the modus operandi of the ideal narrative.

From the archaic era through the Catholic liturgy, this enacted narrative—also known as living speech—has informed the quest for a political realm consisting of unique features that can be shared with other people. But Hannah Arendt is the one who revived this agenda as a political project at the heart of the modern crisis of culture: "The specific revelatory quality of action and speech, the implicit manifestation of the agent and speaker, is so indissolubly tied to the living flux of acting and speaking that it can be represented and 'reified' only through a kind of repetition, the imitation or *mimesis* which according to Aristotle prevails in all arts but is actually appropriate only to the *drama*, whose very name (from the Greek verb *dran*, 'to act') indicates that play-acting actually is an imitation of acting."[146] Acting, seeing, recollecting, reaching the recollection through the narrative are all steps along the royal path to the disclosure of the "who," which adds up to a veritable politics of narration in Arendt's work.

The narrator's gaze, which Arendt considers to be essential to narration as she rereads Aristotle, and which could be deemed "theatrical" or "political," is not the same thing as the quiet astonishment of the philosopher confronting the unnamable, which invariably turns out to be death. The gaze is neither the *bios theōrētikos* of pure thought nor the solitary disclosure of pure poetry, but the contemplation of the actions put into words in the city-state. In an exceptionally obscure passage in Aristotle that has already been discussed at length, Arendt sees a communal realm made up of political concerns that are in some ways pre- or posttheoretical, a realm that admires neither man himself nor the mortal being but the capacity of the narrated action to immortalize the living.[147] Arendt remarks, "The famous passage in Aristotle, 'Considering human affairs, one must not . . . consider man as he is and not consider what is mortal in mortal things, but think about them [only] to the extent that they have the possibility of immortalizing,' occurs very properly in his political writings. For the *polis* was for the Greeks, as the *res publica* was for the Romans, first of all their guarantee against the futility of individual life, the space protected against this futility and reserved for the relative permanence, if not immortality, of mortals."[148] "We" are immortalized by becoming a "who" that acts within the political realm, and only then by crafting a memorable narrative.

Why does speech that recounts action enjoy such a privileged role? First, because it is in action, in the sense of a capacity for beginnings, that the human condition of individuation can be realized. The "living flux of acting and speaking" is manifested in mimesis, which, according to Aristotle (and as emphasized by Arendt), does not signify the imitation of an isolated character but an "imitation of acting"—through "the plot."[149] Whereas for Plato, mimesis allows itself to be trapped, like a slave to appearances, and whereas *The Sophist* rejects "the plot" or *muthos* as being infantile, Aristotle, in considering the tragedy, discovers a unique *mimesis praxeōs.*[150] The characters of a tragedy are not reified as such because the members of the choir, who "do not imitate," devise a commentary about the characters that responds to hubris (excessive pride) through *phronēsis* [wisdom]. Further, the "composition or writing of the play" effects an imitation that occurs only when it is represented, and thus acted out, as theater. All these actions endow language with the movement of life and with public wisdom. As Aristotle put it, "Tragedy is not an imitation of men but of actions and of life. It is in action that happiness and unhappiness are found, and the end we aim at is a kind of activity, not a quality; in accordance with their characters men are of such and such a quality, in accordance with their actions they are fortunate or the reverse. Consequently, it is not for the purpose of presenting their characters that the agents engage in action, but rather it is for the sake of their actions that they take on the characters they have. Thus what happens, that is, the plot, is the end for which a tragedy exists, and the end or purpose is the most important thing of all." The prototype of this disclosure through action is, as we have seen, the "drama" that takes "what is acted out" and puts it into words. Arendt summarizes her reading of Aristotle in these already cited remarks: "This is also why the theater is the political art *par excellence;* only there is the political sphere of human life transposed into art. By the same token, it is the only art whose sole subject is man in his relationship to others." This notion belies the vision of the power of poetic speech to disclose, a vision Arendt encountered in the works of Heidegger: "However, thinking is poetizing. . . . Thinking says what the truth of Being dictates; it is the original *dictare. Thinking* is primordial poetry."[151]

Yet Arendt is not engaging in some sort of naive return to Aristotle in order to restore a putative original purity. A reader of Nietzsche and Heidegger who is attentive to their successive "dismantlings" of metaphysics, Arendt returns to *phronēsis* and the narrated action only to respond to questions that the two men already posed about action, its freedom, and its practical limitations. In the wake of her predecessors and in a way all her own, Arendt's goal was to find respite in a world capable of being shared with other people.

Solitary and withdrawn, the philosopher's ecstatic *Dichtung* shows Being sheltering its nothingness through a solitary decision [*Entscheidung, Entschlossenheit*], retains what already exists, and anticipates the future with a nod toward the present [*Augenblick*]. Arendt, on the other hand, emphasizes that action is impossible in isolation. Only the sovereign is isolated, and an innovative actor is not necessarily a sovereign. At once an agent and a recipient, the hero is innovative and takes initiative. New, infinite, and unforeseen, action adapts itself in the heart of plurality, and, inversely, enables plurality to ensure *eudaimonia,* this "blessedness" or rather this "living well" that accompanies each man throughout life but that is visible only to others. Thanks to myth and drama and to tragedy and comedy, in the realm of the polis, the hero is the one who sets an example by summing up all his life in a single deed, "so that the story of the act comes to its end together with life itself." Action and life thus depend on the narrator, who has a passionate drive "to show [himself] in measuring up against others."[152] Whereas the Socratic school stood apart from politics

and action and occupied the world of the prepolitical, Aristotle, whom Arendt follows in this instance, advocates the "sharing of words and deeds,"[153] which in turn increases "the
chances for everybody to distinguish himself, to show in deed
and word who he was in his unique distinctness." Arendt
would later suggest that the political narrative was, during the
age of Pericles, the only way to construct an "organized remembrance" as "a remedy for the futility of action and speech."[154]

Arendt's reconsideration of *Nichomachean Ethics* and the
Poetics can be read only in the context of Heidegger's earlier
reading of Aristotle, one that gave rise to his 1924 course on
Plato's *Sophist*—a course that counted a young Hannah Arendt
among its members. It has often been noted that Heidegger, by
reading Aristotle, learned to contrast Husserl's primacy of consciousness with the primacy of practical existence and thus to
found the study of existential analytics (the first part of fundamental ontology). It is less well known that Heidegger's reading betrays metamorphoses, exaggerations, and obliterations of
certain essential features of Aristotle's thought.[155] Heidegger
appears, for example, to absorb Aristotle's distinction between
poiesis and praxis (between fabrication and action). The difference that he establishes between *Umwelt* and *Welt* could be
read to mirror Aristotle's separation (between the public environment, the impersonality of the "they," preoccupation, prov-
ident circumspection, *Wozu* [in light of what?], on the one
hand; and the domain of Being, the self, the concern, the resolution, *Worumwillen* [in view of itself, or of nothing], on the
other). Whereas the world of specific discovery that surrounds
poiesis is the *technē* [expertise] evoked by *herstellen* [to produce, to fabricate] and enlivened by a specific clairvoyance or
prakitsche Umsicht, praxis is an end by itself. That is also the
case with *Dasein*: "*Das Dasein existiert umwillen seiner.*" For
Aristotle, however, clairvoyance, tailored to praxis, is a *phronēsis* [discernment, prudence, or judging insight]. Therein lies
the origin of Heidegger's modification: the absent *phronēsis* is

replaced by *sophia,* in the sense of a view toward Being and not toward the "web of human relationships."

In truth, for purposes of Aristotle's debate with Plato, *sophia* cannot be applied to the frailty of human affairs, which, because they cannot be encapsulated by a solid body of knowledge, require an intellectual, emotional, and moral capacity that is the province of each person, not of specialists. *Sophia* develops through varied deliberations within the space of appearance known as the polis. Although Aristotle emphasizes the preeminence of the examined life, which is the only one that displays "something within him that is divine," he distinguishes between *sophia,* theoretical wisdom, and prudence, which is indispensable to "the affairs of men and [to] things that can be the object of deliberation."[156] The object of *phronēsis* is not only the universals but also the singulars "since the thing to be done is an ultimate particular thing . . . which cannot be apprehended by Scientific Knowledge, but only by perception."[157] Is this not the same *phronēsis* [judging insight] that Arendt scrutinizes through Kant's "aesthetic judgment," which she, like the German philosopher, will use at the end of her life as the basis for a political philosophy?[158]

Phronēin [thinking soundly] indicates, "in an indissolubly intellectual, emotional, and moral sense, sound thinking and appropriate discernment."[159] Aware of its own limits, a human quality that can be contrasted with the *noesis* of the gods, *phronēsis* is particularly apparent in tragedy.[160] In fact, wisdom acknowledges that tragedy, as a catastrophe, arises when the powerful simply conflict,[161] thus exaggerating their features when it would more prudent to observe the *mesotēs* inherent in *phronēsis* and to forbid everyone from declaring himself the master and imposing a dogmatic point of view. In this sense, the representation of tragedy is indispensable to public life, to a *bios politikos* in which speech stages conflicts with an eye toward resolving them in the public realm and with a spirit of equality.

Arendt invokes the tragedians when she wishes to show that a conflict is implacable, particularly the conflict between the "thinking Self" and the "real Self," *bios theōrētikos* and *bios politikos,* and when she finds it necessary to maintain the conflict as such without any artificial resolutions or specious endings. Richard III, the Shakespearean sovereign, thus displays a "conscience," a capacity for "critical thinking," only *after* the crime—following the example of Socrates, who, though a fervent admirer of public life, did not "meet the other fellow" who made him "examine things" until he had returned to his home in solitude.[162] But if Socrates had been obliged to refuse to occupy any public office so he could devote himself entirely to his role as a goading thinker, he would have had to destroy the *doxa* and to align himself with an Oedipus who was "left without any *doxa,* in its manifold meanings of opinion, splendor, fame, and a world of one's own."[163] Similarly, Arendt delves into *Oedipus at Colonnus* and expounds upon Sophocles' double-sided message. On the one hand, the tragic flaw deprives the hero of the "world" and leaves him to ponder the nonbeing, the "not to be born," as well as the risk of returning to it. On the other hand, from the mouth of Theseus emerge words that help us endure the burden of life: "It was the polis, the space of men's free deeds and living words, which could endow life with splendor." As Aristotle put it, "for what appears to all, this we call Being."[164] In Aristotle's footsteps, and in appropriating the Being that appears to us all, Arendt concludes that the space of appearance has the potential to be a political realm made up of diverse actions and exchanges.[165]

With Heidegger, on the other hand, the resolution of *Dasein* is private; it operates beyond the domain of public opinion, far removed from the comprehension of other people and the indulgence that characterize *phronēsis.* The *Gewissen* [the conscience] is an intimate form of knowledge through which *Dasein* in its power-to-be belongs only to itself. By suppressing plurality, *Dasein* hones in on the encounter between the alone with the self, in a "resolved assumption of 'being-for-death'" that encompasses *Gewissen*. At that point *Dasein* becomes that haven for unique intelligibility, that pedestal for the *science* of Being that is known as metaphysics. This scientific bent results from the removal of internal plurality from Aristotle's *phronēsis* and from the promotion of Platonic thought as the authentic experience of action or praxis.

In fact, from *Was ist Metaphysik?* (1929) to his writings contemporary with his bout with the occupational authorities, Heidegger claims to be a follower of Plato's *Republic.* Even if Heidegger was not wrong to remark that Aristotle's Being is modeled on a being and that Aristotelian ontology thus tends to be confused with theology, and even if he was right to warn against an ontology of the world in the sense of a *phusis* and of presence and constancy so that he might revive the totality of temporality—based not on *phusis* but on *Dasein*—he still remained attuned to the conflict and plurality of Aristotle's praxis as well as to its innate modes of discourse: the myth, the story, and the tragedy. The end result is not only a solipsistic unification of action in thought only, but also a transposition of the solipsism of the *sophia* that will replace *phronēsis* even in the public domain. Accordingly, Heidegger will consider the public domain itself not as a temporary plurality that remains to be perfected but as a unanimous and mystical passion: the passion of the people. And once we identify the thinking of Being with praxis, we are steered toward a coercive "scientific" commitment and to a voluntarist day-to-day action of the people. The total disregard for plurality and for the depth and the fleetingness that characterize that radicalization turns it by definition into a species of tyrannical thought and, in the worst case scenario, a dictatorial action.[166] Even after the *Kehre*, Heidegger's reversal, or turnabout, during the mid-thirties, and even after suffering the philosophical, if not political, consequences of his errors, particularly for having abandoned metaphysical "science," Heidegger was no less inclined to continue assimilating action and thought, inasmuch as thought "corresponds initially" to language: "Thinking is the most fundamental characteristic of acting."[167] Loyal to the Platonism that he nevertheless "dismantles" in his *Nietzsche*, Heidegger persists in distancing himself from Aristotelian plurality. In contrast, Arendt's entire philosophical and political trajectory emphasizes the distinction between the power of Platonic ideas and their tyrannical latency that comes to the fore when the thinker applies them while acting in a political capacity, and the opening up of "authority" that Aristotle—that other philosopher of "ways of life [*bioi*]" and "one of the most consistent and least self-contradictory great thinkers"—was the first to consider. For Aristotle, it was an "authority" that was founded not on the notion of "domination" but on the notion of a "nature" made up of "differences."[168] We must not forget, then, that the discourse that belongs to this other authority that Arendt strives to restore beyond modern secularism is, quite simply, the narrative.

This rapid return to Aristotle by way of Heidegger was necessary not only to understand the implicit exchange that Arendt had with her former professor from Marburg, often without mentioning his name and while adopting an arguably "ironic" tone, but also to see their interplay in the Platonic sense of a dialogue or a displacement that is in no way a Voltairian mockery, a display of scorn, or a caricature. And yet Arendt, who decried Heidegger's refusal to read her books or to discuss them with her, could have said the same thing about Heidegger that she often said about Plato by way of the following remarks of Cicero: "I prefer before heaven to go astray with Plato rather than hold true views with his opponents."[169] At the same time, her affinity for thought and for Plato endures in the importance she gives to *theōria*, which is what enables men to remove themselves from the cycle of birth and death, and, by aligning themselves with praxis, to leave behind the futility of everyday affairs and to approach the divine. Without disposing of this conquest of thought or of *bios theōrētikos* and without denigrating the contributions of Heidegger's work, Arendt seeks to reveal its "fallacies" and, significantly, to restore the plurality of action—as well as some ways in which its manifestations can be disseminated—by referring to Aristotle.

Arendt's meditation on action and the narrative reveals that she found the Homeric universe indispensable for crafting a conception of the life of language as *muthos*-fable by honoring the excellence of a hero such as Achilles, and as a drama, by drawing attention to the inherent energy of speech.[170] Her meditation also inspired her to consider metaphor at some length,[171] with the result that she essentially affirmed that philosophical concepts at first, and all forms of human language in the end, refocus the mind on the world of the senses: "The metaphor provides the 'abstract,' imageless thought with an intuition drawn from the world of appearances whose function it is 'to establish the reality of our concepts' and thus undo, as it were, the withdrawal from the world of appearances that is the precondition of mental activities," thereby illustrating concepts through "examples" based on "common-sense reasoning." Relying on Plato's *Seventh Letter* (which Heidegger discussed in his course on *The Sophist*) but especially on the Aristotle of the *Poetics,* Arendt grants metaphor the privilege of transforming thinking into a phenomenon and of reconciling it with "perception" and "common sense." Metaphor, which can be "overwhelming" and even dangerous but which allows "the world of appearances [to insert] itself into thought quite apart from the needs of our body" since language is itself metaphorical, partakes in the flux of surprising and innovative births: "The sheer naming of things, the creation of words, is the human way of *appropriating* and, as it were, disalienating the world into which, after all, each of us is born as a newcomer and a stranger."[172] Because the life of the mind is always already grasped by a language that is metaphorical, sensorial, and divisible, it is not just a *thaumazein,* what Plato calls an ineffable, unspeakable [*arrēton*] wonder and what Aristotle calls a speechless [*aneu logou*] one. On the contrary, the only appropriate metaphor for the "disalienated" life of the mind is the sensation of being alive. On that score, Arendt quotes this well-known passage from Aristotle's *Metaphysics*: "The thinking activity [*energeia* that has its end in itself] is life."[173]

Arendt intersperses her rereading of Aristotle with frequent references to Saint Augustine in an effort to formulate an indelible bond between the deed and the word, a bond that culminates, above and beyond the poetic word, in the supreme "revelation" of the "uniqueness" that makes human plurality into the "paradoxical plurality of unique beings": "With word and deed we insert ourselves into the human world, and this insertion is like a second birth, in which we confirm and take upon ourselves the naked fact of our original physical appearance."[174] At that point, Arendt transforms the gravity of Heidegger's Being-toward-death, which finesses the asceticism of the self into the disclosure of language, into a series, more radiant than desolate, of ephemeral strangers who fade away only when they are dismissed by the unforeseen births of newcomers: "Human action, like all strictly political phenomena, is bound up with human plurality, which is one of the fundamental conditions of human life insofar as it rests on the fact of natality, through which the human world is constantly invaded by strangers, newcomers whose actions and reactions cannot be foreseen by those who are already there and are going to leave in a short while."[175]

We can now understand more easily why Arendt is such a supporter of the historical narrative (the memory of human plurality in Herodotus and Thucydides, personal confession in Saint Augustine), as the historical narrative joins word and deed. The narrative is a memory of action that is itself a perpetually renewed birth and strangeness and that acquires its ontological potential from the very fact of our birth. Heidegger's *Sein und Zeit*, on the other hand, makes only a single reference to myth, to the fable of Care (via Caius Julius Hyginus, written in Rome during the age of Augustus and communicated by Herder to Goethe, who included it in the second *Faust*), as well as declaring Thucydides to be superficial.[176] Having asserted that not only words but grammar in particular are unable to grasp the "entity" in its Being, Heidegger contends that only the "complexity of concepts" and the "harshness of our expression" can provide a remedy. The philosopher locates them in the "ontological sections" of Plato and Aristotle, which he compares favorably with the "narrative section from Thucydides": "We can then see the altogether unprecedented character of these formulations which were imposed on the Greeks by their philosophers. . . . It is one thing to give a report in which we tell about *entities,* but another to grasp entities in their Being."[177] Arendt notes that Heidegger, after his "reversal," "seems no longer interested in stressing the very close relation between philosophy and poetry" but instead veers toward "something he has said nowhere else," a riddle: "thinking must poetize on the riddle of Being."[178] Under her terminology, is it an enigma-drama, an enigma-narrative?

Still, unlike her master, Arendt relies on the "famous words of Pericles in the Funeral Oration" as reported by Thucydides to praise the "scene" and the "witness" that the polis shapes in the glory of the hero through the intermediary of the memorable narrative, such that "those who forced every sea and land to become the scene of their daring" have no need for "either Homer [or for] anyone else who knows how to turn words."[179] "Men's life together in the form of the *polis* seemed to assure that the most futile of human activities, action and speech, and the least tangible and most ephemeral of man-made 'products,' the *deeds and stories* which are their outcome, would become imperishable."[180]

We can now understand the implicit dialogue between Arendt and the above passage from Heidegger's course on "The Reversal" that assimilates thought, action, and language.[181]

Arendt's main point here is that if thinking is *sophia,* political action accompanies it and transforms it into a *phronēsis* that knows how to partake of the plurality of the living. It is narrative, and not language itself (although language is the pathway to narrative), that provides the mechanism for innately political thinking. It is through the recounted action that makes up narrative that man corresponds to life or belongs to life, inasmuch as human life is invariably a political life. The narrative is the first dimension in which man lives, through *bios* and not through *zōē,* a political life and/or an action recounted to other people. The initial correspondence between man and life is the narrative. Narrative is the action that is the most readily shared and, in that sense, the most intrinsically political. Through narrative, it turns out, the "initial" is whittled away into the estrangement that pervades the infinite nature of narration.

THE TALE OF THE TWENTIETH CENTURY

Arendt broached the subject of narrative more concretely in her studies of twentieth-century authors. She favored writers who wrote stories that bore witness to the course of history and that revealed the hidden meanings of history to their contemporaries. Arendt liberally quoted poets in her texts—among them her friends Randall Jarrell and Robert Lowell, as well as Rilke, Yeats, Emily Dickinson, W. H. Auden, Mandelstam, Valéry and René Char—not for their brilliant words themselves but for the wisdom they imparted. The theoretician was attracted not to narrative prowess or stylistic singularity, but to "narrative themes": brief narrative sequences that condense the personal testimony of historical experience into a metaphor.

Marcel Proust—whom Arendt read with both patience and passion—took Swann, Charlus, and the Guermantes and painted a portrait of the intrinsically anti-Semitic philo-Semitism that infused the French salons in the years before and after the Dreyfus Affair. The Arendtian art of citation extracted from *In Search of Lost Time* one of the "superimpositions" that Proust adored, one that targets the assimilated Jew but other "clans" as well—including French society as a whole—through the famous phrase: "The question is not, as for Hamlet, to be or not to be, but to belong or not to belong."[182] Through her interpretation of Proust, Arendt asserts that the secularization of "Judaism" into "Jewishness" entails abandoning "identity" ("to be") in favor of "belonging" ("to belong"), and she shows that this transformation had tragic consequences for European Jews in the twentieth century and that it culminated in the Holocaust: "Jewish origin, without religious and political connotation, became everywhere a psychological quality, was changed into 'Jewishness,' and from then on could be considered only in the categories of virtue or vice."[183]

An immense photograph of Franz Kafka adorned Arendt and Blücher's New York apartment at 95 Morningside Drive. Kafka is represented, in Arendt's thinking, by a parable, "He," which describes the "time sensation of the thinking ego," the "battleground where the forces of past and future clash with each other." Arendt first draws attention to the "extreme parsimony of Kafka's language" by linking Kafka's parable to Nietzsche's allegory of the "now" [*Augenblick*]— which is itself represented by a gateway between two paths. She then turns to Heidegger's interpretation of the image, according to which the view of the "now" is granted not to a beholder but to "the one who *himself* is the now."[184] Arendtian reading is constructed as a true literary mosaic that interlays stories from Kafka, Nietzsche, Heidegger—and Arendt herself. The philosopher does more than observe, however, for she also becomes the "battlefield" for thoughts and for the history of her century in her language.

In an earlier study on Kafka (1944), Arendt began by praising the author's "absence of style" and his "absence of love for the words themselves, to the point of coldness." Although the critic obviously abhors "all manner of experimentation and affectation," her rather simplistic study of Kafka's writing makes two important observations.[185] First, she affirms that "what is wrong with the world in which Kafka's heroes are caught is precisely its deification, its pretense of representing a divine necessity": can evil, then, be "divine"? More significant, and more in line with a literary perspective, is Arendt's interpretation of Kafka's hero: he may "lack all the many superfluous detailed characteristics which together make up a real individual," but he is more than the simple reflection of a bureaucratic universe in which society functions as a machine that the hero struggles to destroy. In Arendt's view, Kafka does not present realistic characters—made famous by the bourgeois novel—but "models." It is not their "reality" that interests the writer, but their "truth," which is "the product of thinking rather than of mere sense experience."[186] Kafka, who is more of a thinker than a naturalist novelist because he thinks what he feels, sketched out models for thinking where the reader expects to find characters.

In reading the *Autobiography of Stefan Zweig,* the political theorist returned to the story she had recounted in her life of Rahel: the drama of an assimilated Jew who hoped to overcome his ambiguous status and to distinguish himself as a celebrity in Viennese society—only to endure in the end the humiliation of rejection. Zweig's rejection forced him to confront the reality of the Jewish people, but because he was incapable of political engagement, this "exile from the paradise of cultural enjoyments"—as Zweig described himself—could contemplate only the quiet despair of suicide. Zweig provided us with an incomparable demonstration that "from the 'disgrace' of being a Jew there is but one escape—to fight for the honor of the Jewish people as a whole."[187]

The Arendtian pantheon of contemporary storytellers was completed with Hermann Broch for the "earthly absolute" and the musical "abstraction" that characterized his style; Walter

Benjamin for his "bad luck" and his "gift of *thinking poetically*" through paradoxes that drove him to suicide; and Isak Dinesen, alias Karen Blixen (one of the rare women who—along with Nathalie Sarraute and Rosa Luxembourg—found favor with Arendt's pen in these "dark times").[188]

Behind the man's name Isak Dinesen (which reminds us of the photograph taken in the 1950s of a boyish Arendt) hid Karen Blixen, whose life was not without similarities to the life of the woman who chose her as her subject. Karen Blixen was the daughter of an emancipated mother (a suffragette, as Martha was not—but then didn't Martha know Rosa Luxembourg?) and a father who died too young (Karen was ten years old, whereas Hannah was seven when Paul Arendt died). The novelist married a man who had syphilis (like Hannah's father) and suffered the terrible effects of that disease herself (no parallel in Hannah's life). Karen-Tania, who went by Titania, believed that women were unsuited for the glare of public life. She hated the trap of "writing" and detested people who took themselves too seriously. Like Hannah, she loved to laugh: by adopting "Isak" as her pseudonym, she chose not just any man's name but a word that means in Hebrew "the one who laughs." A mere analogy becomes a veritable twin when Arendt recalls that it was a *"grande passion"* (like Rahel's? like Hannah's?) for the unclassifiable and impossible Denys Finch-Hatton that determined the course of Titania's life as well as her desire to narrate and then to write. Titania was unable to put her life together until she had lost everything, and only then could she put everything into words. Our wily reader discovered, however, that her Sheherazade was in love—as Shakespeare would have it—with nothing more than the head of an ass. A word to the reader: it would not be a good idea to force the comparison between these two women. And yet a sort of twin emerges when Arendt draws attention to one of Isak Dinesen's essential thoughts, an idea that could just as well have been her own: "Without repeating life in imagination you can never be fully alive; 'lack of imagination' prevents people from 'existing.'"[189] Hannah elaborates upon Dinesen's idea: "If it is true, as her 'philosophy' suggests, that no one has a life worth thinking about whose life story cannot be told, does it not then follow that life could be, even ought to be, lived as a story, that what one has to do in life is to make the story come true?"[190] The epigraph of the chapter "Action" in *The Human Condition* comes from Dinesen: "All sorrows can be borne if you put them into a story or tell a story about them." From Rahel to Titania, the pattern is complete: at the time Hannah wrote the article (in 1968), she already knew that her own life would become a real story as well as a recounted one.

Blixen-Dinesen's lover was the sort of man who rejected the world. Arendt considered extremists—whether conservatives or revolutionaries, thinkers or criminals—to be united in their common refusal to accept the world. The reader recalls Arendt's philosophical master, the former Nazi and the solitary poet. Meanwhile, the nonconformist storyteller neither accepts nor rejects the political life but is happy merely to be acting through speech. But what traps are laid in this enacted narration. And those pitfalls are just as fascinating to our philosopher, who concludes her study of Dinesen with an extended recapitulation of her stories. Elsewhere, Arendt appears ready and willing to devote herself to teaching litera-ture: "If I were a literary critic, I should go on from here to talk about the all-important part the sky plays in Brecht's poems, and especially in his few, very beautiful love poems."[191] But Arendt is neither a Sheherazade nor a literary critic: she is "nothing but" the embodiment of political vigilance—one who was the first to take notice of none other than Louis-Fer-dinand Céline.

Arendt was indeed one of the first critics to discuss Céline, whom she believed exemplified an "alliance between the mob and the elite."[192] Céline's thesis "contain[ed] exactly the ideo-logical imagination that the more rational French antisemitism had lacked," she wrote in *The Origins of Totalitarianism*, citing the anti-Semitic pamphlets of sinister memory.[193] She expanded upon her analysis and concluded by suggesting that the formalism of artistic elites—avant-gardes like those in the Bauhaus movement—gave rise to a cult of technique and anonymity. In her view, the elites scorned the "grandeur of man" proclaimed by Robespierre, and they were prepared to pay a price, the "destruction of civilization," for the sake of destroying "respectability." To the elites' "desire for the unmasking of hypocrisy" might be added an "aversion to the philosemitism of the liberals": thus a "fictitious world" for the rootless masses is born out of the elites' "lack of a sense of reality."[194] Arendt's analysis is no doubt perfunctory, but it is not without relevance to the field of "human affairs."

Kipling and his origin myth, Lawrence of Arabia and his English Self, Barrès, Maurras, and others as well (including the oft-mentioned Péguy) complete Arendt's universe of narrative references: the true "origins" of her *Origins of Totalitarianism*.[195]

Nathalie Sarraute was the only contemporary author to whom Arendt devoted a complete study. Arendt found herself seduced by a narrative that departed from the canons of the classical novel to "crack open the 'smooth and hard' surface of these traditional characters" and to succumb to "psychological vivisection."[196] Arendt acknowledged that she preferred Sarraute's tropisms about this "inner life" to the ripples that might spread out from the psychoanalytical couch. Arendt delighted in the cruelty and irony with which Sarraute explored the catastrophic interiority of the selfish "I": each word becomes a "weapon" when it is not a "commonplace" expression or a cliché. Meanwhile, the family and society break up and descend into the futility of multiple incarnations of the "They." And the most insignificant "They" is none other than the so-called intellectuals. Once again, Arendt's analysis engages with narrative, only to bypass technique in favor of disclosing social mechanisms—and, here, the psychosocial comedy. There is a "moment of truth" in Sarraute in which the clash of two subconversations generates a "metamorphosis"— the fleeting glimpse of an unsustainable revolt. Arendt finds that this "moment of truth" has a dramatic quality that is unique in contemporary literature. Even so, and even though this "Age of Suspicion" amuses her greatly, she hesitates to embrace its radical disenchantment. In its place, she would rather save the "common world" and "natural kinship"—even though the antinovelist's bitter tales reveal the duplicity of such human communities. Ten years before she wrote *Lectures on Kant's Political Philosophy*, Arendt encountered Sarraute's barbs on the subject of "taste," which Kant considered to be the foundation for social ties.[197] But Arendt preferred to conclude on an optimistic Kantian note: against the false "They," there may nevertheless exist a possible "We," a valid community of reader and author, so fragile and yet so strong.

Finally, Arendt broached the subject of Brecht. She admired Brecht's melancholy genius, but she warned against the expectation that the irresponsibility endogenous to poets (like philosophers?) could be at all politically relevant: poets are adept at thinking but are incapable of judging. Since their work sanctions what Arendt calls "the chronic misbehavior of poets and artists," they need not seek the public's approval. Although poets deserve our aid and forgiveness, they "can sin so gravely that they must bear their full load of guilt and responsibility."[198] The most crushing of these burdens, which was borne so dramatically by Brecht, is no less than the death of talent itself.

We might fault Arendt for failing to grasp that the poetic language of a narrator—such as Proust—is a way to join the "thinking ego" and the "self as it appears and moves in the world." More effectively than any philosophical concept or mystical vision, poetic language of this sort can translate the *nunc stans* of the senses and breathe life into a recovered past.[199]

We might be worried by Arendt's Lukács-style sociology that allows her to declare of Kafka, a bit too hastily, that "style in any form, through its own magic, is a way of avoiding the truth";[200] to announce that the complex destiny of the classical novel could only "presuppose the decline of the citizen" as understood by Kant or the French Revolution; or to propose that, in the face of a world ruled by hidden powers, Kafka wanted nothing else than "to be a citizen" and a "member of a community." Our beloved Kafka is supposed to "frighten" to the point of inspiring cabalistic interpretations, even satanic theology, when in fact he dreamt only of becoming a "citizen."[201]

We might further regret that Arendt did not recognize the need for rebellion—an intrapsychic need but a historical one as well—that led the century's avant-garde to an unprecedented reevaluation of narrative structures, of the word and the self. This need for revolt was accompanied not only by melancholy and "desolation," as Arendt explained, but also by psychosis. And these borderline states (experienced by individuals as well as by the "mob") were expressed in the work of an author such as Céline, who proved to be their most representative witness, if not the most prudent or the most clearheaded. Art, and in particular the art of narrative, has a history that does not repeat past problems and old solutions. Today's narrative is more akin to clinical protocol than to moral judgment. It is up to us to discover the causes and the fate of this history, not to stigmatize it.

But that is not what really interests Arendt, who seeks the optimal solution to the "frailty of human affairs." Through this political lens, narrative art is subordinated to the just act that it may or may not illuminate. The illustration of just action may even consume narrative art: aesthetic privilege and greatness of the work simply are not enough to make Arendt forget the Aristotelian ideal of *hou heneka*: the ideal of a life that is both beautiful and good.

In Arendt's view, the artist, and the modern artist in particular, is the quintessential *homo faber*: a deeply mediocre form of humanity who embodies the modern tendency to regard contemporary works as opportunities for commercialization and consumerism. Taken to its logical extreme, might not the greatest work be, for Arendt, a nonwork—a work not written, a work that has not taken the trouble to "reify" itself into a "product"? Socrates dedicated himself to the endless search for true judgment in a perpetual interrogation of the self and of other people, without neglecting a polis in which disparate opinions and lives could conflict. Arendt cannot credit Socrates—that anti-Plato, stinging gadfly, birthing midwife, paralyzing torpedo-fish—with being the source of "the opposition of truth and opinion . . . certainly the most anti-Socratic conclusion that Plato drew from Socrates' trial."[202] Far from being a benefactor of the city, even though he believed virtue could be taught, Socrates left to the historian an example of thinking in motion, of a *bios theōrētikos* whose permanent questioning should always challenge "public affairs" themselves:[203] "The meaning of what Socrates was doing lay in *the activity itself.* Or to put it differently: To think and to be fully alive are the same, and this implies that thinking must always begin afresh."[204]

In Arendt's vision of the "narrated life" as a "quest" for shareable meaning, she has no interest in a total or totalizing work. But neither does she yearn for the creation of a political space that might in itself be an "artwork," a "collective artwork." Imagining the essence of politics in terms of a welcoming phenomenality, a place of pure appearance free from the schemes of domination, would amount to an aestheticization that would run counter to Arendt's thinking.[205] The aesthetic reification of politics observed in National-Socialism does not reveal the nonpolitical essence of politics, as some might suggest, but rather the death of politics. For Arendt, political life may be inseparable from the narrative that makes its conflicts visible to each spectator [*dokei moi*], but only to the extent that political life can resist its own aestheticization, can be conceived as an "activity" (praxis) that cannot be reduced to its "product" [*poiēsis*], and can allow itself to be shared by the irreducible plurality of human beings.

In other words, art is not necessarily the essence of national aestheticism, which in turn is presumed to be the essence of Western politics. A certain cult of poetry and myth, deploying the genius of a national language, may seem to lead invariably to national aestheticism. But Arendt "dismantles" this thesis. By focusing on narrative and the novel, Arendt demonstrates that narrative can partake in another politics—the politics of a memory that is opened, renewed, and shared, which she calls a life of the "who." That the narrator (Céline or Brecht) may speak true or false is another problem altogether, but it is one that does not undermine the structural potential of narrative: its potential to be a political action, unlimited and dehiscent, that is offered up to the judging discernment of the *inter-esse*.

Throughout her life, Arendt remained a fervent reader of poetry,[206] but she was always drawn most to the narrative: a narrative inextricably linked with action, which in the end is always political. We should keep in mind that Hannah Arendt wrote poetry herself, notably during the difficult episodes of her youth, in the ordeals of passion, and in the depression that followed it.[207] Arendt's poetic experience was undoubtedly one part self-preservation and one part self-destruction. Poetry locked her into the very state of "desolation" that she was so prone to criticize—and that she tried to defeat—when she analyzed the solipsistic writing of Rahel Varnhagen and when she later ironized the "melancholia" of the "philosophical tribe." Yet Arendt's adherence to narrative should not be deemed a denial of poetry. Although she obviously never explored the complexities of style or prosody, she recognized that poetry was intrinsic to the narrated word: how could poetry be brutally separated from narrative when, according to Arendt, the prototypical "word" for the "deed" is Homer's?

Nor, it would seem, did Arendt subscribe to Adorno's well-known proposition that "to write a poem after Auschwitz is barbaric."[208] Her rejection of that notion owes nothing to her professed aversion to the philosopher himself.[209] For Arendt, in fact, it is only by summoning the imaginary, including through the poetic deployment of narrative, that we are capable of thinking about horror. At the same time, Arendt would not have endorsed Primo Levi's contrary view, which asserts that poetry alone can descend to the depths of the hell of incarceration.[210] Levi's diatribe betrays too much of the tragic desolation and irreparable disenchantment with human plurality that in the end led to his suicide. Arendt, who also suffered from melancholy and who struggled with its temptations, rightly proposed the possibility for transforming hubris and morbid obsession into the *phronēsis* of narrated action: an action constantly renewed and strange, and for those very reasons resurrecting.[211] Poetry's functioning, though different from the elaborative activity of story or history, confirms "the everlasting glory of the English language."

Can narrative—myth, tragedy, or history—ever hope to escape the traps put in its path? Narrative might ignore the wisdom of professional philosophers and the utilitarianism of artmakers, but only if it is able to maintain the tension between *bios theōrētikos* and *bios politikos* without retreating into arid speculation, without taking delight in the banality of the vital process, and without destroying one with the other. Where are they, those gadfly narratives that sting but that also generate a new life? They might turn out to be the Arendtian experience itself: the plurality and paradoxes of a process that has never stopped questioning itself.

It is thus through the narrative itself, and not through some particular understanding, analysis, or rationalization of that narrative, that Arendt believes we will be able to contemplate the horror of the Holocaust. The only possible "reflection" on hell is the "fearful imagination" of those who can relay their memory of Auschwitz.[212] Arendt keeps her distance from any philosophy of irrationality: she defends narrative as rationality writ large, freed from the constraints of a quibbling reason.

"I have never, since a child, doubted that God exists," Arendt told her friend Alfred Kazin (who had recommended her *Origins of Totalitarianism* to the publisher Harcourt Brace).[213] And yet her insistence on the narrated action and the acting narrative reveals, in the end, a rare atheism that is devoid of nihilism. Arendt advances this atheism subtly, with a nod to Aristotle and his appreciation for the *logos-phronēsis,* the field of human praxis beyond the nous reserved as a retreat for the gods. "Logos as distinguished from *nous* is not divine."[214] What Hannah Arendt is devoted to is this nondivine, living word that transforms the life of the mind into the life of politics.

What Heidegger found compelling is altogether different. Although in 1938 the "official" version of his philosophy affirmed that "there is nothing to being," in the "Contributions to Philosophy" (written between 1936 and 1938 and never published), Heidegger professed a different view: "Let us have the courage for the direct word. . . . Being is the trembling of Godding. [*Das Seyn ist die Erzitterung des Götterns*]."[215] Though she always remains in close proximity to her master, the student keeps her distance.

And what about the woman? With or without Isak-Titania Dinesen-Blixen? Another mythic tale, from the long list that Arendt invokes, recounts the well-known story of Orpheus and Eurydice. The man of imagination, musician-poet-thinker, fails to wrest his dead beloved from the grasp of hell—for when he arrives in the land of the living and turns back around toward her, she vanishes. Arendt's analysis, which involves thinking, but also creating "the fictitious characters of a story," requires a desensing.[216] The creative imagination manipulates the elements of the visible world, but only after those elements have been desensed, evaporated, killed—in a word, disappeared, like Eurydice's body, from the perceptions of sense and sight.

Does Arendt-Orpheus demolish Hannah-Eurydice? This commentary does not give the reader the impression that our author identifies with a sacrificed Eurydice, nor that she regrets Orpheus's productive imagination. Perhaps it is because the only way to save the elements of the sensory realm, and to start with, femininity, is to make Eurydice into an Orpheus who is capable of recounting the story of desensing. Only in this way, through a narration of this sort, can the story of desensing somehow become sensitive to each of the participants in the action. To accomplish this eminently political act, we must operate from two sides at the same time, and we must possess, of course, a healthy dose of reflective wisdom, but especially of political *phronēsis*.

In that sense, Eurydice, the sensory realm, and femininity do not evaporate under the pen of our politically minded narrator. Instead, they make a comeback, less as "concepts" than as recurring metaphors that organize her thinking and that express its presuppositions and turning points: the origin, the condition, and natality. In Arendt's writings, those metaphors reflect the tension between the *vita activa* and the *vita contemplativa* as well as the sensing-desensing process that makes a woman into a thinker of genius.

In the end, though, because no label truly applies to Arendt's energy or to the anxiety that motivated her never-ending project of deconstruction, "genius" suits her no better than any other term. She has already stated her objection: the phenomenon of genius, which was unknown to the ancients and which was invented by the Renaissance, is the ultimate justification for *homo faber*. Frustrated by the idea that he might vanish into what he produces and thus what eradicates the "who," modern man searches for something that might transcend both his trade and its object. And so he finds himself reifying that longed-for transcendence into a manufactured "genius": "The idolization of genius harbors the same degradation of the human person as the other tenets in commercial society." Exit the "genius"! What remains, then, is Arendt's energy, which constantly informs us that "the essence of who somebody is cannot be reified by himself."[217]

Nietzsche once invoked a philosophy of a life fully lived: "I only allow the greatest men to philosophize about life. . . . One must want to *live* the weightiest problems through the body and the mind." In her own way, Hannah Arendt was perhaps the only twentieth-century philosopher to actualize this philosophy of life, an expressly political philosophy that she experienced through the lens of her "status" as both a woman and a Jew. Her work as a political thinker shows this to be the case, as does her reflection on the narrated life or, rather, on a narrative that is essential to life, as at once its precursor and its double. As Arendt and Aristotle have told us, there is no life without politics, and as Arendt and Augustine have informed us, there is no life [*bios*] without a rebirth in and through narrative.

SUPERFLUOUS HUMANITY

TO BE JEWISH

Hannah Arendt owes her fame to *The Origins of Totalitarianism,* a work of political anthropology that endeavors to retrace the crystallization of an absolute evil: the notion, put into practice in the twentieth century, that humanity is superfluous. By relying on economics, political science, sociology, and even social psychology, and by drawing from literature and philosophy, Arendt recounts an era of history made up of individual and collective stories. "Facts" are conveyed through the imaginary and then exploited by the most deadly ideology humanity has ever known—an ideology that eventually declares that some people are superfluous. Is it just *some* people or, under the

pressure of utilitarianism and automation, are we *all* superfluous in the end? Arendt unabashedly fears the latter.

Arendt's goal of unearthing the "origins" or "nature" of this
horror is held in check by her intellectual convictions. Because
"causality" is a concept foreign to history and political science,
Arendt simply lays out the "elements," which "become origins
of events if and when they crystallize into fixed and definite
forms. Then, and only then, can we trace their history back-
ward. The event illuminates its own past, but it can never be
deduced from it."[1] The author realizes, then, that the "crystallization" she discovers at the core of such events when she looks
into the past for portentous "elements" is essentially an imaginary process. Didn't Stendhal describe the beginnings of love
as a "crystallization"? Arendt also reveals her intent to uncover
"the elementary structures" of totalitarianism.[2] Claude Lévi-
Strauss had just published *The Elementary Structures of Kinship*
(1949), and structuralism was all the rage, along with its desire
to analyze the elements comprising "savage thought."

Only when "elements" are dramatically transformed into
"events" do they disclose the ingredients of those events. When
Arendt addresses the crystallization process itself, she limits
herself to telling its story, which is based on indisputable facts
as well as on interpretations determined by its own implica-
tions, political choices, and personal judgments, which in the
first instance are not moral but which stem from a whole host
of factors. Arendt takes issue with all forms of "engagement" as
the term was understood by Sartre or by the other members of
the New Left. Her only goal is to enact the role of a "spectator"
removed from the action itself. For Arendt, only the spectator
can judge action impartially, which is the only way a judgment
can be transformed into an action.[3] Arendt's insight into this
relationship and her passion for truth, which for her was both
a personal truth (the truth of a Jew who escaped the Holocaust)
and a universal historical necessity (the necessity of a judgment
that is as informed and rigorous as possible because it is not

content simply to be coherent but is founded upon a moral imperative that is nothing less than the love of other people), elevate her book into a work of unparalleled testimony. Today, with the benefit of hindsight, and without ignoring the relevance of the historical analyses in Arendt's book or the vigor of its moralist tenets, which have met with both criticism and praise since the book was first published, it appears that the book's most important feature lies in the art of recounting the novel of the century. *The Origins of Totalitarianism* is shaped as a series of individual and collective stories interspersed with the personal story of the narrator, who finds herself still grappling with crystallization.[4]

"The word 'Jew' never came up when I was a small child," recalled Arendt in an interview. Raised by her mother to be "completely a-religious," Arendt was "enlightened" about her Jewish identity only because of the anti-Semitic remarks she heard children making in the street. Her mother's response was to advise Hannah to defend herself rather than to hide her head in shame. Martha was more concerned, on the other hand, about the anti-Semitic remarks made by Hannah's high school teachers: "I was told to get up immediately, leave the classroom, come home, and report everything exactly." Her mother would then write a certified letter in protest, and Hannah would be granted a day off from school.[5]

It is not enough to say that Arendt's was a secular, nonreligious definition of Jewish identity: I do not define myself as someone who is part of a religion, but I assume my identity by defending myself all alone, and I write—we write—formal letters of complaint because I believe—we believe—that it is possible to judge injustices. In a famous exchange with Scholem following the scandal that erupted over her reportage on the Eichmann trial, Arendt revealed her doubts about a putatively secular rejection of religion on the part of certain Zionists who wished, rather openly, to transfer the religious spirit to the cult of either the state or the providential people: without God, the people are our God. Avoiding such an approach, Arendt offered a unique perspective on the question: while rejecting nihilism, she rethought the religious tradition ("believing in God") by constantly questioning transcendence. In Arendt's view, that was the only way for each person to be respected and reborn within the confines of a diverse political community.[6]

All the while believing that we are reborn upon each act of our thought, Arendt considered herself to be a product of her parents' education and her mother tongue. To that conviction she added her belief that Jewishness is a "fact" and a "look," which is what makes it appear the way it does in the ever-politicized realm of other people.[7] Neither a biological determination, which never really interested her (and which she must have considered to be a simple *zōē* that every being transforms into a *bios* in an effort to humanize itself), nor a psychological particularity (which she called a "vice" when she accused both the assimilated Jews and their falsely philo-Semitic assimilators of reveling in so they could more readily pursue the intruder should the opportunity present itself), Jewishness is one of the facts bestowed upon us when we are born that demand our appreciation and judgment. Arendt considers Jewishness to be a "political problem": "I just noticed your question again about whether I'm a German or a Jew. To be perfectly honest, it doesn't matter to me in the least on a personal and individual level. . . . Politically, I will always speak only in the name of the Jews," she wrote Jaspers. Arendt reiterated this position later on: "But now, belonging to Judaism had become my own problem, and my own problem was political. Purely political!"[8]

As merciless as she was with the enemies of the Jewish people, Arendt was no more generous with her own kind, as the Eichmann affair proved beyond cavil. In fact, if it is true that we judge only from the inner world of public realm and only when we are in the company of other people, "judging" is a way of "thinking." And when we think, we are "nowhere." The crux of Arendt's intellectual adventure teeters between main-

taining the absolute need to think, on the one hand, and showing concern for the particular, on the other—a struggle that
illuminates the complexity and tensions that drove her and
that have also been interpreted as ambiguous beliefs on her
part. In the end, Arendt was less interested in intellectual
purity than in remaining loyal to the essence of the life of the
mind that consists of combining the abrasive force of solitary
questioning (speaking the truth) and the greater community of
judgment (doing justice for her people within the bounds of
humanity). The by-product of all this is a radical estrangement
that pokes holes in the various sanctuaries of identities or
groups but that Arendt adopted without abandoning her own
identities and group affiliations. She was convinced she could
preserve them as they are and, by doing justice to them, that
she could make them even more just—though certainly not by
"accommodating" them. Although this strain of her thought
does not expressly refer to the Hebraic tradition with which
Arendt in any event does not appear to have been too familiar,
it is inextricably linked to the essence of Judaism as the political theorist defined it when she spoke of Judah Magnes: "The
man simply cannot be replaced. He was an unusual mix of typ-
ically American common sense and integrity along with a genuine, *half-religious Jewish passion for justice.*"[9] These words suit
Arendt just as well.

On that front, two anecdotes illustrate the tension and
demands of the Arendtian experience. In Arendt's first postwar
letter to Heidegger (February 9, 1950), she wrote, "I have never
felt like a German woman, and for a long time I have no longer
felt like a Jewish woman. I feel like what I really am—a maiden
from afar."[10] *Ein Mädchen aus des Fremde* [The maiden from
afar] is the title of a Schiller poem that Heinrich Blücher used
to refer to his wife.[11] Heidegger himself wrote Hannah a poem
on the same subject.[12] The second anecdote is a Jewish story.
In response to the order from the sultan Saladin to "Come forward, Jew!" Nathan the Wise simply replied, "I am a man!"[13]

Although Arendt did not deny her difference and even struggled to ensure that it would be recognized politically, she refused to be trapped into any one identity and refused to join the cult of a people, even a chosen one. As a reader of Aristotle, she understood that the examined life enjoys the highest place in the city-state, not to forge together a compact and more easily governable people under the authority of a god, but to sustain the distance that guarantees a political arena constituted of individuals. Arendt reminds us that the Greek terms *hekastos,* which means "every one," is derived from *hekas,* "far off,"[14] and that *bios theōrētikos* is fundamentally a *bios xenikos,* a life apart, which means "leaving the company of his fellow-men."[15] She goes on to translate these abstractions into political realities that were germane to the realities of her day: "We would do best not to settle down too permanently anywhere, not really to depend on any nation, for it can change overnight into a mob and a blind instrument of ruin."[16]

In response to Scholem, who criticized her for failing to love the "Jewish people" [*Ahavat Yisrael*], she retorted, "I found it puzzling that you should write 'I regard you wholly as a daughter of our people, and in no other way.' The truth is I have never pretended to be anything else or to be in any way other than I am, and I have never even felt tempted in that direction. It would have been like saying that I was a man and not a woman, that is to say, kind of insane."[17] A woman and a Jew: for Arendt, it would seem, both these terms are "political consequences."

And as for love, not only does Arendt believe that we should be wary of it so we can maintain the Homeric impartiality that makes it possible to appreciate the exploits of the Greeks as well those of the barbarians, but she adds, "I have never in my life 'loved' any people or collective, neither the German people, nor the French, nor the American, nor the working class or anything of that sort. I indeed love 'only' my friends and the only kind of love I know of and believe in is the love of persons."[18]

At its core, then, love, which distances itself from the good as well as the bad qualities of the person who is loved, destroys the in-between that relates us to others while separating us from them; love is "unworldly," "not only apolitical but antipolitical, perhaps the most powerful of all antipolitical human forces."[19] Accordingly, Jewishness, which Arendt, as we have just seen, considers to be a political problem and thus what else exists in the world, cannot be approached in terms of "love," but simply of "friendship" and "respect."

Did this generous humanist fail to love herself? How should we interpret the following words, taken once again from her same response to Scholem: "I cannot love myself or anything which I know is part and parcel of my own person." Even if we accept that the "facts" of a Jewish birth are "part and parcel of my own person" and that the complex "person" has roots in this fact, but particularly in friendship, respect, and *philia politikē* toward other people, was Arendt not implicitly acknowledging a tendency toward reveling in "self-hatred"?[20]

Several incidents suggest that she was not. In 1932–33, for example, Arendt wrote Heidegger a letter that infuriated him, a letter in which the word "Jew" was used for the first time, first by her and then by him. Were the rumors true, Hannah wanted to know, that he excluded Jews from his seminars, ignored his Jewish colleagues, and refused to direct the dissertations of Jewish students—in sum, that he was acting like an anti-Semite? Heidegger responded with indignation: not only did he love her, a Jew, but he regularly granted extraordinary favors to Jews as well. Was this not a sarcastic way of acknowledging that he "clearly distinguished between Germans and German Jews"?[21] We can only speculate about Hannah's reaction to this ambivalent letter, given her intense idealization of her master, but "it is conceivable that Heidegger's ambivalent letter to her . . . sealed Arendt's decision to leave Germany in August 1933."[22]

In Paris, where she would spend eight years, Arendt learned Hebrew because "I want[ed] to know my people." She worked as a secretary in the offices of the Agriculture et Artisinat, an organization that helped young Jews emigrate to Palestine by training them in farming and crafts, and later at the Youth Aliyah, where she became the *secrétaire générale* of the Paris office. She went to Palestine in 1934, and although she was enthusiastic about the opportunities it presented to Jewish settlers, she was opposed to what she later termed "Palestine-centered Zionism."[23] After returning to Paris, she immersed herself in French culture, political as well as literary. She took a particular interest in Proust, Clausewitz, and Simenon, and she met Russian intellectuals including the famous philosopher Nicolas Berdyaev. She also became friends with the group of leftist German intellectuals, including the Cohn-Bendits, whose younger son she would contact in 1968. Arendt was particularly fond of Walter Benjamin and Heinrich Blücher.

When the French government decided to intern male German nationals, Blücher was ordered to report to a camp for *prestataires* (who worked for the French military) in Villemalard, near Orléans. Exhausted and ill, he was released from the camp through the efforts of some "well-placed friends." The lovers were married in January 1940. In May, Arendt, who went by "Mme Stern" after her first marriage but who kept her maiden name after her second marriage to emphasize her Jewish origins, was called to appear at the Vélodrome d'Hiver following an announcement by the *gouverneur général* of Paris. She was then sent to the camp of Gurs, which had been used since 1939 for Spanish refugees and for members of the International Brigade.[24] Over the course of the summer, nearly two-thirds of the internees left the camp of Gurs. Hannah fled and then decided to join her friends in Montauban. As chance would have it, while Blücher was wandering around southwestern France, he passed through Montauban. The two lovers were thus reunited after having lost all hopes of seeing each other again. After a stay in Lisbon, Arendt and Blücher set sail for New York, where they arrived in May 1941. One year later, they learned about the extermination camps and that those interned at Gurs had been sent to Auschwitz.

In New York with her mother, Martha Beerwald, and her husband, Heinrich Blücher, Hannah Arendt assumed the role of head of the household. She learned English and found work; encouraged by Salo Baron, a Jewish historian at Columbia University, she began to work on a study of the Dreyfus affair. Luck came her way when she was hired as a columnist for the German-language newspaper *Aufbau,* the news bulletin of the German Club that was run by Manfred George. She published important articles in *Aufbau,* including "The Jewish Army— The Beginning of a Jewish Politics?" and "Can the Jewish-Arab Question Be Solved?" These reflections on the Palestinian question (which would soon became the Israeli-Palestinian question) laid the foundation for the reflections that would culminate in *The Origins of Totalitarianism.*

To summarize, Arendt's Zionist ideas, which were inspired by Kurt Blumenfeld, the dedicatee of *The Origins of Totalitarianism,* grew out of positions taken by Judah Magnes at the Biltmore Conference. Arendt rejected Manfred George's proposal for a Jewish Commonwealth that would give minority status to the Palestinian Arabs, but she also condemned a proposal for relocating Arab populations because it would require "fascist organization."[25]

And yet, when Judah Magnes called for a binational state in which the Jews would have minority status and which would be incorporated into a federation and affiliated with an Anglo-American union, Arendt resisted it, recommending in its place a Palestinian entity that would make no distinction between the majority and the minority. She thought that an Arab federation would be "nothing but cover for an Empire." She dreamed of a federation without a majority or a minority like the United States or the Soviet Union, even a *Commonwealth* if it was sufficiently distinct from the British Empire![26] Arendt's independent and impractical recommendation meant that she had no hope of influencing political decision makers. At the same time, however, her intellectual influence was exploding. She taught at Brooklyn College and Columbia University, then later at the New School for Social Research, in military education programs, and at Princeton University, where she would eventually become the first woman ever to earn the rank of full professor. Little by little, invitations came in from all over the country: the RAND Corporation, Berkeley, Yale, the University of Chicago, and elsewhere.

In 1944 Arendt began to prepare a "Tentative List of Jewish Cultural Treasures in Axis-Occupied Countries," published in *Jewish Social Studies* and incorporated into *The Origins of Totalitarianism*. Having accepted the senior editorial post at Schocken Books, she worked steadily on manuscripts by Walter Benjamin while publishing Bernard Lazare, Kafka, and Scholem. In this literary environment, the academic struck up a friendship with Hermann Bloch, whose advances she would learn to decline. Increasingly affiliated, even integrated, with the New York intellectual milieu, particularly with the set at *Commentary* and *Partisan Review,* where she published several of her articles, Arendt also became interested in French neo-Catholic thought (the Action française group, Georges Bernanos, and Jacques Maritain).

Three centers of interest profoundly influenced the period in which she prepared for her *Origins of Totalitarianism*: the Israeli-Palestinian debate, the current state of America and the Cold War, and European culture with its benefits and burdens.

Arendt was constantly adding to her output on the "Palestinian" (and then Israeli-Palestinian) question, and she remained in a critical dialogue with Judah Magnes. Arendt respected Magnes's political party, the Ikhud Party, which she believed presented a viable political opposition to a powerful Jewish Authority. After the 1947 U.N. resolution to partition Palestine (which contravened the proposal of Andrei Gromyko, the Soviet Union's representative to the United Nations, to form a binational state), Magnes accepted the State of Israel without abandoning his dream of Jewish-Arab cooperation. In the May 1948 issue of *Commentary*, Arendt published an article well received by Magnes entitled "To Save the Jewish Homeland: There Is Still Time." Her essay denounced the dangerous bias of the prevailing discourse propagated by the new state. Arendt took on the anti-Americanism and the "childishly" pro-Soviet leanings of the new state, and she spared neither the "cynicism" and "racist chauvinism" inherent in the idea of a "master race" nor the "mass unanimity [that] is not the result of agreement, but an expression of fanaticism and hysteria" and that is pledged "not to conquest but to suicide."[27] The dramatic, even mocking, tone of these remarks and the brutality of her unsubtle and undiplomatic attacks incited virulent critiques of her piece, as evidenced by Ben Halpern's reply in the August 1948 issue of *Jewish Frontier*. Halpern's rejoinder foreshadowed the violent reaction Arendt would experience upon the publication of her book on the Eichmann trial: he accused her of having an "*enfant terrible* complex," of writing a text that was no more than "outrageous scandal-mongering . . . for the sole (sub-conscious) purpose of discrediting such conventionally, and hence disconcertingly 'successful' Jewish figures as Herzl, Weizmann, and Ben Gurion," and so forth.[28]

The accused stuck to her guns. On the one hand, she considered the creation of the Jewish state to be indispensable in counteracting the absence of politics that she believed characterized the Jewish tradition: a "worldlessness," as she would later call it, that, as a result of its exile and then of its status as a pariah, acquired personal qualities of justice, generosity, and mutual aid but that neglected the need for a "space of appear-

ance" that respected uniqueness and bonds with other people—the fundamentals of any democracy. On the other hand,
although Arendt resisted any notion of "collaboration," a label
applied to her by critics who compared her to those who "col-
laborated" with the Nazis, she believed it was extremely important to encourage "cooperation" with the English and the
Arabs in order to keep the young Zionist state from taking
refuge in a permanent military mobilization against "the solid
threatening opposition of many millions of people from
Morocco down to the Indian ocean." With her extreme rationality and her total absence of realism or diplomacy, Arendt had
already turned into what she would later declare herself to be
to Scholem: "I don't fit. . . . I am independent. I do not belong
to any organization and always speak only for myself. . . . I have
great confidence in Lessing's *Selbstdenken* for which, I think,
no ideology, no public opinion, and no 'convictions' can ever
be a substitute."[29]

In 1952 she did not shy away from advocating yet another
entrenched position. After the Israeli government passed a
Nationality Law that excluded a large majority of Arabs living
in Israel from Israeli citizenship, and after the several attacks
that ensued, including one by the Israeli Defense Ministry that
left fifty-two Arabs dead, Arendt reacted strongly: "I decided
that I no longer wanted anything to do with Jewish politics."[30]
Her intransigence did not prevent her from contributing generously to the United Jewish Appeal and the Israeli Emergency
Fund, particularly during the 1967 war in the Middle East.[31]

AMONG THE ELEMENTS IN THE STRUCTURE

Arendt's host country, the welcoming and disarming America,
was not spared the vigilant observations of its new citizen.
Imbued with European customs and culture, but impressed by
the freedoms that American federalism bestows, Arendt drew a

useful contrast very early on: she found the Americans to be politically independent but socially conformist.[32] She had concerns about the anti-Communism of the Republican Party, but also about the blindness of the Left, which called itself anti-Stalinist but then failed to disavow Communism as a viable political-economic option and to denounce its totalitarian roots. She also took issue with the Left's failure to oppose the totalitarian elements of the American system itself (the conformity of individuals who identify with their work and who seek success above all else, the overemphasis on publicity, and so forth). On the other hand, she criticized the European Left's allegiance to Communist parties and to nationalism as well as its systematic opposition to American anti-Stalinism. In her view, all these positions missed the subtleties of international politics, and they automatically transformed many European intellectuals into "fellow travelers." Her analyses—which were supported by her reading of works by Eugen Kogon (*The Theory and Practice of Hell*), David Rousset (*The Other Kingdom* and *Les Jours de notre mort*), and an anonymous writer from the Russian camps (*The Dark Side of the Moon*, with a preface by T. S. Eliot)—led Arendt to the hypothesis that Nazism and Communism were two sides of the same coin. Arendt was moving toward a new idea: the two sides of totalitarianism that both led to the same phenomenon—the concentration camps—and to the same disdain for human life.[33] This vision, which remains controversial even today, shows Arendt's to be a brave, independent mind that hunted down fascism in all its forms and that has inspired nonconformists of all stripes ever since.

Arendt's concerns about American society did not stem solely from McCarthyism and from the virulent anti-Communism campaigns that outraged Blücher. She also railed against racism against blacks, which she saw as the counterpart to the anti-Semitism that she had personally experienced in Europe, in a highly explosive piece on racial integration entitled

"Reflections on Little Rock."[34] Arendt's essay reiterated positions she had already taken in *Origins* and *The Human Condition,* but because her ideas were recast into concrete terms that were contemporaneous with a pressing current event, her essay proved very controversial. She was accused of being "unsympathetic" and "callous," labels that would be applied to her once again upon the publication of her book on the Eichmann trial. The main point of Arendt's argument was to advocate the toleration of racial differences in the social realm to prevent them from spilling over into the private and political realms, where they could become destructive. She denounced the miscegenation laws, but she warned against enforced school integration because she thought it was abusive to try to make children into the avant-garde of integration. Arendt wanted black children to feel "pride," which she defined as "that untaught and natural feeling of identity with whatever we happen to be by accident of birth,"[35] and which she distinguished from racial, ethnic, or national pride. All her arguments still hold sway today, particularly in the debate in France about a "new secularism" that would respect differences without running the risk of eradicating them too quickly in the name of universalism. But few critics appreciated the genuinely nonconformist value of her positions, which were considered at the time to be ultraconservative or arch-Republican.

Long after she wrote *Origins* but without abandoning its fundamental themes, Arendt continued to be an attentive "spectator" of "her" America. She commented on the Kennedy assassination in the *New York Review of Books,* and she analyzed the repercussions of the Arab-Israeli conflict in several articles and interviews.[36] Her irritation with America, though it did not erase the positive image she still carried from her readings of Jefferson and de Tocqueville, drove her so far as to consider, during the Vietnam War, repatriating to Switzerland or reinstating her German citizenship![37]

But it was Europe that remained at the heart of the developing crystallization that underlies *The Origins of Totalitarianism*: a fascinating Europe and a repellant Europe that Arendt would never leave behind in her thinking, and a Europe that she would encounter again during a trip she made between August 1949 and March 1950. Germany clearly caused her the most pain, as suggested in her article "What Is Existenz Philosophy?" where Arendt mocks "the real comedy" of Heidegger's itinerary in tracing out "exact parallels" between the conduct of the philosopher and "German romanticism." The vitriolic nature of this "parallelism" suggests that it is in no way haphazard, for it hints at another comparison, one between Hannah and Rahel the Romantic. Heidegger is described as being the last (one would hope!) of the wonderfully gifted Romantics, along the lines of a Friedrich Schlegel or an Adam Müller, someone "whose complete irresponsibility was attributed partly to the delusion of genius, partly to desperation."[38] To this rigid and grandiloquent egotism, which she accuses of neglecting men and their community, Arendt contrasts the work of Jaspers, who from that point on became her mentor in matters moral.

In his book *The Guilt of the German People* (1946), Jaspers asserts that "the criminal is always the individual" but that "each citizen finds himself jointly liable for the acts of the State to which he belongs." At the same time, Jaspers believed in neither a "collective moral culpability" nor a "collective metaphysical culpability." These remarks, which were poorly understood at the time, invited suspicion and even slander.[39] The discussion between Jaspers and Thomas Mann heightened the tension and further complicated the debate. And yet the German novelist, a celebrated anti-Nazi who left Germany voluntarily once Hitler rose to power, declared in 1945 that he did not seek to divide Germany in two but to "show solidarity with the German calamity." Although Arendt and Blücher were "very much in agreement" with Jaspers, they wanted the next German constitution to include a provision guaranteeing that any Jew, no matter where he was born, could "become a citizen of this republic, enjoying all rights of citizenship, solely on the basis of his Jewish nationality and without ceasing to be a Jew."[40] At the same time, Arendt wrote Jaspers later that year that she, unlike Jaspers's wife, "never felt myself, either spontaneously or at my own insistence, to 'be a German.' What remains is the language."[41]

THE EXAMPLE OF FRANCE

More than England (which nevertheless warranted extensive treatment because of Disraeli the "potent wizard" and because Arendt had much sympathy for its two-party system), France is the country that enjoys the most privileged role in the crystallization described in *Origins of Totalitarianism*.[42] Turning her attention toward the old continent that generated the absolute horror, Arendt claimed to be "homesick" only for France, and once a year on May 8, she always cracked open a bottle of champagne with "Monsieur," as she affectionately called Blücher, to celebrate the day that Paris was liberated. For better or for worse, France is the *"nation par excellence."*[43] France, whose language Arendt spoke, and its "authors," whom she cited liberally—Bernard Lazare, Péguy, Clemenceau, Zola, Proust, and Céline, along with such neo-Catholics as Maurras, Barrès, Bernanos, Gabriel Marcel, Raïssa and Jacques Maritain—became her unavoidable landmarks as she retraced the crystallization of anti-Semitism in the nineteenth and twentieth centuries.

With the Dreyfus affair marking the beginning of modern anti-Semitism, Arendt cites Roger Martin du Gard in the epigraph to "Antisemitism," the first part of Arendt's *Origins:* "This is a remarkable century which opened with the Revolution and ended with the *Affair!* Perhaps it will be called the century of rubbish." Not surprisingly, Arendt targets the army and the clergy, who tried to outdo each other in their devotion to anti-Semitism during the Dreyfus affair. What is much more surprising—and what is one of Arendt's more original, or perhaps more candid, showings—is her attack on the French Left. Arendt reminds us that in 1845, fifty years before the affair, Toussenel published *Les Juifs, Rois de l'Epoque,* which unleashed a flood of insults against the Rothschilds and was enthusiastically received by the entire Left-wing press, which served as a mouthpiece for a lower middle class whose "sentiments . . . were not very different from those of the young Marx."[44]

The nonbelievers versus the believers: Arendt does not fail to point out that this Franco-French debate was used as fodder for anti-Semitism. "French anti-Semitism . . . is as much older than its European counterparts as is French emancipation of the Jews, which dates back to the end of the eighteenth century. The representatives of the Age of Enlightenment who prepared the French Revolution despised the Jews as a matter of course; they saw in them the backwards remnants of the Dark Ages, and they hated them as the financial agents of the aristocracy. The only articulate friends of the Jews in France were conservative writers who denounced anti-Jewish attitudes as 'one of the favorite theses of the eighteenth century.'"[45] This quotation is from Joseph de Maistre, whom Arendt supports, in this particular instance, against Charles Fourier. Adopting de Tocqueville's historical analysis, Arendt enjoys exposing the rising tide of French anti-Semitism, from the Comte de Boulainvilliers, a freethinker and antinationalist who prepared his country for civil war by pitting the Franks, who considered themselves noble warriors of Germanic origin, against the Gauls—and who was an unlikely promoter, before the English as well as the Germans themselves, of the idée fixe of German superiority—to Arthur de Gobineau and his *Inequality of Human Races* (1853); and to Valéry, whom Arendt criticizes in a footnote for having signed, *"non sans réflexion,"* a call by military officers and others to adopt a new set of solutions for the hundred thousand Jews living in France at that time.[46]

Even so, Arendt points out exceptions to this anti-Semitic parade. In addition to Zola, whom she warmly praises,[47] Arendt mentions Diderot as the only Enlightenment philosopher who was not hostile to the Jews: the author of the article "Juif" in the *Encyclopédie* is said to have recognized in the Jews "a useful link between Europeans of different nationalities." On the German side, Arendt mentions the insightful Wilhelm von Humboldt, who remarked that the Jews risked losing their universality upon being changed into Frenchmen, as well as Nietzsche, who referred to the Jew as the "good European" and who thus avoided "the pitfalls of cheap philosemitism or patronizing 'progressive' attitudes."[48]

Throughout all Arendt's writings, various patches of French culture are closely examined or merely evoked in passing, ranging from Pascal, Fontenelle, and Fustel de Coulanges to Jean-Pierre Vernant on the Greeks and the Romans; from Georges Sorel to the sociology of Alain Touraine, and passing through the philosophers Henri Frenay, Bertrand de Jouvenel, Jean Wahl, Malraux, and finally Camus, whom Arendt prefers to Sartre.

A more than honorable place is accorded to the "great Montesquieu" and to his "divine writings": was he not the one who realized that the reason tyranny is the only regime that self-destructs is that it rests on isolation and not on participation in the public realm so dear to Aristotle?[49] Arendt points out that, at least ten years before the French Revolution, Montesquieu's *Spirit of the Laws* broached the subject of the constitution of political freedom, with the word "constitution" in no way implying a negative limit on power but a "grand temple of federal liberty" that must be based on "the foundation and correct distribution of power."[50] That conception of politics explains the predominant role Montesquieu played in the American Revolution, whereas the French Revolution remained enthralled with Rousseau. Montesquieu was also the object of Arendt's attention when she contrasted him with the American "transcendentalists" and when she joyously cited the following excerpt from *The Spirit of the Laws*: "Man, this flexible being, who submits himself in society to the thoughts and impressions of his fellow-men, is equally capable of knowing his own nature when it is shown to him as it is and of losing it to the point where he has no realization that he is robbed of it."[51]

And what can be said about poor Voltaire, who merits only a single ironic mention (is it because he was considered an anti-Semite?)? Did he not, following Lucretius, heap scorn on the eminently human predisposition for desiring to see (and thus to know, speculate, and appear) by dismissing it as a cheap curiosity that man shares with monkeys and young dogs?[52] That is, unless this attack on the famous satirist is another one of those double-edged swords so pleasing to Arendt, who uses Voltaire to mock the "fallacies" of a few humorless "professional thinkers" caught up in a certain *Augenblick* [the now] if not a *durchschauen* [looking through, piercing, penetrating] or even in a certain "conflict with the occupation authorities"? They are "specialists" who are content to "see" by thinking rather than by living the life of the mind in the "space of political appearances," a space that, incidentally, is as Greek as it is French.

More subtly, however, Arendt denounces the secularization and universalism of the rights of man as the hidden source of—if it is not the principal French contribution to—modern anti-Semitism. Although she recognizes the "perplexities of the Rights of Man," she elaborates upon Burke's critique of the notion: in the name of universality, the ideology of the rights of man is a paradox because it reduces the "person" to a "human being in general"—"without a profession, without citizenship, [and] without an opinion." This ideology therefore deprives individuals of their political community, which is the only "common world" in which they can express themselves.

As result, they lose all significance and thus lose their rights. Universalism eradicates historically constructed religious and political differences and hierarchies and thus provides a path to a universe made up of natural differences, a universe governed by the brutal findings of the private sphere (differences in intelligence, color, and so forth), and not by the bonds of justice interwoven with time in the "space of appearance." If the species man is all that we have, the species does not contain politically constituted individuals but natural specimens such as Negroes and Jews.[53]

This excessively naturalist interpretation of the rights of man is also the ill-fated legacy of the Enlightenment, although its origins go back, as Arendt tries to show in *The Human Condition,* to the very essence of the human being or at least to the central role the human being plays in Western metaphysics. That is why Arendt concludes her section on imperialism by stating that while civilization is not threatened from the outside, the conditions of the savage "from its own midst" produce the barbarity, already underway today, of a "global, universally interrelated civilization."[54]

Beyond Enlightenment universalism, and beyond even the totalitarian regimes that provided a home for twentieth-century imperialism, the reality of globalization in the beginning of this third millennium is the most plausible target of Arendt's apocalyptic words. And yet the violence of this critique of universalism will be superseded, or at least held in check, by Arendt's return in her later work to Kantian thought and to the notion that an "enlarged mentality" and a humanity that possesses "common sense" and "cosmo-politics" provide the only possible foundations for judgment and the only viable criteria for just political action.[55] In like manner, her exploration of Christian thought, which reaffirms, along with Saint Augustine, the dignity of each man as he is born, is a sort of political reading of Christianity in which the rights of man are a legacy to be shared and an impassable apotheosis.[56]

Arendt was strangely unaware of the complexity of the French Enlightenment; she forced its various tenets (materialist, sensualist, libertine, and so forth) under the rubrics of "secularization" and "universalism." In her discussion of the burgeoning philosophy of the eighteenth century, her focus is primarily, if not exclusively, on the French Revolution of 1789. In fact, in her subsequent and sometimes ambiguous *On Revolution* (1963), what she admires most of all is the constitutional spirit of the American Revolution, which was founded on the biblical covenant of the Protestants. These well-to-do property owners, who were ready and willing to federate, were able to develop a contractual, moral, and ultrajuridical society. Arendt admired John Adams and Thomas Jefferson, unmistakable heroes and political thinkers above anything else. She was more reticent, on the other hand, about the French Revolution, which she described as being motivated by a Rousseauesque, sentimentalist, and debased enthusiasm that was trapped in the centralism of the Jacobins and that degenerated during the Terror. With a more generous spirit, she also praised the cult of "public" happiness extolled by Abbé Siéyès and Saint-Just. On that front, Arendt noted the way the French revolutionaries recognized the "people" and "misery," and she emphasized the invention of new forms of political life by the ephemeral "sections" and "clubs," which were soon destroyed by Robespierre's revolutionary apparatus that substituted the sacred unity of the people or the nation for God or the king. The reader of *On Revolution* has the impression that Arendt never stopped debating with herself: is it possible in the end that what characterized the French Revolution was the fragile resurgence of political debate in the public realm and those popular, even ephemeral, initiatives of a deliberative citizenry as well as the permanence of the revolution, and not its institutional sacralization? Who can know for sure?

France clearly intrigued Arendt with its taste for the *petit bonheur,* that inimitable "charm." Was she merely drawn to the decline of the aristocratic "greatness" of yesteryear and its quiet reduction to the irresistible enchantment of an entire people? Charm is "the world's last, most purely humane corner," of course, but "it does not constitute a public realm" because it remains essentially private.[57] At the very least, it is a question that deserves to be asked. It would have been interesting to turn Arendt's question back to her: What if these French "elements," these public *and* private "small things"—resolutely private yet displayed in public because they need the very public that made them possible—were among those rare elements that are capable of communicating in the modern world the deliberative and enchanted mind, the *eudaimonia* of the Greek polis so appreciated by our heroine? And what if this occurred in a way that was different from, but perhaps more effective than, the legalism of the Puritans whom Arendt was already beginning to criticize for the manipulation of their politicians and their media, manipulations that are increasingly apparent today to the point of discrediting and destroying the entire democratic system?

"In the contest that divides the world today and in which so much is at stake, those will probably win who understand revolution," she adds, as if she were not certain that she had said everything important about the revolution and its pleasures in light of her remarks on the limitations of centralism, of the cult of the nation, and of the supreme Being that once embodied French-styled universalism.[58]

WHAT IS MODERN ANTI-SEMITISM?

It appears that Arendt was the first person to distinguish between pretotalitarian anti-Semitism and totalitarian anti-Semitism. Although the history of Christianity is tainted by both a hatred toward the people of the Bible, who are considered deicidal, and the pogroms, and although the "Protocols of the Elders of Zion" has a "ludicrous story," this past cannot explain why "the totalitarian claim to global rule, to be exercised by members and methods of a secret society, should [have] become an attractive political goal at all" in the twentieth century. The philosopher shows that modern anti-Semitism, contrary to conventional wisdom, is the product of neither traditional nationalism nor the conflict with the religious and spiritual values of the past. Instead, anti-Semitism has grown in proportion as the nation-states have declined and as the Jews have become assimilated.[59] Arendt even dares to write, in the wake of the Holocaust, that some Jews concerned with the survival of their people were prone to "hit on the consoling idea that anti-Semitism, after all, might be an excellent means for keeping the people together."[60]

As a backdrop to her belief in the necessity of founding a Jewish state as the only cure for this absolute evil, Arendt sets up one of her main points: that the lack of Jewish politics played a role in this crystallization: "The lack of political ability and judgment have been caused by the very nature of Jewish history, the history of a people without a government, without a country, and without a language. Jewish history offers the extraordinary spectacle of a people unique in this respect, which began its history with a well-defined concept of history and an almost conscious resolution to achieve a well-circumscribed plan on earth and then, without giving up this concept, avoided all political action for two thousand years."[61]

How did the nation-states create anti-Semitism out of this worldlessness? Going as far back as the seventeenth century, Arendt points out that the expansion of economic activity and its concomitant need for capital led at first to the emancipation of the Jews. The system gave rise to legal and political equality, which was first accorded to individuals, and then to isolated communities, and then to the Jews as a whole. The court Jews financed the transaction of the state, but the nation-state preferred that the Jews remain a small distinct group and that they not become integrated with the class-based society. The Jews, for their part, had an interest in surviving as a separate group and did not participate in the burgeoning capitalist enterprise (and so the Rothschilds, who shunned the key positions of the capitalist society, set their sights on the world of finance instead). After the revolution, the states summoned the Jews of central and western Europe, who entrusted their assets to several Jewish bankers. Made up of a unique family, but divided among five nationalities, the House of Rothschild enjoyed a monopoly on the issuance of government loans. The Rothschilds made it easier to access Jewish capital on a large scale, and Jewish wealth was able to partake in the states and in a new European cohesiveness.[62]

This phase reached its apogee at the end of the nineteenth century, when expansionist imperialism began to undermine the foundation of the nation-state. Jews who had formerly enjoyed a monopoly in government transactions were replaced with businessmen who were more amenable to imperialist expansion. In an imperialist world, the wealth of the Jews lost its importance, and the European Jew became an object of universal hatred as a result of his "wealth without visible function" because it was without political power. Arendt relies here on de Tocqueville's conclusion that the French began to hate the aristocrats at the same time that the aristocrats began to decline in power, even though their political decline did not correspond to a concomitant decline in their wealth. In like manner, "antisemitism reached its climax when Jews had similarly lost their public functions and their influence, and were left with nothing but their wealth." These powerless groups, in the throes of losing their influence but not their fortune, were deemed to be "parasites."[63]

The court Jews had established relationships with the nobility based on personal loyalties, and although they did not insinuate themselves into political life, neither were they excluded from it. Imperialism put a stop to these relationships, replacing them with a hateful liberal anti-Semitism directed toward the Jews, who were affiliated with the nobles and who were considered to be enemies of the bourgeoisie. The role of the powerful Jewish "banker" or "adviser" existed only until the time of Bismarck and Rothschild, and it was replaced for a brief moment by the role of "communicator," a role that Disraeli occupied with much aplomb during the 1870s. Disraeli was one of those "exceptional personalities" plucked from the Romantics and criticized by Arendt in her study of Rahel Varnhagen. Proclaiming himself to be a "chosen man of the chosen race," Disraeli lent his genius to the service of the Queen of England, who took pride in her "exception Jew" and his racial theories.[64] Around the time of the peace treaties of Versailles, the Jews made their last appearance as advisers in the person of Walter Rathenau, the foreign minister of the Weimar Republic. Once the relationships between the various nation-states had deteriorated, the role of adviser no longer served any purpose: as long as the aim of war was not peace or a modus vivendi with the enemy but rather the extermination of the enemy, "the Jews could no longer be of any use."[65]

At the same time, the Jews, who continued to be adept at distribution and who were unable or unwilling to join the world of industrial production, came to be perceived as an obstacle to capitalist development: "Jewish interests were felt to be in conflict with those sections of the population from which a middle class could normally have developed" because the Jews "formed a middle class without fulfilling its productive functions." Anti-Semitism first flared up in Prussia at the time of a "revolution from above" that no longer needed financial help from the Jews and that, by granting equality to the Jews, made them cease to exist. In any event, this emancipation concerned only those wealthy Jewish groups who were already endowed with civic rights. By linking the fate of the Jews to the fate of an emancipating state, however, the reform inspired a liberal and aristocratic anti-Semitism, the likes of which had never been seen before. These anti-Semitic strains assimilated the Jews en masse to the revolutionary ideals and to the egalitarian state, and they assimilated the "powerful Jews" to the power of the state.[66]

The idea that the Jews were superfluous—that there were not enough of them or that they were too nationalistic—was beginning to take hold. Arendt would later suggest that this idea of "superfluity" was inherent in Marx's notion of the force of work (which produced "surplus value") and, more generously, in Nietzsche's notion of the very luxury of life. The perversity of the new anti-Semitic ideology, on the other hand, was that it localized this superfluity in a group of people and then designated the group for extermination, as if the "superfluous" could simply be eradicated. This burgeoning sociohistorical crystallization assigned the Jews the role of scapegoats in the logic of horror, even if other peoples or groups could have occupied that role just as well and even if the intricacies of Arendt's analysis reconstruct a process much more complex than the mere irrational designation of an expiatory victim.

The first financial scandals that shook Germany, Austria, and France were caused, in Arendt's view, by an overproduction of petty capital in which the Jews served only as middlemen.[67] The petite bourgeoisie, however, who were gravely damaged because the scandals caused them to lose all their savings, suddenly turned anti-Semitic based on the fact that many bankers were Jewish. These developments gave rise to the first anti-Semitic parties, which in reality were supranational movements.[68] In response to the growing number of national parties, these movements claimed to represent the entire nation as if they were a mystical unity fending off a "Jewified" state, and they immediately latched on to a supranational structure. The Jews' situation in Europe, on the other hand, which could easily have provided fodder for socialist federalism, was not exploited in that way because "socialists were so concerned with class struggle and so neglectful of the political consequences of their own inherited concepts that they became aware of the existence of the Jews as a political factor only when they were already confronted with full-blown antisemitism as a serious competitor on the domestic scene. Then they were not only unprepared to integrate the Jewish issue into their theories, but actually afraid to touch the question at all."[69]

Against the backdrop of this general politicoeconomic context, Arendt devoted part of her study to the phenomenon of France. That the Third Republic was bereft of authority did not keep people from attacking both the Jews and the government. The socialists, who had internalized the anti-Semitism of the Enlightenment, waited until the Dreyfus affair to take a stand against anti-Semitic propaganda.[70] In the egalitarian ideology that was a product of Enlightenment universalism and in the assimilation of the French Jews that this ideology permitted, Arendt detected a pernicious breeding ground for a burgeoning anti-Semitism that could not be explained by economic circumstances alone: the political equality afforded by the republic would remain a mere abstraction were it not accompanied by the recognition of a social equality.

How did things get so out of hand? The "Jews' political ignorance"[71] brought on a novel situation: "man for the first time confronted man without the protection of differing circumstances and conditions."[72] In society as it actually was, social differences were no longer coded according to the religious values of yesteryear; even worse, they were outright denied by political egalitarianism. But although these differences did not evaporate completely, the only real difference with the past was that they now functioned in a state of nature without any protection. Accordingly, the Jews' only options were to remove themselves from the national arena while preserving their uniqueness, on the one hand, or to associate themselves with it without ever being seen as anything more than an intruder, on the other. Pariah or parvenu: that was the dilemma put forth by Bernard Lazare,[73] a dilemma that Arendt had already confronted in her book on Rahel Varnhagen. Once again, and this time by way of sociological arguments, Arendt denounced the secular assimilation that, in her view, is destined to transform religion (Judaism) into a psychological vice (Jewishness), a move that would entail more disastrous consequences than ever before: "Jews had been able to escape from Judaism into conversion; from Jewishness there was no escape. . . . A vice can only be exterminated."[74]

In Arendt's view, it was not only the decline of the nation-state but also the abandonment of religion that paved the way for the cold rationality and exterminationist tendencies of modern anti-Semitism, to the extent that it played the role of an ersatz religion and orchestrated fantasies without the relative protections offered by religious codes. Proust's masterpiece, the most insightful of all on this point, illustrates Arendt's analysis of the sociological and, one might say, psychological crystallization that transforms economic and political elements into absolute evil. In the end, assimilationist universalism and enlightened philo-Semitism are more dangerous than the hatred and the national religious wars of the past. Those elements are the essential beginnings of the crystallization of totalitarian evil whose alchemy is elucidated by our historian. More clandestine than before and invisible to the lens of economics and history, they entrench themselves in the opacity of "social factors" that poets and novelists have portrayed with great alacrity: "Social factors . . . changed the course that mere political antisemitism would have taken if left to itself, and which might have resulted in anti-Jewish legislation and even mass expulsion but hardly in wholesale extermination." And as Arendt also points out, "social 'philosemitism' always ended by adding to political antisemitism that mysterious fanaticism without which antisemitism could hardly have become the best slogan for organizing the masses."[75]

That leaves us to explore the psychological components of this "fanaticism," which Arendt believes underlies "universalism." Arendt did not complete this task herself, but she suggests how important it is because she includes it in the politicoeconomic model of causality that she outlines in sweeping terms. It is true that the third part of *Origins*, "Totalitarianism," makes a few important remarks about the psychology of the masses that totalitarianism made into fanatics. But Arendt refrains from delving into the complexity of the problem, which remains a fruitful line of inquiry today. If we resist the traditional safeguard of religions, with their focus on admonishment, guilt, and consolation, how can our individual and collective desires avoid the trap of melancholic destruction, manic fanaticism, or tyrannical paranoia? The absence of a psychoanalytic anthropology is clear here, and the least we can say about it is that it is currently being developed—but Arendt curiously appears not to see why it even matters. Instead, her interests lie in drawing conclusions from the Dreyfus affair, particularly in emphasizing the only thing that remains perpetually "visible": the birth of the Zionist movement that Arendt herself joined, as we have seen, with some resistance and ambivalence.[76]

IMPERIALISM . . . AND TOTALITARIANISM

The nation-state, of which France, in Arendt's view, is the example *"par excellence,"* is an autonomous structure that has existed since the French Revolution, that solidified during the nineteenth century, and that has created a new variety of social being.[77] As it is the product of several centuries of monarchy and enlightened despotism, the structure and consequences of the state are ambiguous. By proclaiming the universal rights of man while considering itself to be sovereign, that is, to be bound by no universal law, the French nation-state, Arendt informs us, has revealed its inherent paradoxes ever since the time of the Revolution: the French nation replaced "man" with the "citizen" as early as in the 1798 Declaration of the Rights of Man and passed laws against foreigners before going up against the aristocracy during the Terror.[78]

The "perversion" that the Romantics would later introduce into the idea and the practice of the nation, moreover, culminated in an identification of the nation-state with a "national soul" or with a sort of "supreme individual." By binding together the centrifugal forces produced in such a society, particularly through the class struggle that has been downplayed ever since, nationalism, which provides the only link between individuals and their nation-state, protects against "the consequences of its social atomization and, at the same time guarantees the possibility of remaining in a state of atomization."[79]

In Arendt's view, Hobbes and his *Leviathan* (1651) provide the precursor and the justification for the tyranny of the nation-state. With rampant overaccumulation and overproduction taking place, capitalism was already under way. Marx would later analyze it and reveal its superfluity as a law of the "surplus value" that provides a basis for "capital" as well as for "man's exploitation of other men"—a phenomenon that has culminated, one might add, in the "virtual" economy of the new world order that characterized the end of the twentieth century. For the time being, the "superfluity" that drives Arendt is manifested only as a dehumanization of social bonds in favor of an uninhibited, even solicited, violence in human relationships: the one who accumulates the most through the help of the tyrannical Leviathan-state is the one who wins it all. In Arendt's view, Hobbes theorized the social bond among "animals" who are devoid of any moral precepts, "cleansed of [Christian] hypocrisy," and wholly unscrupulous.[80] Once we assume that people need to manage the accumulation of surpluses, tyranny as a sort of political behavior becomes inevitable. Without becoming an apologist for tyranny, Hobbes predicts the likelihood of exterminating forms of violence, including those grounded in racial doctrines.

Arendt, for her part, analyzes racism as an ideology that improperly claims to be a science and that uses nineteenth-century Darwinism to deny the solidarity and equality that form the basis for the Christian humanity of the nation. Racism is one of the figures that characterize the decline of the humanist concept of the "nation" in favor of the "record of patriotism" that would be the Nazis' "racial nationalism."[81] A certain indifference toward the excluded, the marginalized, and the discarded members of every social class; the eroticism of the dregs of society; the admiration for what is "fundamental"; and the attraction to what is "deep" all played a role in this crystallization of the archaic, the tribal, and the instinctual into an ideology that dominated Europe, particularly Germany.[82]

Arendt draws an important distinction here between political nationalism of the French variety and "tribal nationalism," which is mystical and inherently totalitarian. She asserts that a powerful administration of the nation-state "entrenched itself like a parasite" in the body politic of the French nation, but that the French people "never committed the fatal error of allowing it to rule the country—even though the consequence has been that nobody rules it. The French atmosphere of government has become one of inefficiency and vexations; but it has not created an aura of pseudomysticism."[83]

In central Europe and the former Soviet Union, on the other hand, "masses who had not the slightest idea of *patria* and patriotism, not the vaguest idea of responsibility for a common, limited community," and who were forced by history to migrate and to uproot themselves, latched onto a tribal nationalism that defied legal and political organization as well as governments and parliaments in order to demand a traditional community devoted to God.[84] Pan-Slavism and pan-Germanism thus developed into religious movements as well as pan-movements that had to forgo the option of colonial expansion that was provided to the western European countries. The "national soul," which was presumed to be innately divine, was hostile to the nation-state: it counted on popular demand and turned the Jews into its main target soon thereafter.

Through what Arendt calls a "perversion of religion," this mystical tribal nationalism was identified with the chosen people: the Jews turned out to be the perfect model for a nation without a state and without perceptible institutions that the new mystical nationalists tried to imitate and used to fight to the death. "Guided by their own ridiculous superstition, the leaders of the pan-movements found that little hidden cog in the mechanics of Jewish piety that made a compete reversion and perversion possible, so that chosenness was no longer the myth for an ultimate realization of the ideal of a common humanity—but for its final destruction."[85]

Two-party rule in England, on the other hand, enjoys Arendt's blessing, as do the "Rights of Englishmen" that she, along with Disraeli, "the potent wizard," appears to prefer to the French "Rights of Man."[86] Even though Arendt was fully aware that English nationalism is based on what Burke called the *"entailed inheritance* derived to us from our forefathers," as well as on the racist supremacy of the white man that exploits the theories of Darwin and that culminates in the cult of the colonial hero (such as Lawrence of Arabia), in the end she concludes that the two-party system in England maintains the desired functioning of the nation-state.[87] It guards against the excesses of patriotism and racism that run rampant in the ideology and "movements" on the continent. Accordingly, even though England experienced the harsh effects of unemployment more than other countries did, it never dissociated "men," in the sense of independent metaphysical entities, from the state, which exploited them and which they would try to destroy. In the two-party system, only one party identified tentatively with the state, whereas the other party, the opposition party, subjected the first one to a degree of control whose effectiveness was enhanced by the certainty that it would remain in power. In other words, the opposition itself is what preserved the integrity of the whole package. The political logic behind two-party rule precluded any possibility of a single-party dictatorship and nullified the antiparliamentarian and antistatist movements that were fomenting among the masses.

To this analysis, Arendt could have added the observations she made in *On Revolution* concerning the role of Protestant and Puritan religion in maintaining the British social pact as an indissoluble political pact in the sense that it manifested God's will here on earth.[88] In a similar vein, one could point out that certain features of orthodox Christianity, which underestimates the uniqueness of the individual as well as the individual's political independence and which is inclined to subordinate the individual to a mystical community, were transposed onto totalitarian Communist ideology. Those "elements" could have buttressed Arendt's analysis of the "emergence of mass society" and the "loneliness" endemic to Soviet totalitarianism.

In this way, the history of imperialism—as an economic development and as a form of secularization, universalism, assimilationism, colonialism, and racism—led the European nation-states to a decline manifested most clearly by the waning of parliamentarian regimes, the growth of movements that came to replace them, and the "status" of minority groups, which belied the principle of equality before the state. All these developments paved the way for the deadly institutions of the totalitarian regimes.

The various movements, which wished to exist above the fray of parties as well as social classes, embarked on a national reconstitution that was hostile to discredited political institutions and then announced their plans for a supranational, European, and even worldwide mission. The "pacifism" of the Right and the Left that remained steadfast during Hitler's rise to power, the hypocritical reactions during the Munich crisis, and finally the collaboration with the Nazis were all evidence of the deep crisis brewing in the party system.[89] The crisis was dramatically exposed in the German-Russian nonaggression pact, which reacted to the disintegration of national politics by exhibiting the "resilient unity of fascist and Communist movements."[90] In truth, neither the members of these movements nor their leaders were troubled in any way by these spectacular reversals of fortune even though they were uprooted from their national identity and also deprived of their capacity for moral judgment, given that they were so fanatically absorbed by their own ideology. The political consequences of these movements can also be explained by the fact that immigration seriously undermines national homogeneity. In the space of a few years, France became a country that was totally dependent on foreign labor.[91] The social and political status quo, which was perceived as an admission that parliament had lost its power, incited a fear and a panic that overcame and surpassed the fear of the Nazis or the Communists.[92] To these sociopolitical causes, Arendt wisely adds analyses in the third part of *Origins* ("Totalitarianism") that describe more explicitly the psychology of the masses as well as the methods used by the various movements to control them, such as propaganda and, once the masses gained power, the police. The effectiveness of these movements and their attendant methods penetrated deep into postwar society, as Arendt warned: "The movements have survived the last war and are today [in 1951] the only 'parties' which have remained alive and meaningful to their adherents."[93] It is possible that the waning of movements as faux religions and the waning of the totalitarian strains that lurk within them became a reality only upon the fall of the Berlin Wall in 1989. Did that mark the end of imperialism? Or at least of its totalitarian strains? Probably so. We will see later in this book that Arendt's analysis of the human condition, an analysis that is no longer historical but historicizing, far from disarming our vigilance, incites us to note the barbaric side of "superfluity," "reification," and "movements" under those appearances, both new and old, that may appear innocuous at first blush.

In the end, the European nations' readiness to believe that they had solved the minority problem played no small role in the hideous "crystallization" of "superfluity." The first *Heimatlose* or *apatrides*, the category created by the peace treaties, "were for the most part Jews who came from the succession states and were unable or unwilling to place themselves under the new minority protection of the stateless people."[94] We now know the results of that system: the Jews, who were at first a minority unrecognized in Germany and then a stateless people whom the nation-state evicted from its borders, in the end were gathered together in the concentration camps. Before that point, however, and beginning with the peace treaties of 1919 and 1920, minorities and refugees had attached themselves to the newly established states that were created in the image of the nation-state. Hannah Arendt, who was herself a stateless woman before she became an American citizen in 1951, the same year that *Origins of Totalitarianism* was published, was convinced that the inability of the nation-states to treat the *apatrides* like lawful persons and the effort to deprive them of the legal status accorded to citizens destroyed the very essence of the nation-state, which is founded on equality before the law. The minority problem, which eventually culminates in an "anarchic mass of over- and underprivileged individuals," contributed to the crystallization of totalitarianism.[95]

Arendt's reflections cannot help but remind us of the "migratory flux" occurring today and of the status of undocumented aliens. If those problems remain unresolved by the political, economic, and legal measures enacted by the nation-states and the European Community, they may very well lead to crystallizations comparable to those incited by minority groups before World War II. Arendt's apocalyptic insight has lost none of its urgency.

Little by little, then, from economics to sociology and political science, Arendt paints a striking picture: human beings, "rejected" for good from their familiar haunts and from their memories, removed from their own soil and thus ungrounded, are the favorite target of once-promising fantasies that prove to be deadly strains of fanaticism. The breaking up of national, political, and religious bonds through the rise of movements and "statelessness" lent mid-twentieth-century Europe an odd sort of humanity. Throngs of people who remained apathetic and indifferent to the duties and responsibilities of citizenship and who were drawn to a life geared exclusively toward commercial success or failure lost all their personal will and ambition. Forming "one great unorganized, structureless mass of furious individuals" for whom "the source of all the worries and cares which make human life troublesome and anguished was gone," this sort of humanity displayed the "lack of self-interest of masses who are quite prepared to sacrifice themselves."[96]

The propaganda of Nazi and Communist movements, beginning with their inception and to an extreme degree when they exert power, ably targets this sort of humanity, whose members are attracted (as noted by de Tocqueville, whom Arendt cites liberally) to "absolutist systems which represent all the events of history as depending upon the great first causes linked by the chain of fatality, and which, as it were, suppress men from the history of the human race."[97] To socialist and nationalist ideologies already eviscerated of their utilitarian content, totalitarian propaganda adds the rhetoric of an "infallible prediction" and thus combines scientificism and prophetism ("everything follows comprehensibly and even compulsorily once the first premise is accepted"). In this sense, propaganda fabricates an ideological nonreality that nevertheless adorns itself with the entire artifice of logical consistency: unknown to "common sense," "ideological supersense" constructs a supposedly coherent world that proves to be a paranoid delusion that seeks to compensate for social atomization and depression.[98] Science is forcefully mobilized to fabricate these ideologies, which are emancipated "through certain methods of demonstration," "independent of all experience," and founded on the "tyranny of logicality" that is implacable and that culminates in a coherence that in reality does not exist.[99] In sum, the universe of the ideology that Arendt probes is tantamount to madness. The masses of atomized individuals become caught inside this world after they lose their "common sense" because of the destruction of the political realm and under the weight of the manipulations to which totalitarian regimes subject them: a legalistic aberration in Germany and a self-critically confessional aberration in the former Soviet Union that the "organization" puts into the hands of the "masses."

The sole party and its satellite organizations, which Arendt calls "fellow-travelers," enlist the population in every phase of its life, the very possibility of persuasion having been tempered from the beginning by constraint and coercion.[100] Arendt creates a veritable anthropology, even a political psychology, of totalitarian massification by describing the destruction of the psychic space of humans under totalitarian regimes, proof of which may be found in the fact that when movements lose their power, their formerly fanatical supporters immediately stop believing in the dogma and throw themselves instead into the quest for another promising fiction.[101]

A highly perceptive analyst and a close reader of Alexandre Koyré, Arendt described totalitarian movements as being "secret societies established in broad daylight."[102] By imitating the apparatus of secret societies without ever trying to keep their own goals a secret, these movements, just like secret societies, suppress dissenting opinions and seek "to safeguard the fictitious world through consistent lying," as manifested, for example, in the Nazis' "racial selection," the Bolsheviks' "dictatorship of the proletariat," and the infallibility of the leader combined in various groups with an incredulous rank-and-

file.[103] The most effective fiction, shared by the two totalitarian regimes in different ways but on parallel tracks, was the
invention of a worldwide Jewish conspiracy.[104] From the "family tree"—a "means . . . [of rationalizing] the essentially futile
feelings of self-importance and hysterical security" of the atomized masses—to the rediscovery of the "Protocols of the Elders
of Zion," Nazi propaganda proceeded by negatively identifying with an enemy slated for death while at the same time imitating him with a hateful fascination. In that sense, the Protocols' saying, "Everything that benefits the Jewish people is
morally right and sacred," becomes, for the Nazis, "Right is
what is good for the German people."[105]

Terror and the police, the two pillars of these regimes, bring
all their powers to bear as they put the finishing touches on the
work of destruction. The traditional police would proceed
through "provocations" in order to manufacture guilty parties.
The secret service of the totalitarian police, on the other hand,
did not identify the Jews in Germany and the older classes of
Soviet Russia as "suspects" but simply declared them to be such
by labeling them with the cliché of the "objective enemy,"
which varied according to the whims of the prevailing climate
of the day. Arendt analyzes on many levels the purges that
sought to destroy people as well as their infrastructure, the
splitting of the power-laden organizations (the state and the
party), the psychology of the double agent, the conspiracy of
the outsider, the various medical experiments, the overwhelming distrust, and the proliferation of departments that
destroyed the sense of responsibility and competence. In so
doing, she embraces collective psychology without being afraid
to employ the psychoanalytic terminology that she otherwise
rejects (she uses the terms "hysteria" and "perversion," and she
comes close to the notion of the unconscious: "To be sure,
totalitarian dictators do not consciously embark upon the road
to insanity").[106]

How are the two totalitarian regimes different from each

other? Without abandoning her customary humor that she displays throughout this survey of horror, Arendt takes a stab at several "narrative themes." Thus Hitler's "final solution" would be the equivalent of the commandment, "Thou shalt kill," and one could decode Stalin's orders as "Thou shalt bear false testimony."[107] In another context, she points out, tongue-in-cheek, that because the totalitarian man is incapable of trust, "Stalin trusted only one man and that was Hitler."[108] The czarist regime and Russia's economic and political impediments do not hold Arendt's interest, nor does she associate Stalinism with the ideas of Lenin that preceded it and, in many respects, that articulated it.[109] Preoccupied with the similarities between the two totalitarian regimes, Arendt did not hone her analysis of their differences. In her preface from 1966–71, however, she did remark upon the signs of change in the Soviet Union; without predicting an end to the regime, she noted that the rebirth of arts and letters during the last decade, and the fact that dissidents like Andrei Sinyavski and Yuli Daniel could be tried in court, showed that "we deal here no longer with total domination."[110]

By invoking the events of history, Arendt also examines the essential destiny of humanity in order to diagnose the worst offenses of totalitarianism as being none other than the eradication of the human being. The process was set in motion by the fabrication of soulless men "who can no longer be psychologically understood" because their psyche is destroyed before their bodies are destroyed: "only the fearful imagination," like Solzynitsin's, "can afford to keep thinking about horrors."[111]

The process then culminated "naturally" (Arendt scoffs at attempts to reduce humanity to a "nature" deprived of "meaning") in the concentration camps, "laboratories where changes in human nature are tested."[112] It is a sinister path from Hades to purgatory and then back to hell: from the ghetto to the gulags and then the Nazi camps. These are artifices "outside of life and death," economically futile and even harmful, originating in "another planet" in which "the human masses sealed off in them are treated as if they no longer existed."[113] The juridical personhood of the deportees was destroyed when they were mixed in with the other prisoners; their moral personhood was destroyed by destroying the bonds of human solidarity. The concentration camp "embodies" hell:[114] "Here the night has fallen on the future."[115] Is it because "one" has lost faith in the final judgment? Because "one" is no longer consumed with hope and fear? Transcendentalist historians and political scientists will ask Arendt to elaborate upon those points.

Arendt rails against an even more dramatic occurrence: the "organized oblivion" rampant in the camps that erased every trace of the deportees by pretending that the victims had never existed and that "robbed death of its meaning as the end of a fulfilled life."[116] But the true horror began with the enactment of a cold and systematic destruction based on the principle that men are beasts.[117] This historical naturalism, which captivated Darwin and Marx and which seeks to "stabilize" men and to secure their "nature" in order to free the forces of nature and history and thus to "manage them more efficiently," culminates in something no less dramatic than the reduction of man to "One Man of gigantic dimensions." This sort of scientific and technocratic vision of humanity deprives the individual of his space: the interdiction against any form of movement or communication with the outside world invariably entails the destruction of "the space between men as it is hedged in by laws" and "the living space of freedom."[118]

The metamorphosis of men into "nature" serves to transform them into "living cadavers" because the "nature" of man is "human" only to the extent that it gives him "the possibility of becoming something highly unnatural, that is, a man."[119] Spontaneity, with its characteristic unpredictability, which is the image of the capacity to begin that is bequeathed to us by birth, is what allows man to act out his unnaturalness, his essential estrangement from nature. And this human essence, which Arendt endorses in spite of her historicism, brings her back to her thesis on Saint Augustine by way of an impassioned plea for the respect of both emerging life and thinking. In that sense, Arendt presents us with an unexpected equivalence that she would later elucidate in *The Life of the Mind*. Thus in the wake of the terror of the totalitarian regimes that destroy thinking *and* life, it is politically paramount—because it is philosophically indispensable—to insist on freedom, which Arendt identifies with birth: "This freedom . . . is identical with the fact that men are being born and that therefore each of them *is* a new beginning, begins, in a sense, the world anew." Terror, on the contrary, eliminates "the very source of freedom which is given with the fact of the birth of man and resides in his capacity to make a new beginning."[120]

"To begin": that is what guarantees spontaneous uniqueness. A "common space": that is the precondition for a politics that can be shared. By suppressing our internal ability to begin, and by destroying the common space in which we can move and which is the political space, totalitarian terror, "lest anybody ever start thinking," ultimately targets the human quality par excellence that is thinking, which is synonymous with birth and rebirth: thinking is "the freest and purest of all human activities."[121]

We should keep this reflection in mind, as it will guide the political theorist's discussion of the Eichmann trial. Arendt is moving toward a definition of thinking that is not reasoning (thereby alluding to Kant's distinction between *Verstand* and *Vernunft*): thinking is not content with mere evidence, with internal consistency and truisms that have no need for other people or the world, that "[do not] reveal anything," and that constitute the object of the logico-positivism in question, which becomes an unconscious partner of desolation.[122] The totalitarian world is an antiworld because it is a world in which thought falls into a progressively narrower path that destroys the political space; it is a world of loneliness, of uprooting, and of the emergence of mass groups, as suggested in the play on words [seul/sol] inherent in the French word dé-solation—which combines "melancholy" and "being deprived of soil or space." "What we call isolation in the political sphere, is called loneliness in the sphere of social intercourse."[123] On the other hand, "only because we have common sense, that is, only because not one man, but men in the plural inhabit the earth can we trust our immediate sensual experience."[124]

And yet sharing is not the only possible or effective guar-antor of free thinking. The supreme quality of sharing demands an ability to engage in a dialogue with the self in the midst of a fertile solitude such as the solitude of a philosopher as distinct from Epictetus's "lonely man" [eremos].[125] In truth, never are we less alone than when we are engaged in a dialogue with ourselves. At the same time, and although Arendt vigor-ously defends the demanding solitude of the thinker that is threatened by modernity, she also warns of its hidden danger of desolation that may be realized if the thinker inadvertently finds himself losing the gift of friendship. Our ever-alert critic of totalitarian imperialism thus lays out several "fallacies" endemic to philosophy: is she suggesting that the limit expe-riences of the philosophers, verging on melancholy or psy-chosis, were an experimental form—as if in a microcosm of a laboratory—of the impending desolation of the rootless masses who pave the way for totalitarianism? We are reminded, for example, of Hegel's solitude as he whimsically declared, "Nobody has understood me except one; and he also misunderstood." And we are also reminded of Nietzsche's painful split as expressed and resisted by his Zarathustra: "Noon was, when One became Two." Arendt concludes by noting that "man loses trust in himself as the partner of his thoughts."[126]

Arendt thus suggests that the philosophy that developed dur-ing the crystallization of totalitarianism in the nineteenth and twentieth centuries explored with unparalleled brazenness the antidote to totalitarianism known as thinking. That said, she also acknowledged the risks of melancholia and psychosis because they operate close to the boundary of a stabilized delirium. Is the "professional thinker" a willing precursor of the totalitarian instincts of the present and the past? Or on the other hand, does he display a symptom that allows him to contemplate those instincts more effectively? Before returning to this fundamental question that she had just uncovered, Arendt concludes her essay on totalitarianism by rereading Saint Augustine through a political lens: to the "end in history" she contrasts a "new beginning": "Politically, [the new beginning] is identical with man's freedom. *Initium ut esset homo creatus est*— 'that a beginning be made man was created' said Augustine." Before this beginning becomes a political event, it is harbored in each new birth. The third section of Arendt's essay, "Totalitarianism," ends with a plea for renewed human uniqueness whose very last words are "every man"—"every man" against terror, against the mass groups and extermination that stemmed from the idea and practice of human "superfluity."[127]

THE BANALITY OF EVIL

It has been said that Arendt denied that evil existed, that she did not believe in it, and that she trivialized it.[128] And yet the development of her thought shows that from the time she wrote *The Origins of Totalitarianism*, she posited that radical evil, though clearly not an original sin, is a historically and politically "crystallized" way to reduce men to a mere "superfluity," with the effect that it annihilates their spontaneity and thinking and encourages them to destroy mercilessly a segment of humanity. Arendt believed in the existence of an "incalculable evil that men are capable of bringing about," as she wrote in an essay entitled "Organized Guilt and Universal Responsibility."[129] She associated this radical evil with what Kant called "absolute evil," although she also criticized Kant for trying to make absolute evil intelligible to the extent that he attributed it to a "perverted ill will."[130] Arendt maintained, for her part, that totalitarianism ultimately escapes human comprehension because its horror, beyond its anti-Semitism alone, is in the realm of the unreal.[131] Only the "fearful imagination" of those who have not suffered the desperate terror but who have been "aroused" by the "reports" they have heard and by the "series of remembered events" are capable of "dwelling on horrors."[132] Beginning in the 1950s, when she first begin thinking about Auschwitz, the political theorist identified radical evil, as we have seen, with what she would later call the "banality of evil" because whether it is manifested in a totalitarian system or an Eichmann, radical evil always entails the destruction of thinking (a destruction that is surreptitious, generalized, imperceptible, and thus banal, though it is also scandalous), which prefigures the scandalous annihilation of life. It is clear, then, that one would have to be operating in bad faith or be completely unfamiliar with Arendt's earlier texts to claim that she somehow exonerated or trivialized Eichmann's crimes.

Otto Adolf Eichmann was the former chief of the Gestapo's Jewish Office, which in 1943 was the only operation still engrossed in the task of "eliminating the Jewish adversary." Eichmann was captured in a Buenos Aires suburb on May 11, 1960, extradited to Israel, and put on trial in Jerusalem in 1961. Arendt proposed herself as a trial reporter to *The New Yorker*. Because she had missed the Nuremberg Trials, she thought that "to attend this trial is somehow, I feel, an obligation I owe my past."[133] And as she told Mary McCarthy, "I wrote this book in a curious state of euphoria."[134] In 1963 the five articles published in *The New Yorker* were reprinted in a book entitled *Eichmann in Jerusalem*, but the controversy surrounding her work had already begun and would only intensify as time went on.

Many people criticized Arendt for her "flippant" tone, but

their main target was three major themes of her book: first, her accusation that the Ben-Gurion government as well as Gideon Hausner, Eichmann's prosecutor, put on a show trial to be used as propaganda; second, her criticisms of the European Jewish councils [*Judenräte*] for having participated in the deportation and, eventually, in the extermination of those who shared their faith; and third, her portraying Adolf Eichmann in a way that downplayed his criminal personality and focused on an abstract construction for which he served as the intellectual proof: the "banality of evil." In Gershom Scholem's view, Arendt lacked what he called *Herzenstakt,* or sympathy. Many vituperative articles appeared that twisted Arendt's thinking around and accused her of anti-Semitism. The most dramatic and widely publicized of these events, in the opinion of Elisabeth Young-Bruehl, was a speech by Hausner and Nathan Goldmann, who was at that time the president of the World Zionist Organization, on the eve of the book's publication by Viking Press. Goldmann told an audience of nearly one thousand people that "Hannah Arendt had accused European Jews of letting themselves be slaughtered by the Nazis and of displaying 'cowardice and lack of will to resist.'"[135] With the exception of a few positive letters that were written almost exclusively by young people and a warm welcome by some Columbia University students on July 23, 1963, the campaign of attacks against her, which reached the point of slander, lasted three years.[136] The attacks even penetrated the mind of her old friend Kurt Blumenfeld. Hospitalized with illness, Blumenfeld had not read her *New Yorker* articles but appears to have been influenced by close associates of his who misrepresented Arendt's work to him. Right before Blumenfeld's death in May 1963, Arendt went to see him in Israel, but she was apparently unable to convince him completely of the validity of her position. In France, *Le Nouvel Observateur* published on October 26, 1966, a letter signed by prominent Jewish intellectuals entitled "Is Hannah Arendt a Nazi?" Only with the passing of time and with the restoration of the complex memory of the Holocaust—which owes much to Arendt's book, its controversy as well as its content—have we learned to read *Eichmann in Jerusalem* more objectively.[137]

In response to her critics, Arendt defended herself by arguing that her tone, hardly flippant, reflected an anger commensurate with the gravity of the problem, even though she reserved her right to use irony and not just pathos to broach the subject of evil. Arendt also admitted that because of a lack of information or a hasty judgment on her part, she had neglected to point out that the participation of Jewish councils in the Holocaust was gradual and that "it was difficult indeed to understand when the moment had come to cross a line which never should have been crossed." Although she offered overwhelming proof of betrayal (on the part of Kastner in Budapest, for example), her accusation against Rabbi Leo Baeck, whom she described in the first edition of her book as being a "Jewish Führer," incited so many objections that she retracted her remarks, although she declined to endorse the mystique of suffering that the leader of the Berlin Jews thought was inherent in the status of the chosen people.

Contrary to the words her enemies have put in her mouth, Arendt never found fault with the Jewish people as a whole for having submitted to extermination, and she emphasized that "no non-Jewish group or people had behaved differently."[138] But she also insisted to Scholem that "wrong done by my own people naturally grieves me more than wrong done by other people."[139] To the Jewish establishment that experienced her works as a profanation of the Name [*chillul haschem*] even though it was merely what Josef Maier, her friend from the *Aufbau* days, called a "report," Arendt replied, "You have misunderstood me." Finally, the historian considered the problem of the *Judenräte* [Jewish councils] (to which, it has been pointed out, she devoted only ten pages out of a three-hundred-page book) to have been widely known among the Jewish community, but she also believed that the community decided it was necessary to guard the councils as a sort of family secret, particularly because some of the people responsible for the councils still occupied scattered positions of political power. Since 1944, moreover, Arendt had paid homage to the resistance movement in the Warsaw ghetto because it put an end to the pariah status of the Jewish people and because it brought back the glory and honor that had been lost since the Macchabean era. Despite the violence of the attacks against her and the few subsequent modifications she made to her position, Arendt never backed away from her fundamental conclusion: "The whole truth [many critics took issue with this peremptory phrase that sounded exhaustive and unequivocal] was that if the Jewish people had really been unorganized and leaderless, there would have been chaos and plenty of misery, but the total number of victims would hardly have been between four and a half and six million people."[140]

Among the targets of the attacks against Arendt, her main thesis on the "banality of evil," as embodied by Eichmann, was no doubt the most difficult to dispose of. The political theorist makes herself into a narrator here and recounts the biography of an ordinary German, "neither feeble-minded nor indoctrinated nor cynical." This "average," "normal" person upset her during the entire trial because he proved himself "perfectly incapable of telling right from wrong."[141] Arendt notes sarcastically his "heroic fight against the German language" as well as his trite phrases and bureaucratic vernacular: "he was genuinely incapable of uttering a single sentence that was not a cliché."[142] Alongside the itinerary of this displaced man who found potential recognition and a promising career in National-Socialism, alongside his fascination with the "idealism" of the Zionists, and alongside the "good conscience" of a German who thought he could adhere to Protestant or Kantian moralism by obeying the orders of his superiors, Arendt adds some seemingly innocuous observations that some of her readers must have found particularly shocking. She points out, for example, that Eichmann refused to read Nabokov's *Lolita,* which an Israeli police officer offered him to make him more relaxed, because he considered the book to be "unwholesome." In the eyes of our journalist, this was the ultimate proof, if one were even needed, that Eichmann completely lacked spontaneity and thus lacked freedom and a capacity for independent thinking. "The longer one listened to him, the more obvious it became that his inability to speak was closely connected with an inability to think, namely, to think from the standpoint of somebody else. No communication was possible with him, not because he lied but because he was surrounded by the most reliable of all safeguards against the words and the presence of others, and hence against reality as such."[143] Eichmann had the "horrible gift for consoling himself with clichés," and until his death, he was content with emitting fixed expressions, like a discourse handed down to him from above, as if he was repeating words that were ready-made or that came right out of the mouths of his superiors. In the face of so much inauthenticity and obedience, those who followed the trial had in their minds the question "of whether the accused had a conscience."[144]

It is possible that Arendt's observations about the accused's lack of thinking were influenced by the philosophical work of her contemporaries on the relationship between language and thought, a body of work that was beginning to dominate the 1960s. Her observations were no intellectual speculation, however. The "reporting" in *The New Yorker* was a "live" reenactment of the troubling human phenomenon that Arendt had analyzed in her *Origins* as being a "crystallization" of the sociopolitical conditions of Nazi totalitarianism: the eradication of thinking in human beings, their ceasing to think for themselves, and their willingness to obey superiors who gave them orders. Eichmann gave her the opportunity to prove that because the vast majority of those who enacted Nazism were not sadistic monsters or inveterate torturers, they shared this *banal*—because it was widespread and because it was often deemed innocuous—condition of renouncing personal judgment.

"Banality" is therefore not the same as "innocence." The story of Eichmann is in no way the tale of an innocent man: Arendt supports the death penalty because the law is intended to punish the crimes that the man has committed, and not the person incapable of distinguishing between good and evil. What is more, Arendt does not believe in collective guilt because she fears the transformation of justice and morality into propaganda. The goal of her analysis of Eichmann is to question the individual conscience rather than to stigmatize the collective crimes that risk swallowing up the individual conscience.[145] But Arendt, along with others, wanted Eichmann to be brought before an international court, because "the crime against the Jews was also a crime against mankind." And she concludes that her book teaches "the lesson of the fearsome, word-and-thought-defying *banality of evil*."[146]

In other words, Eichmann is a concrete example of the manipulation of humanity that is the hallmark of totalitarianism: without being stupid per se, Eichmann exhibited "sheer thoughtlessness." Did he belong to the class of criminals described in Dostoevsky's *Journals* as "eternally unrepentant . . . and who cannot afford to face reality because his crime has become part and parcel of it"? Even more troubling is this seemingly less dramatic statement from Arendt, who finds banality to be all the more frightening: neither perverse nor sadistic, "frighteningly normal" people, in perfectly good conscience, commit crimes on a whole new scale. Incapable of judging, they take it upon themselves "to determine who should and who should not inhabit the world," and we can imagine that, in the near future, the demands of automation will cause certain "determiners," they too incapable of judgment, to seek to "exterminate all those whose intelligence quotient is below a certain level."[147] Do powerful Eichmanns lie dormant in the "winners" of a hypertechnological society?

Does this conception of evil exclude sadism and perverted evil? Arendt was not unaware that many Nazis had a penchant for perversion and that to the "rational" use of Gestapo torture tactics was added an "irrational, sadistic type" that manifested the "blind bestiality of the SA." But beyond this "concession of the regime to its criminal and abnormal elements,"[148] what concerns Arendt even more is the "kind of Pontius Pilate feeling" that was shared by the vast majority of Nazis and their collaborators: "Who was he [Eichmann] to judge?"[149] That sort of perversion, which in Arendt's eyes is the most troubling of them all, implies a perversion of the moral imperative and of its underlying judgment: it is a "distortion" of Kant: "His guilt came from his obedience, and obedience is praised as a virtue."[150]

Even so, although Arendt recognizes that sadism has a sexual component, she rejects Freud's conception of a radical sadism that depends on the death drive, and she attempts to show that violence is neither "bestial" nor "irrational." She has recently been criticized, in some respects appropriately, for having underestimated this aspect of Nazi barbarism.[151]

In the first place, by rejecting the Manichean or Gnostic doctrine that holds that the battle between good and evil appears in the cosmos and in each man, which is the same doctrine that underlies Freud's dualism between Eros and Thanatos (the life drive and the death drive), the philosopher–political theorist appears to endorse the Platonic and then Christian notion of unthinkable evil.[152] In *The Life of the Mind* she goes into more detail about the philosophical problem of evil, pointing out that Plato's wondering admiration [*thaumazein*] concerns only the good and the beautiful and has no place for evil. In the end, hideous things and ugly deeds serve only to make us retreat out of fear, as they do in Plato's *Parmenides*.[153] The Christian tradition merely carries this reasoning one step further by asserting that there is no such thing as a bad creation, that Lucifer is a fallen angel and not a being created evil, and that evil is merely a privation of the good; in sum, that tradition saw no metaphysical reality in evil. In other texts, however, Arendt distances herself from the philosophical tradition whose variants go back to Hegel and Marx, who believed that "evil is no more than a privative modus of the good, that good can come out of evil; that . . . evil is but a temporary manifestation of a still-hidden good."[154] From that standpoint we can understand Arendt's resistance to dialectical philosophy and to the "power of negation" to bring about something "positive" (the good, freedom, and so forth). In fact, Arendt criticizes this Hegelian vision, which she believes runs the risk of justifying the cynicism of "negative means" that lead to "positive ends" and which she detects in the reasoning of the Zionists (she believes that using our enemies for our own salvation is "the 'original sin' of Zionism").[155]

In her later writings, Arendt appears to forgo any further contemplation of evil and to adopt instead the view held by Heidegger, who reinterpreted Plato by claiming that Being and Nothingness are so close to each other that Being is included *in* Nothingness: "Nobody can think Being without at the same time thinking nothingness, or think Meaning without thinking futility, vanity, meaninglessness."[156] The striking role that Heidegger assigns death as a "shelter" for Being and this sheltering of Being in Nothingness are both accompanied by an unequivocal affirmation that consents to existence, so much so that they appear to be the very precondition of thinking [*denken*], without which thanking [*danken*] would be impossible.[157] At no point, however, does Arendt subscribe to the notion that death is the muse of philosophy, if not the only indispensable condition for thought, which is a notion that can be easily inferred from Plato and Heidegger.[158] Without denying the caesura of death, Arendt ceaselessly returns to birth, as we have seen, by searching in Kant, in Spinoza, or in Nietzsche's "Eternal Return" for a way of thinking about joy, admiration, and *amor fati*, "the highest possible formula of affirmation."[159]

We can detect a trace of this "affirmation" in Arendt's writings when she defines *fate* as a postulation and an acceptance of the good, in this case within the Jewish tradition. In a letter to one of her students, Arendt thus mentioned the thirty-six righteous men whose identities are known to no one, least of all themselves, and for the sake of whom God does not destroy the world.[160] She also evokes the Hebrew Kaddish, the death prayer that says nothing but "Holy is His Name" as a sign of the "silent, all-embracing genius of consent."[161] In a similar vein is Arendt's response to Scholem: "It is indeed my opinion now that evil is never 'radical,' that it is only extreme, and that it possesses neither depth nor any demonic dimension. It can overgrow and lay waste the whole world precisely because it spreads like a fungus on the surface. It is 'thought-defying,' as I said, because thought tries to reach some depth, to go to the roots, and the moment it concerns itself with evil, it is frustrated because there is nothing. That is its 'banality.' Only the good has depth and can be radical."[162]

Arendt is thus of the view that if these various aspects of Western tradition are able to make evil into an abstraction, they can offer us the sheer advantage of preserving the possibility of thinking itself. Believing in the good means more than just an adherence to thought, for it also manifests our very faith in thinking. Such faith adheres to thinking to the extent that it wishes to preserve the best of what that tradition has to offer us: not "values," which even at their best can lead to noxious behavior if we apply them without thinking, but the ability to question each value as a fundamental characteristic of thinking. Still, a philosophical rejection of radical evil is in some ways tempered by the affirmation that Being is "concealed" in Nothingness, which suggests that "Being withdraws into itself" and that the "oblivion of Being belongs to the self-veiling essence of Being." As a result, *Dasein,* which is itself "sheltered in its concealment," finds a place only in errancy: to err and error. Even though it is in the privileged moments that take place from one epoch to the next, "Being qua Truth breaks into the continuum of error."[163]

Let us be specific here about the highly personal way in which Arendt appropriates Heidegger's thought. First, the errancy/error of *Dasein* means that thinking is not tantamount to true action, as Plato and the early Heidegger believe: "thinking and acting do not coincide, . . . to act is to err, to go astray."[164] Arendt rehabilitated this Heideggerian tenet dating from the time of his "reversal," for it is an essential element in obviating, in the face of a society of work and massification, the need to think "beyond" the "interval between birth and death" that gives rise to the "life process" and that is nothing less than "being-toward-death": "death as the shelter for the essence of human existence."[165] Arendt does not stop there, however. Once she accepts this need for thinking, she suggests that given her original affirmation of this joy, which will serve as the foundation of her own faith and which she defines as being a nonreligious joy, it is important not to limit thinking to its solitude but to guide it toward the goal of developing into judgment. In the political space of appearances and of sharing with other people, to think about the good is not to do good. It is not necessary to "engage" or to be a "militant," but rather to reconnect the universal with the particular, to evaluate, and to choose. That is what totalitarianism has destroyed. Going beyond the totalitarian brand of politics that Arendt so violently attacks, her stand on the evil of the century is really quite basic. If she seeks to preserve the otherworldliness of philosophy, it is not so that it can disappear into oblivion in an unnamable, affected, and even potentially tyrannical solipsism, but to infuse the dialogue of thinking into the very political space in which thinking is used as a means for distinguishing between good and evil. Eichmann would later force her, putting aside what she considered to be the *cura posterior* of a Jew engaged in the history of her people, to pursue philosophically the path from thinking to judgment in *The Life of the Mind.*

FAITH AND REVOLUTION . . . IN SOCIETY, THAT SANCTIFIED HEARTH

The work of Hannah Arendt suggests that the loss of religious reference points and the secularization of European society, together with the growth of technology, were the primary reasons behind the crystallization of totalitarianism. The important school of political thought directed by Waldemar Gurian (and of which Eric Voegelin was a member) was of the view that totalitarianism resulted from modern atheism rather than from a sociohistorical process.[166] In Voegelin's view, fascism and Communism stemmed from a "spiritual disease of agnosticism" and from an "immanentist sectarianism [that developed] since the high Middle Ages" and that reached its peak in the eighteenth century. Voegelin also posited that the real rift was not between the liberals (as in the political Left) and the totalitarians, but "between the religious and philosophical transcendentalists on the one side, and the liberal and totalitarian immanentist sectarians on the other side."[167] Voegelin tried to ascribe this position to Arendt as well.

Arendt's response to Voegelin begins by clarifying her conception of a "human nature," the existence of which she appears to endorse as she considers it to have been destroyed by totalitarianism. From the outset, however, she rejects essentialism: "This essence, in my opinion, did not exist before it had . . . come into being." Avoiding the abstract debate between "essence" and "existence," Arendt asserts that human nature is manifested in concrete historical realities. That notion would become her thesis in *The Human Condition* (1958), which she completed less than ten years after *Origins of Totalitarianism* (1951). By going back to the dawn of civilization, Arendt describes the way the concrete sociohistorical organization of human activities and space facilitated the rise of human beings as well as the impasses that they have faced. "Historically, we know human nature only to the extent that it has an existence," she responds to the transcendentalists. Without denying that a strain of atheism played a role in ending ethics, Arendt maintains that the totalitarian phenomenon is unique and that no other prior event, whether in the Middle Ages or during the eighteenth century, could be properly deemed "totalitarian."[168] Arendt is also careful to distinguish her philosophical inquiry from any sort of religious position by associating the political use of the "divine" with the same pernicious nihilism that it believes it is counteracting: "Those who conclude from the frightening events of our times that we have got to go back to religion and faith for political reasons seem to me to show just as much lack of faith in God as their opponents."[169]

Arendt's remarks recall Nietzsche's and Heidegger's opposition to the utilitarianism intrinsic to the "value" of God. Similarly, *The Human Condition* can be read as a sociohistorical demonstration of the metaphysics and "errancy" that are always already in *Dasein*. Didn't Arendt lovingly dedicate her book to Heidegger, "to whom I remained both faithful and unfaithful"?[170]

And yet her unfaithfulness is precisely what carried her forward. The author not only returned to the pre-Socratic universe by consulting literary and historiographic testimonies about the Age of Pericles, and even earlier eras, in an effort to reconstruct this Greek "model" in a way that is not a facile nostalgia but also hypothesized about the premetaphysical world. Even more unfaithfully, in fact, she also believed that the amorphous mass of totalitarian regimes is not a preordained fate of the "ones" to which *Dasein* would be condemned as soon as it abandoned its solitary model to integrate with other people. Arendt believes in "common interests" or, as Cicero would put it, "common 'consent'": *esse* can become *inter-esse,* or interest. *Inter-est* is a "between men," at once the foundation and the aim, the antithesis not only of totalitarianism but also of solipsistic isolation and transcendental utilitarianism.[171]

Ignored when it was first published in France, *The Human Condition* lionizes the public realm as the Other of transcendence because it realizes—at great risk—the immortality that defines human nature. Arendt's reasoning can be laid out as follows. Because "human nature" is coextensive with thinking, it is inherently antinatural. And to the extent that thinking, as a way for mortals to perceive eternity (in the pre-Socratic and biblical tradition), is not reduced to a "calculus of consequences," it discloses what is unknown in the world of the senses (that is, it discloses Being in appearance). It is because we are mortal and because we believe we are mortal that we are able to contemplate eternity. What defines thinking as a disclosure is the fact that it contemplates mortality and Being. The Greeks' *bios theōrētikos*—or the medieval *vita contemplativa,* which is a highly imperfect way of translating the wonder of the Greek sage—guaranteed this activity of thought.

In response to the aporia of mortals contemplating eternity, those mortals, as living beings, strive for immortality in time. Their efforts are manifested in ways that are always imperfect and that are generally futile or fragile: labor, work, and action. *Bios politikos*—which is always translated imperfectly as *vita activa,* the counterpart to *vita contemplativa*—realizes this effort for the *animal laborans,* for *homo faber,* and for political praxis. The *animal laborans* wears himself out through his maintenance activities in a direct connection with nature: an interminable "labor," with no chance of standing the test of time, is what ensures the survival of the *animal laborans* because it provides for his consumption, which, in the end, is what consumes him. *Homo faber,* on the other hand, produces *[poiein]* objects or "creations" that endure, defy nature, and create a "world." Yet although this world fabricates and commercializes, it is merely an exchange among property owners, a transaction involving values and moneys. *Homo faber* believes that he has conquered everyone before he realizes that he has been recast as the *animal laborans* because he shares the same goal as his predecessor: to reproduce the life process. It is only in political action, in the sense of sharing and recollecting the hero's "exploits" (what the Greeks called *arēte* and the Romans *virtus*), that men, through their ability to give shape to a story or to history, are able to survive not only as a species, but as a plurality of "whos" as well. It would be fair to call this praxis a miracle: based on "action" as a "beginning," it manifests within the polis the human condition of natality through the splendor of the act and the uniqueness of the word.[172] Even so, political action, as Arendt understands the term, finds itself gobbled up today by our new conception of politics, one that was entirely unfamiliar to the ancient Greeks: politics as a "process" that governs the world of nature and the whole of humanity.

This state of affairs ensues from the scientific discovery of our mortality, which, though it undermines the foundations of religion, particularly Christianity, is still paired with a search for immortality. In fact, even if secularization, as Arendt reminds us, "meant nothing more or less than that men once more had become mortals," it does not preclude a certain quest for immortality that still remains at the heart of political communities. More concretely, "a strictly human and earthly permanence in this world" or the "potential immortality of mankind," which culminates in Hegel's philosophy of history as "one uninterrupted development of the Spirit," is tantamount to a secularization that revives antiquity by countering Christianity.[173] And yet the political communities in which a history of this sort would tend to be manifested descend into a "fabrication," into a "process" (whether a natural process, a historical process, or the process of meaning itself, or into a "mass-

society [that] is nothing more than that kind of organized living."[174] Put another way, the moderns do not transform such a
history into a new religion, as is often suggested; rather, they
try to reenact the cult of "liv[ing] in a community [*sundzēn*]"
that was so dear to the Greeks.[175]

Still, to seek immortality through a life limited by the interval between birth and death is no small paradox, as recognized
by Aristotle and as explored in all its fullness[176]—from its limitations to its opportunities—by Arendt, all the more because
labor, work, and action encroach upon one another and evolve
as one while breaking down hierarchies and increasing the risks
of reification inherent in each of them. Is it not the case that
the political (and particularly Marxist) vision of history, as if to
put an end to this process, also suggests that "man makes history," thereby reducing history to a utilitarian object, a fabri-
cated product, or a "creation" that ignores the vagaries of
human interaction as well as the dangers of freedom, spontaneity, and uniqueness? "Nobody is the author or producer of
his own life story. . . . Somebody began it and is its subject in
the twofold sense of the word, namely, its actor and sufferer,
but nobody is its author."[177]

Even more important, is it not the case that the modern
conception of a secularized immortality, reduced to the earthly
domain that is "history *made* by men," also disrupts the very
faculty of thought? In fact, can any thought disclosure or revelation still exist if an increasingly automated labor turns the
body onto itself and deprives the laborer of the world, if the
work is reduced to merchandise whose only significance is the
price it extracts to maintain the life process of the manufac-
turer, and if political action is no longer engaged in by people
able to restore its memory and outline but rather by engineers
that "manufacture" it? In sum, are we still able to think if it is
really true that we lost the "common world" and the public
realm *stricto sensu* at the very moment we lost sight of the transcendence that inspired us to aim for an extraterrestrial, virtual

immortality? To remain even remotely in touch with this "world" that both brings us together and keeps us from getting in each other's way, Arendt, though a fierce critic of psychology, proposes theological solutions that would implement a strongly political and ontological strain of psychology: forgiveness and the promise. At the same time, however, she paints a troubling, and sometimes apocalyptic, picture of a human condition that contains within itself the risks of its own eradication, a human condition that from the outset is in danger—if not of losing itself, at least of betraying that which defines its very nature: thinking alongside the public realm.

Evil begins by abolishing the ancient Greek boundary [*horoi*] between the "private" or "one's own" [*idion*], which is centered on the household [*oikia*], and the "public" or "common" [*koinon*] space of the agora. For the ancient Greeks, the private realm is sacred because it sustains life. To do so, however, it harbors labor and procreation—slaves and women, in other words—and invariably finds itself subjected to inequality and to the tyranny of necessity and of arbitrary power. The agora, on the other hand, is the locus of the appearance and of publicness, a space in which the citizen displays himself amid the publicness of free men, welcomes the excellence and marvels of other people, and secures the memory of us all. Once the needs of production surpass the limits of the family and encroach upon the city-state itself, the ensuing flow of household concerns [*oikia*] into the public realm erases the boundary between the private and the public, which puts various sorts of freedom in jeopardy.[178] At that point, public activities are conceptualized according to the model of familial relationships: the "economy" (from *oikia*: "household") is what eats away at the polis and transforms it into a "society." The medieval professional guilds and *confréries* were companies [*cum-panis*] of a familial sort—the family was absorbed into social organizations, and the advent of society was accompanied by a decline in the family itself. The result was that the private was ejected into the intimate, on the one hand, and that politico-public freedom was restricted, if not abolished, on the other hand. In fact, whereas in the polis the goal was to use political action to dominate the instinct of conservation and the biological process, the "society" that replaced it "excluded the possibility of action, which formerly was excluded from the household."[179] "Society equalizes [and] normalizes" to the point where "the most social form of government" is "bureau-cracy."[180] Arendt's demonization of society reaches its peak in her critique of the state, whose decline "had been preceded by a withering away of the public realm" and was "transformed into a nation-wide 'housekeeping.'"[181] By the same token, Arendt does not spare the conservative economists who hope to fix society by privatizing it: their goal is ultimately futile, Arendt believes, because in a society made up of employees, the state is no longer the public's guarantor but quite simply the hostage of "society" in the sense of a familial economy sub-sumed under our needs of life.[182]

Faced with the "private" and even with the "sacred" that it harbors (because both realms engulf the "public" in the form of the "social"), Arendt becomes a very shrewd reader of Machiavelli. We recall that the formidable prince rises up against the church's participation in current affairs more than against the corruptness of the prelates. In the eyes of the mas-ter politician, nothing is more reprehensible than the religious domination of the secular domain, for such domination even-tually effaces the division between the public and the private. As an alternative, the prince proposes the following: "either the public realm corrupted the religious body and thereby became itself corrupt, or the religious body remained uncorrupt and destroyed the public realm altogether." In a word, to seek to preserve the ancient boundary between public and private, Machiavelli, in an apparently cynical move, teaches that we should "not be good" because "goodness" (in its purest form in Christian thought) is not "of this world." His conception of politics also explains his mistrust of "reformed" religions, which are even more dangerous than the other kind because they tell us to be good and "not 'to resist evil,'" with the result that "wicked rulers do as much evil as they please."[183] Arendt responds with applause! Our "Machiavellian" reader suggests, sotto voce, that the priest, as well as the philosopher, does not blend together thinking and acting or praying and governing but preserves their differences and tensions.[184]

We cannot help but admire Arendt's bold critique of a "society" subjected to an economy, given that "the social" has become such a political cliché for the Right as well as the Left. We also find it tempting to link Arendt's diatribe against the social with the psychoanalytic distinction between need, which links the subject to the archaic realm and its dependence on the mother (which Arendt refers to as the vitalist "household," "economy," and "society"), and desire, which affords the dangerous freedom of bonds with other people (which she calls the "space of appearance" and "political action").

A more thoughtful political anthropology might object, however, that the "economy" of the household [oikia] is not limited merely to ensuring survival, and to the simple world of the animal laborans and his painful and servile labors that metabolize nature in order to make the body last. By mirroring its own etymology ("ruse" or "negotiation"), moreover, the term "economy" meant, in late antiquity, in the Gospels, and in the Byzantine era, "plan," "exemption," and "transition" between the invisible universe (the divine) and the visible universe (the human). Is it not true that the term "economy" would later be used to indicate the representation of icons of God: oikonomia-eikōn?[185] The busy household and the bodies of women and slaves it contains were not—and still are not—destined merely for an unhappy life of labor ("travail," from tripalium, "torture"). In fact, it is possible that the oikonomia that characterizes women and slaves is a ruse and a negotiation with immortality, an oikonomia that is different from a political outburst, of course, but that still allows for a softer approach to the invisible. The economy of icons [*eikōn*] was believed to be a divine incantation, which is how representation came to be accepted in the Christian world. Alongside narration and action, images increasingly emerged as the privileged domain of the divine presence in the political realm itself. Taken on its own terms, as a simple "economy" or "icon," the representation that characterized the beginning of the Christian era remained, it is true, stubbornly caught in the Byzantine world, and it eventually had to be replaced by the Roman form of representation and then later by its more overtly worldly and political Renaissance counterpart until the point where images finally became the principal face of modern politics—for better or for worse in a media-driven economy—even though by then they had lost their "economic" bond with invisible eternity.

The point of this digression on the economy and the icon is to emphasize the limitations of Arendt's diatribe against a society that is consumed by the economy and that therefore destroys the freedom of the polis. Other limitations also emerge in her approach to the body as well as in her lack of attention to psychic life and intimacy, which she considers to be hybrid relics of subjectivism and the loss of transcendence. Preoccupied by her project concerning political freedom and by her ancient Greek models, the political theorist managed to neglect the plural and possible economies of prepolitical freedom that disclose "the social" and that are precisely what interest us today. Is it not the case that the dismantling of the "purely political" and the development of its attendant freedoms and of civil society are integral parts of the "dismantling of metaphysics" to which Arendt contributed? In that respect, "the social," which the philosopher denounced so strongly, may still not have revealed all the freedoms that lurk inside it.

Arendt's respectful but radical debate with Marx provides another glimpse of her vigilant insurgence against the society of labor and production. Arendt credits Marx with discovering the "productivity" of labor: human energy is not exhausted by the production of what is necessary to subsist; instead, it produces "surpluses." Through the intervention of the Hebraic tradition that underlies the thinking of Marx—who, rather than indicting labor associated it with reproduction—productivity, considered a "surplus value," is forever recognized as that which constantly reinvigorates production and accumulation. And yet Marx, who uncovered the direct relationship between labor and reproduction and who defined labor as "men's metabolism with nature," dissociates labor from the work and from the way it enables us to reach the world, human plurality, and political freedom.[186] By delving into the *oeuvrièrisme* of Marxian thought, which idolizes "labor" and the "laborer," Arendt unearths the pernicious underpinnings that drove Marxism toward the absence of freedom and totalitarianism. In Arendt's view, the end result of the "consistent naturalism" that underlies the conception of labor in Marx—whom Engels called "the Darwin of history"[187]—culminates in a state in which "everything has become an object for consumption," as with the *animal laborans*: say goodbye to *homo faber,* and especially to political praxis. The "work" itself becomes "labor," the "individual" disappears into "the gigantic subject of the accumulation process,"[188] and the *animal laborans* is "deprived" of a private place of his own to hide because Marx assigns him to a communitarian society in which every producer, including the intellectual, is a "servant." By likening the human condition to a sort of laborer while seeking to avoid exploiting that laborer, Marx gets caught up in paradoxes: he is forced to describe Communism as an abolition of labor that would bring about a mythical leisure society—an essentially "worldless" society of "hobbies" and strictly private activities.[189] Fixated on the *animal laborans* and on the socialized individual who resists the political and the singular, the Marxist universe remains, even in its idealized dream of Communism, a truncated system that lost any opportunity it may have had to respect the individual or to create a shared realm.[190]

Throughout history, while labor and subsistence have consumed the work of art, the technology that has mastered the life process has increasingly come to dominate the human condition, including its political elements. The realm of politics has forgotten its ancient Greek destiny of celebrating what is great through the energy of the living act and the word. Instead, politics is now content simply to assess motives and results. What modernity calls "the judgment of history" hallows victors, but not the actuality [*energeia*] of greatness [*megethos*]. Technology, as the ultimate overseer of the survival of the species, transforms the Platonic and Christian mistrust of the splendid space of appearance into a Puritanism of sorts and reduces politics to administrative intrigue. Science, on the other hand, has brilliantly conquered the universe, but it remains adrift from human relationships.

All the same, Arendt's version of Heidegger's *Gestell,* which leaves little room for human activity to reconnect with thinking as a form of disclosure, seeks neither a resistance to technology nor a reinstatement of religious values. In her view, the only possible remedy is to change our relationship to time. In fact, all of Arendt's proposed solutions modify temporality, beginning with birth as a paradigm of the reconstructive initiatives offered by forgiveness and the promise.

On a more strictly political front, Arendt believes that revolution plays the role of a rupture that shatters the process of reification inherent in the modern human condition and announces—always temporarily—an ongoing renewal. As an experiment in freedom and an experience completely unknown to the ancient Greeks and Romans, revolution is "the experience of man's faculty to begin something new." Even more important, the "bombast of newness" that is the revolutionary rupture is not an insurrection by one group against another, but a demand of happiness for all: "The revolutionary spirit of the last centuries, that is, the eagerness to liberate *and* to build a new house where freedom can dwell, is unprecedented and unequaled in all prior history."[191] Revolution enables thought, which is solitary by definition, to return to the public realm and action. On that point, Arendt cites Malraux: "As Malraux once remarked in *L'Espoir,* revolution came to play 'the role which once was played by eternal life': it 'saves those that make it.'"[192]

Is the search for political renewal, that is, for a secularized humanity, tantamount to what was once known as transcendence? Arendt comes close to thinking as much, although with the caveat that revolution does not seek to adopt the form of a centralized institution, which could only become an arm of the Terror that distorts "the most pronounced political ambition of the people."[193] The basic flaw of the French Revolution, Arendt suggests, was that it believed that its innovative spirit could take hold in an institution despite the fact that it was unable "to find its appropriate institution."[194] While aspiring to construct an eternally terrestrial city-state, the republic manifested, in Arendt's view, a "conviction [that] was so un-Christian" because "in this republic . . . there was no space reserved, no room left for the exercise of precisely those qualities which had been instrumental in building it" and because it "has perverted all virtues into social values."[195] As a result, politics had become a trade and a profession, whereas republican centralism laid bare the "lack of public spaces to which the people at large would have entrance."[196]

Even so, this critique of French Jacobinism, which Arendt compares unfavorably with the federalist constitutionalism of the American Revolution, in no way detracts from the fervent attention she pays to revolutionary temporality—though not to its violence, which she rejects in a move that would result in a no less violent rejection of the modern Left, from Sartre to Mao and even the student protests in May 1968. Those protests did earn some indulgence on her part, however, because of their moral preoccupations and playful tone. Arendt sent a message of sympathy to Daniel Cohn-Bendit in memory of her friendship with the young student's parents.[197] She even went so far as to articulate the following hope for intellectual rebels: "The really new and potentially revolutionary class in society will consist of intellectuals, and their potential power, as yet unrealized, is very great, perhaps too great for the good of mankind." At the same time, Arendt did not hesitate to associate all left-wing movements with a destructive force, thereby stubbornly refusing to see the way those movements evinced a desire for renewal and renaissance. Instead, Arendt saw only a pallid rejoinder to the technological violence that is rampant in a society paralyzed by atomic bombs and that is unbalanced by the constant weakening of political power.[198] It thus comes as no surprise that the American and European Left, particularly in Germany, found Arendt's views to be wholly reactionary. In truth, though, Hannah Arendt's radical focus on the moral front rather than the political one dissatisfied all the establishment groups, from the Left to the classic liberals. She would not allow herself to be classified as "empathetic"; at most she saw herself as being perhaps a bit out of the ordinary. Her attitude was disturbing. But was it also empowering?

Arendt's sympathies remained drawn to the revolutions of the eighteenth century, with their expression of renewal, joy, and public happiness. In that sense, although she criticized the third-world utopias and the naively antilibertarian infatuations of the New Left, and although she declined to vouch for either "capitalism" or "Communism," Arendt admired the enduring "people's utopias" that consist of the "council systems" that have been organized spontaneously in every revolution but that have also been smothered by the parties and the bureaucracy. Were the council systems not "the single alternative that has ever appeared in history, and [that] has reappeared time and again"?[199] Coming from Arendt, who is often classified as a "conservative" thinker, this statement is surprising. But one cannot understand Arendt's political thought if one forgets that the reason she involved herself in the political realm was to expand and refine moral philosophy and ethics.

This tribute to revolutionary renewal also reveals the mark of Heidegger's reading of the Anaximander fragment, which Arendt reinterprets. After Heidegger had his "reversal," he abandoned the "History of Being" [*Seinsgeschichte*] that is enacted behind the back of acting men.[200] At the same time, Heidegger continued to believe in transitional moments during which "a kind of history" takes on an ontological difference.[201] The continuum of time is broken up into different eras in such a way that the errancy of beings produces privileged moments of transition from one epoch to the next.[202] At such moments, "Being qua Truth breaks into the continuum of error, and the 'epochal essence of Being lays claim to the ecstatic nature of *Dasein.*'"[203] Freedom, then, is merely the time of the breakup, a freedom-scansion: just like the appearance of freedom according to Saint Augustine's *City of God,* an appearance that emerges in the briefest moments of beginnings. Arendt reshapes this "ecstatic nature,"[204] however, and, by returning to its ontological expression, she is eventually able to grant it a political significance that resonates with the wonderment and happiness [*eudaimonia*] of free citizens during the Age of Pericles as celebrated by Aristotle: "The joys of public happiness and the responsibilities for public business would then become the share of those few from all walks of life who have a taste for public freedom and cannot be 'happy' without it."[205]

All the same, and putting aside the fact that "the revolutions of the modern age appear like gigantic attempts to repair these foundations, to renew the broken thread of tradition, and to restore, through founding new political bodies, what for so many centuries had endowed the affairs of men with some measure of dignity and greatness," this "salvation," in its purest Western form, descends into restoration or tyranny.[206] In the end, the freedom-revolution is merely an "abyss,"[207] a simple "hiatus" between liberation and the constitution of liberty that our Western tradition[208]—which is known to be the only tradition that makes freedom the very reason for politics to exist—disguised by defining the new as an improvement upon the old. Mistrustful, in sum, of revolutions, Arendt still tries to rehabilitate the meaning of the dangerous rupture that Saint Augustine modeled on the only affirmative mode ever known—"birth"—by grounding ontologically the political philosophy that she strives to extend. And it was in expressing herself on Lessing that she returned to her thinking about "revolution" at the crossroads between the critical mind and the concern about the world: "His attitude toward the world was neither positive nor negative, but radically critical and, in respect to the public realm of his time, completely revolutionary. But it was also an attitude that remained indebted to the world. . . . We can apply what Lessing once said about the man of genius in two of his finest lines of verse. . . . 'What moves him, moves. What pleases him, pleases. His felicitous taste is the world's taste.'"[209]

The attachment to political *energeia* (in the sense of "actuality") as well as to the "joy" of the world endemic to it, served as the primary force behind Arendt's interest in Catholicism. Outside the realm of a religiousness that she did not indulge in, it was the *energeia* and the *eudaimonia* of "living well"—undiscoverable in any form of production but only in pure actuality—that she came so close to admiring in Pope John XXIII. Indeed, while vacationing in Rome during the summer of 1963 following the publication of her book on the Eichmann trial, Arendt wrote an essay on the heels of the Pope's funeral. The observer described him as a man with a good sense of humor, with a "quasi-Voltairian mind" that was capable of tripping up a diplomat who wanted to embarrass him by showing him a photograph of a naked woman: "Roncalli looked at the picture and returned it to Mr. N. with the remark, 'Mrs. N., I suppose?'" Arendt believed that the Pope spoke "his greatest words" on his deathbed: "Every day is a good day to be born, every day is a good day to die."[210]

The unusually casual style of these minor Arendtian tales confirms that she did not adhere to a particular religion, ideology or political vision but to the joy of the human condition. It is a joy that, despite the reifications she denounces that have appeared in human society since the beginning of time and that have become increasingly menacing in modern history, allowed her to praise the uniqueness of revolutionary beginnings no less than in the simplicity of each life, each birth, each death, and each day.

When Jaspers posed the following question: "Hasn't Jahwe faded too far out of sight [in your *Origins of Totalitarianism*]?" Arendt responded, "No more than I've been able to find one to my own demand from the final chapter. On the personal level, I make my way through life with a kind of (childish? because unquestioned) trust in God (as distinguished from faith, which always thinks it knows and therefore has to cope with doubts and paradoxes). . . . All traditional religion as such, whether Jewish or Christian, holds nothing whatsoever for me anymore. . . . Evil has proved to be more radical than expected. . . . The greatest evils or radical evil has nothing to do anymore with such humanly understandable, sinful motives. . . . This happens as soon as all unpredictability, which, in human beings, is the equivalent of spontaneity, is eliminated."[211] Arendt preserved for herself, during her entire life and throughout a body of work that never stopped beginning anew, a confidence in the unpredictability that may well have been the most successful—and the most trying—manifestation of her "faith . . . in humankind." In that sense, Hannah Arendt was without a doubt a woman of God—and of a certain God that she would eventually call, as did Kant, *Menschenverstand*: a "humanity" adorned with "judgment."

THINKING, WILLING, AND JUDGING

THE "WHO" AND THE BODY

It is impossible to appreciate the originality of Arendt's concept of political action without understanding that she considers such action to be an actualization of a "who"—a hypothetical, hazardous actualization that is dedicated to hope rather than founded upon an implausible law. Although the current state of liberalism and technology condemns to failure any action that pretends to alter alienation, reification, or "inspection," Arendt's personal and political experience inspires political actions to direct their attention as well as their criticisms toward the space of a modern world seen from the perspective of an appropriation of a fundamental ontology that is centered on the "essence of man" and to see within themselves the beginnings of the "who." Thinking, willing, and judging guide Arendt toward some reflections that appear philosophical but that in fact dismantle philosophy as well as politics itself, reflections that lay out a new, and specifically Arendtian, approach to freedom. The aporias of the "who" and the "body" will lead us into what Arendt deemed to be the final deconstruction of metaphysics: the rewriting in *The Life of the Mind* of the opposition between philosophy and politics.

"*Who* are we?" as opposed to "*what* are we?": that is the revelation whose inherent tension enlivens Arendt's political and philosophical work. Before Arendt came Heidegger's "*Who Is Dasein?*" In contrast to solitary reflection, however, Arendt moors the acts and words that reveal the "who" in the plurality of the world. Did Arendt "anthropologize" fundamental ontology in the manner of her reading of Kant, which some have criticized as being "abusively sociological"?[1]

Arendt's thinking returns to and evaluates the Heideggerian revolution. The "who" is extracted from the transcendental life of consciousness that is the locus of Husserl's ego; it opens up to beings as well to itself, and it achieves its own being through excess: it is through "sight" [*Sicht*] that *Dasein* appropriates Being. By doing away with intraworldly preoccupations and by replacing them with "care" [*Sorge*], moreover, *Dasein* moves toward its most characteristic possibility: its own finitude. The anxiety of *Dasein's* being in the world reveals its own mortality as its defining potentiality-of-being. This revelation, which Arendt in no way undermines, is at the very heart of her distinction in *The Human Condition* between "who" and "what."

"What" someone is can be reduced to social appearance and biological attributes. Even though a person's "qualities, gifts, talents, and shortcomings" may make him unique, those particularities reflect "what" he is, in the sense of a specimen that loses itself in the anonymity of the species or in life as the term is commonly understood, that is, as a biological life from which humans must extricate themselves in order to achieve their own specificity. "Who" someone is, on the other hand, is the separate being, the Greek *daimōn* that "appears so clearly and unmistakably to others" but that "remains hidden from the person himself."[2]

Although the "who" acts in the space of appearance, it does not become entrenched in the fixation of vision alone or in poetic utterances, nor does it become reified in life in the sense of *zōē* or social utilitarianism. In Arendt's estimation, however, neither is it a solitary self. When Heidegger traces the transcendent movement that draws the entity toward Being, he describes it as an excess [*Überschuss*] that culminates in a purging of the *Selbst* ("the self in the sense of ipse"), "an authentic potentiality-for-being-Self," and an "intimate knowing."[3] The *Selbst* welds together the phenomenon and the logos, and the only disposition it allows for is an anxious one symptomatic of pure uncanniness [*Unheimlich*], a radical forlornness that coincides with the fact of being thrown into the world.[4] Without abandoning the excess of the "who" that is revealed to its own being, Arendt locates this transcendence in action and in speech with other people. The "who" is a hidden self, but it is hidden more from the person than from the memory of other people. The "who" as "someone's life" thus appears to be essential, but only in the narrow sense of the word: as an essence that is actualized within the time of the plurality specific to other people. If the "foreign girl" whom Hannah Arendt always remained could relentlessly proclaim her uniqueness, even angrily, it was so she could think, act, and live her singularity in the heart of diverse human beings in a mutual "reliance." In fact, Arendt believed that the "who" did not manifest itself to a *Selbst* in an "intimate knowing" separate from *Mittsein* but rather in its dynamic exceptionalness that could not help blossoming before the multitude of other people—the given reality of diverse individuals who are born that way, and who receive and interpret the acts of each newcomer by implicitly asking him the question, "*Who* are you?"

Neither a life of the species nor a solipsism, the "who" is as removed from nature and society—which objectify it as an element of either the species or a "domestic" society of producers—as from the isolation of self-appropriation. The "who," which to some extent is distributed in human plurality and in the infinite temporality of human narratives, is manifested as a dynamic actuality, an *energeia* that transcends its own doings and activities and that is opposed to any effort toward reification or objectification. "Its disclosure can almost never be achieved as a willful purpose, as though one possessed and could dispose of this 'who' in the same manner he has and can dispose of his qualities." The "who" is disclosed only in an "action" (which is distinguished, as we recall, from "labor" and the "work") to which the "'who' is attached." From the moment action "transcends mere protective activity," the "who" is thus a "source" of creativity, though one that remains outside the actual work process and that is "independent of *what* [artists] may achieve."[5]

By broaching in this way the thorny problem of an "essence" or a "human nature,"[6] Arendt reshapes the ideas of the master of Marburg as well as his reading of Aristotle and the church fathers, which she enriches with her own worldly political experience. In Arendt's view, the excess of the "who" replaces the enigmatic "essence." What is more, this excess is neither a pure thought nor a pure language that discloses Being. The "who" arrives in the midst of life's conditions, which are the conditions of activities with other people, although they do not unilaterally determine what the "who" will be. The "who" as an excess is achieved through a constant attack on biological life, against the metabolism with nature, and against the reification of "works" and other "products." Although the "who" can appear to be a "source," it is formed as something indefinite and after the fact: the "who" is decoded, like one of Heraclitus's signs, through what various witnesses recount when *quid* is no longer. "In other words, human essence—not human nature in general (which does not exist) nor the sum total of qualities and shortcomings in the individual, but the essence of who somebody is—can come into being only when life departs, leaving behind nothing but a story. . . . Even Achilles . . . remains dependent upon the storyteller, poet, or historian, without whom everything he did remains futile."[7]

Because the "who" knows that it is mortal and that it belongs not to the survival of the species but to the spoken memory of multiple and conflicting opinions, it ceases to be a "what" [*quid*] and attempts to transform "labor" as well as the "work" into an "action," which is itself spoken, projected toward the past and the future, and shared with other people. Arendt cites Dante in that context as she praises action for the way it discloses someone's unicity: "In every action the primary aim of the agent, whether it act because its nature compels it to or as a matter of free choice, is to reproduce its own likeness. . . . Nothing acts unless it has the qualities which are to be communicated to the thing acted upon."[8]

The sign of the "who" at the heart of the actuality of action is nothing less than extraordinariness, not in the sense of an arrogant exclusiveness but as the distinguishing feature of the Greek *hērōs* that all citizens are presumed to share,[9] which the theological tradition, following Saint Augustine, developed into a "uniqueness." Arendt's horror in the face of totalitarian mass groupings is expressed here as a passion for the uniqueness of the "who" as evidenced in the works of Duns Scotus. Arendt is passionately devoted to the position of John Duns Scotus, which is that "only particular things (*res*), which are characterized by 'thisness' (*haecceitas*) can be said to be real for man," as well as to his *principium individuationis,* which is what makes man the singular being par excellence. Duns Scotus's appreciation for "*this* particular man" places that man at a higher rank not only than the species but also to the idea of mankind that precedes him thanks to the universality of thought.[10] Even more important, by rejecting the primacy of intellect over the will, Duns Scotus not only individualizes the power of the mind, but he also adorns this power with desire and reasoning and endows the unique man with an untold freedom, which is in stark contrast to any notion of causality that condemns human affairs a priori to a discredited contingency. Finally, because the roots of intellect meander into intuition, the grasping of a thing in its "thisness" [*haecceitas*] is always imperfect and wanting. By contemplating the *summum bonum,* the "highest 'thing,'" however, willing is changed into loving and thus finishes the path begun by Augustine: "*Amo: volu ut sis.*" "Love is understood as an activity," Arendt writes, but it is not merely a mental activity: the primacy of *haecceity* means that "its object is no longer absent from the senses" and it remains "imperfectly known to the intellect." This coalescence between thinking and action, which Arendt traces back to the heroic Greeks, is manifested in Duns Scotus's beatitude through the intermediary of *haecceity:* "Beatitude . . . consists in the full and perfect attainment of the object as it is in itself, and not merely as it is in the mind."[11] Through his philosophy of liberty and his preference for the contingency that he restores, Duns Scotus offers Arendt a chance to refine her mediation on the uniqueness of the "who" and on the tension between thought and sensory perception that lies at the boundary between willing and loving. In this spirit, Arendt also comments on the work of Petrus Johannis Olivi, the thirteenth-century Franciscan philosopher of the Will who transcended the sheer "givenness" at the heart of the other version of uniqueness of the "who" that he called an *experimentum suitas,* "an experiment of the self with itself."[12]

In the midst of seeking the revelation of the "who" in "the frailty of human affairs," Arendt's questioning follows two parallel tracks. On the one hand, she tries to anchor fundamental ontology in the agonistic relations of the public realm so it might better affirm and preserve the dignity of the "who." On the other hand, she contends that the political thinking that results from this effort can only dismantle that which we know as "politics." As Arendt wrote Judah Magnes shortly before his death, "Politics in our century is almost a business of despair and I have always been tempted to run away from it."[13] Those words would be followed, however, by the act of immersing herself not only in politics but also in its underlying anthropology.

As opposed to the "who," the body is deemed by the philosopher to be the agent of the life process through both fertility and labor. Ensuring the metabolism of nature, the body accomplishes both the reproduction of the species and the satisfaction of its needs. Women and slaves personify this body in labor, which is the zero degree of the human and is the primary expression of biological life or *zōē*. The body never transcends nature; it avoids the world so it can remain exclusively a sphere of privacy. Confined to the species and to its survival, this body thus emerges as "the only thing that we cannot share" and it becomes the paradigm of private property. Because labor—as well as the body that sustains it—is withdrawn from the world, it counts among the "least common" of the human characteristics and becomes the object of a pathos whose violence can be measured only by recalling the *amor mundi* that Arendt professes in contrast.

Just as important, a body of this sort does not appear capable of sensations and perceptions. In the end, by reminding us that men *are* only to the extent that they appear, Arendt draws attention to the sense of sight that subsumes the other senses, and she includes perception in the very structure of language, as fundamentally metaphorical as it is.[14] Arendt also invokes Merleau-Ponty's notion that as long as our universe is a chiasmus between the visible and the invisible, it is impossible to dispel the "illusions of appearances" or to settle on a unique truth.[15] And yet in *The Human Condition,* where the theorist's goal is to rely on production, reproduction, biology, and labor to clear the path toward the "who," the body becomes a primary target of this removal from *zōē*, if not a sworn enemy—which is the most basic paradigm of alienation.

As a result, the only experience that this universe of "drudgery" reserves for the body is pain. Pleasure is mentioned only so that it can be assimilated into pain: both of them "go . . . on within the confines of the body," enjoying no external object and being consumed exclusively in a sort of autistic enclosure: "Nothing . . . ejects one more radically from the world than exclusive concentration upon the body's life, a concentration forced upon man in slavery or in the extremity of unbearable pain." Arendt often returns to the theme of an objectless, exclusively corporeal, and incommunicable pain. Showing the signs of a melancholic experience, such a pain is dissociated from any communicable sexualization and from any possibilities for seduction that might have insinuated themselves in, say, sadomasochism. As a parallel to this desexualized pain, Arendt embraces the Stoic vision of happiness—happiness as merely an "absence of pain" that is achieved only in isolation. That conception, which is common to hedonism and to sensualism, is one that Arendt considers to be both the most consistent and the most evocative of the "non-political, totally private" character of bodily sensations.[16]

Not merely apolitical, the Arendtian body is also generic, which is yet another argument, if one is even necessary, as to why the body is the polar opposite of the "who." Swept along by this declaration, which is founded on Aristotle's *De Anima*, Arendt considers both our inner psychic ground and our inner organs always to be the "same," with individual differentiation occurring only through a discourse enunciated in the space of appearance.[17] In sum, if organs as well as the soul are hidden from view and never appear, why would they need to be personalized? They both belong in some ways to the general order: since they do not appear, they are fundamentally "apolitical." It would be easy to take issue with our impassioned pamphleteer and to point out that the most hidden biological body, particularly its DNA, is in fact extremely personal, and that her goal of saving the public realm as a realm of difference, though admirable, relies on arguments that do not always withstand close analysis.

For the moment, let us simply note that Arendt relegates the body to the role of an uninteresting generalization—because it is biological and because it is incompatible with the uniqueness of the "who"—so that she can rid herself of psychology and psychoanalysis. Using medicine and physiology, which she believes are interested in what our organs have in common— and she is right, though that is not the end of the story!—as a basis of comparison, Arendt is quick to condemn "psychology, depth psychology or psychoanalysis, which discovers no more than the ever-changing moods, the ups and downs of our psychic life" and whose "results and discoveries are neither particularly appealing nor very meaningful in themselves." The phrase "neither particularly appealing" is without a doubt the most revealing of them all. If psychoanalysis is not "appealing," does that mean that it breeds fear? That it scares her? Arendt goes even further, describing "the monotonous sameness and pervasive ugliness so highly characteristic of the findings of modern psychology." Monotony and ugliness? The "urge is always the same, . . . only disorder or abnormality can individualize them."[18] Who's afraid of ugliness, repetition, and abnormality? Even more important, it is simply not true, except perhaps in the case of a psychoanalytic vulgate not worthy of Arendt's seriousness of purpose, that psychoanalysis remains at the level of the "general" at the cost of "discourse." Quite the contrary, Freud's discovery has shown that psychic life becomes a life only when it represents itself in a unique way—in the particular discourse that constitutes a veritable poetics and maieutics of the individual subject. Psychoanalysis invokes a representation that endures until it reaches the "ugliness" of the urge, an urge that is unambiguously sexual or deadly and that, in the analyst's mind, exists only if someone puts it into words in his own particular way.

What we are seeing here are Arendt's defenses. Her approach to personal and historical experience led her to sublimate the "frailty of human affairs" that she characterized as heterogeneous ("action *and* speech") as well as agonistic. She refers to this sublimation as a *politics,* thereby expanding broadly the scope of that concept and practice. In truth, the goal here is to preserve what is unique as well as the complex temporality of other people—all the while making sure not to deprive that temporality of its ontological vigilance and not to close it off in the solipsism of that vigilance. The grandeur of this project demands respect, so much so that it would be unfair to expect its author to have done what she has not done or to explain the reasons behind her failing or her protective device.

We should remember, however, that the refusal to contemplate the uniqueness of the body and the psyche is what drove Arendt to refuse to acknowledge the role played by sadomasochism in the experience of violence, particularly in the political violence that accompanies totalitarianism as well as the movements of the modern Left.[19] The theorist located the political causes of modern violence in the decline of political power, which engenders coercion to compensate for its weakness and to gain strength, and in the heightened development of nuclear warheads and other technical methods of extermination. And yet, the psychological element—sadomasochism in particular—would have enriched her analysis with an important element that would help us grasp more effectively the "conditions" or the "crystallization" of the phenomenon she describes.

Arendt touches upon the theme of sadomasochism when she delves into the Christian concept of authority, particularly the fear of hell that is its basis. She correctly considers the interplay between rewards and punishments, as well as the arousing fear that stems from its being a substratum of faith, to be "the only political element in traditional religion."[20] And yet she concerns herself with neither the psychological foundation of this dynamic nor the indispensable support that it offers the political bond as such. Are perhaps all political bonds based on an arousing fear? Nor does Arendt analyze the specific fate of the alchemy between fear and authority that operates at the heart of the secularized modern world, which has clearly left the fear of hell behind but which has in no way diffused the sadomasochistic spirit of what Arendt cautiously refers to as the "frailty of human affairs." That is an element of the equation that she prefers to ignore not only for reasons that she would no doubt deem "personal" but also as part of an effort to sustain the consistency of her thought. Her main goal is to preserve the freedom of the "who" at the heart of an optimal political plurality and to avoid subjecting it to an unchecked unconscious. In so doing, she runs the risk of depriving the "*who* of someone" of its body, making it cumbersome, perhaps, but also incredibly flexible.

Arendt's defenses and cautiousness do not fade when she analyzes the genesis of judgment. In Kant's view, as endorsed here by Arendt, the faculty of judgment, which is a central activity of the political realm because judgment is what allows thought to leave its solipsism behind and to partake in the "enlarged mentality" and "common sense" necessary to pursue the "good" of the plurality, is rooted in *taste*. The most intimate of the perceptions, and one that mobilizes an orality and a sense of smell that are far more internal than are the other senses (sight, hearing, and touch), taste nevertheless possesses the capacity to be shared. Judgment seizes upon taste through imagination and extends it into the political realm. And yet, before taste can be shared with other people, it is nothing less than the faculty of sharing, the faculty of discriminating between pleasure and displeasure. And there we have it! Is Arendt encountering, in her final work, the body and its capacity to enjoy pleasure? Is pleasure finding its way into the theorist's pen as a criterion of judgment? We have not yet reached the point where we can say it is. Arendt, like Kant, quickly passes over the pleasure that distinguishes in order to choose and that appears to be the prototype of judgment. In its place, she focuses solely on its translation into "approbation/disapprobation," which incites a different sort of "pleasure": "The very act of approbation pleases, the very act of disapprobation displeases." What is the criterion of this "additional pleasure" and of the choice that it demands? Arendt affirms that it is no less than "communicability" and "publicness."[21] Throwing herself quickly (too quickly?) on the path of the "imagination" that prepares for "the operation of reflection," the theorist has forgotten the first pleasure, the pleasure of the tasting body. And yet we have no guarantee that judgment itself has completely "forgotten" the tasting and distasting body. After Kant, Freud became fascinated with the dynamic of the first pleasure of the oral drive. Arendt, for her part, preferred to remain in ignorance: such prepolitical "ugliness" is clearly not "appealing."[22]

From this perspective, the female body no longer demands Arendt's attention. We would be doing no violence to Arendt's thought were we to assume that if the philosopher had tried her hand at contemplating femininity, she would have put the female body at the forefront, that is, at the heart of the natural process from which human beings must extract themselves if they wish to transform *zōē* into *bios*. Is it not the case that the political realm, the only noble realm that exists, is designed to fight against the biological life, against women and slaves? And yet Arendt's reasoning is more complicated, for what is a "given" (like the body) plays a role in the tension of the "who" and thus deserves our "thanks" and "affirmation." In that sense, Arendt finds in her own femininity, as well as in her own Jewishness, an irrefutable "given" that she treats as if it were a piece of evidence: "The truth is I have never pretended to be anything else or to be in any way other than I am, and I have never even felt tempted in that direction. It would have been like saying that I was a man and not a woman, that is to say, kind of insane."[23] If we add to her serenity the attention that she gives to the "acquiescence in one's self" [*acquiescentia in seipso*] of a Spinoza that derives from a reason capable of "liv[ing] with myself in peace," we can safely assume that a sort of confidence, even faith, underlies Arendt's accepting her body as it is. Implicitly, and apart from the internal contradictions in her thought, Arendt suggests that the body, though servile, is also a gift and an act of grace: it is a sort of "individual," an "ego" distinct from the "thinking ego" to which consciousness as well as thinking acquiesce "if and when you come home."

With the same tone of elliptical and understated modesty, Arendt asserts that the distinction between the two sexes is already apparent in the Book of Genesis (1:27). God may have created Adam, but the creation story also indicates that "God created male *and* female." According to the philosopher, this text suggests that human diversity is an essential precursor for action, with the original difference between man and woman at the very beginning of any plurality. She adds that Jesus referred to Genesis 1:27 because Jesus believed faith was closely related to action. As a result, Jesus felt a need to remind us that, from the beginning, God "made them male and female" (Matt. 19:4), whereas Paul, for whom faith was primarily a function of salvation, preferred to say that the woman was created "of the man" and hence "for the man" (1 Cor. 11:8–9).[25] Accordingly, femininity would not be merely an original given, but an intrinsic difference that is indispensable to the action that Arendt considered, as we have seen, to be the essence of politics. Femininity does not confine itself to a body in serfdom; rather, it constitutes from the very beginning the plurality of the world in which it participates.

Arendt did not pursue this theoretical germ regarding the place that femininity might occupy in *amor mundi*.[26] She was content, if we dare say so, to proclaim the difference of each person while protecting herself from any hint of an assimilation into any movement or group that might be tempted to efface each person's uniqueness as a "who": "Plurality is the condition of human action because we are all the same, that is, human, in such a way that nobody is ever the same as anyone else who ever lived, lives, or will live."[27] What better lesson can be learned, indeed, from totalitarianism? In my feminist years, I entitled a piece about the difficulty of being a woman "Unes femmes": how to preserve each woman's uniqueness within the plurality of the group. The text was published by Les Cahiers du GRIF, a journal directed by Françoise Collin, one of the first people to be interested in the passion and sensitivity of Hannah Arendt's work.[28]

THE DIALOGUE OF THE THINKING EGO: THE "SPLIT," MELANCHOLY, AND TYRANNY

While discussing The Origins of Totalitarianism, Arendt professed a goal that she would achieve only with The Life of the Mind: "One compelling reason why I took such trouble to ·isolate the elements of totalitarian governments was to show that the Western tradition from Plato up to and including Nietzsche is above any such suspicion."[29] Her meditation on thinking is presented explicitly as a dialogue with Heidegger's "Was heisst Denken?" and she cites his definition of thinking in the epigraph to The Life of the Mind: "Thinking does not bring knowledge as do the sciences. / Thinking does not produce usable practical wisdom. / Thinking does not solve the riddles of the universe. / Thinking does not endow us directly with the power to act." Arendt's book, which employs an occasionally didactic tone, embraces well-known references to Plato and Kant, and sometimes gets carried away by intuitions that force "life" and "thought" into the same experience, develops her own conception of thinking with all its risks and opportunities.

Written and spelled out (like her other postwar writings) in English, that is, in a foreign language that Arendt mastered, though never completely ("I still speak it with a very heavy accent, and I often speak unidiomatically"[30]), this thinking about thinking in no way adopts the Heideggerian approach to thinking that builds up words only to knock them down. Arendt's own predilections, buttressed by her reliance on a foreign idiom, keep her "life of the mind" within the realm of argumentation. The author clarifies, summarizes, connects, tailors, objects, shapes, and transforms without perverting, but also without shying away from pithy turns of phrase and bursts of thought.

The fate of thinking in another language appeared to her as a "human condition" that modernity was imposing and expanding as never before, a condition that she accepted in her own interrogatory style ("I don't fit?"). Although she was able to write fluently in English, she claimed to remain "at a certain distance" from that language and continued to be consumed with German. "The German language is the essential thing that has remained. . . . It wasn't the German language that went crazy." Others are more adept than she at conforming to a borrowed code, but then again, "one cliché chases another because the productivity that one has in one's own language is cut off when one forgets that language." The theme of "forgetting" one's mother tongue, which is tantamount to "repression," caused Arendt to speak, immediately thereafter, the language of Auschwitz. It may well be the case that the German language is not mad, but we do have to address the question of Auschwitz. The Jewish people had not been treated as war enemies; instead, "it was really as if an abyss had opened."[31] Though the "comprehender" denied the madness of language, her unconscious association stumbled upon an implacable logic: the notion that the primordial habitat, the mother language, and thought describing humanity all came apart at the same time. Under such inhuman conditions, certain people will defend themselves by forgetting or by repressing something as deeply felt as their mother tongue: "I have seen it in people as a result of shock. You know, what was decisive was not the year 1933, at least not for me. What was decisive was the day we learned about Auschwitz."[32]

Does this mean that speaking another language is a way of protecting oneself from the disintegration of the primordial bond? Is it a way of maintaining a repression that begins by transforming the brutality of the drive into a linguistic sign? Is it a way of intensifying the repression in order to live—or to survive? That would be a strange defense indeed. And at what price does it come?

Arendt neither forgot nor repressed, however. She remembered the German language as she remembered horror: "In German I know a rather large part of German poetry by heart; the poems are always somehow in the back of my mind. I can never do that again."[33] But she put these words at a distance and refused to immerse herself in them: she spoke and wrote in English. Heidegger's thinking in the wake of his "reversal," on the other hand, got closer to this *Grundsprache*, this turmoil that is inherent in the human condition precisely because the thinker sets out to disintegrate the signs of his language while providing himself with identifying safeguards (such as Being, the habitat, and serenity). Heidegger's goal was to reconstruct the paths of meaning by bringing them closer to vocal memory, though always within the isolation of a poetic solitude that likens itself to the trembling of the gods, but without getting caught up in the political or historical conditions of the "abyss" that is discarded as if it were a simple *Dummheit* [mistake].

In a very different way, and while remaining within the confines of her foreign status, Arendt invoked that which can be shared by integrating her concerns about the "who" with a pedagogical, even educational, reflection. Arendt's "life of the mind" carried out her own "dismantling" of metaphysics, but she also transmitted it into the "new world"—the political world, the technological world, and the English world. Thinking, which is described in terms of the founders of "continental philosophy," is discussed in a foreign language and in the form of an applied, even academic, commentary that is nevertheless adorned with the qualities of a polemic. At the same time, on a dialogue with texts from the past, Arendt superimposes a tireless, unsettling, and lively conversation with herself. Her reading of philosophical texts can be associated with her attachment to the idea of authority (*auctoritas*, from *augere*, "to augment"), as distinguished from her idea of *power*, which is considered to be its indispensable complement. Far from underplaying the "augmentation" necessary for any initiative or radical reform, Arendt suggests that we should respect that authority, even as we destroy it, in particular, by scorn and laughter—which are other well-known weapons in Arendt's arsenal.[34]

Her train of thought here in some ways reflects the tendency of women to preserve the bond, that is, the bond of original repression that introduces the signs of language along with the mother's status as an object of communication, sorrow, and love.[35] Because she shares the sex of her mother, the woman internalizes the mother's desire as well as her rejection of the "primordial object" and her language, all the while trying to preserve them in the face of a threat of losing her own identity. In truth, even when a woman risks her freedom, it is easier for her to do so by challenging than by dissolving (the mother, language, the bond, and authority). Accordingly, her thinking finds itself drawn to the realm of incarnation made up of men and women who are being born and who are acting in ways all their own, rather than to an asexual universalist logic or to a poetic dissemination—it, too, neutral—of meaning and of bonds with other people. Without exploring the sexual difference that in her view provides the basis for the action but considering it instead to be a "given," Arendt places her thought in the regime of incarnation, which, she believes, is the regime of political history. Even so, political experience, understood to be an in-between of "living essences," is in no way a sociological by-product that precludes the existence of a being based upon itself (a notion for which Arendt has been criticized). Instead, political experience shows us how to be plural, rather than merely a Being, while remaining within the flux of action and language—and with the "who" illuminating its era rather than simply being conditioned by it.

The first stage entails appreciating the "activity" that consists of the nonaction of thinking and that *The Human Condition* does not sufficiently emphasize: as Cicero put it, "never is a man more active than when he does nothing, never is he less alone than when he is by himself."[36] The activism of the modern world is not the only thing that endangers that strange activity, the most human activity of them all, known as thinking. Even before Nietzsche, Hegel had demonstrated that "the 'sentiment underlying religion in the modern age [is] the sentiment: God is dead.'"[37] But Hegel's impression stems fundamentally from "death" as it is commonly understood, that is, as a distinction between the sensory realm and the suprasensory realm. From that perspective, it is the very locus of the invisible that is in danger—which is nothing less than the locus of thought as a paradigm of spirituality. "The experience of the activity of thought is probably the aboriginal source of our notion of spirituality in itself, regardless of the forms it has assumed."[38]

Arendt resurrects the various philosophical tenets that have thought about thinking, and she then goes on to propose an analysis uniquely her own. Indeed, "the metaphysical fallacies contain the only clues we have to what thinking means to those who engage in it—something of great importance today and about which, oddly enough, there exist few direct utterances." Kant's distinction between *Verstand* [intellect or knowledge and *truth*] and *Vernunft* [reason or thought and *signification*] attracts our author's attention.[39] Reason, the second face of this Janus, is what displays the essential features of the paradoxical activity that Arendt revisits and that she rehabilitates in the face of the "thought-trains" encouraged by modernity, particularly in scientific reasoning. The "relentlessness inherent in sheer thinking" is what produces science, itself a form of "common-sense reasoning."[40] In a different way, however, thinking protects us from the never-ending march of scientific "progress," that "string of verities, each one in its time claiming general validity even though the very continuity of the research implied something merely provisional" that is at once self-destructive and infinitely antiauthoritarian because of its questioning stance.[41]

Intellect is of this world, the world of necessities and not of freedom, whereas thinking is merely an "appetite for meaning," a constant source of questions without answers.[42] When Kant reserved a space to replace the knowledge that he believed he was abolishing, it was not for faith but for thinking itself—as well as for the dangers that thinking entails. Because thinking does not evolve in the world of phenomena, it generates non-sense and meaninglessness.[43] In a pedagogical style, though with a bit of impatience, Arendt lays out dichotomies intrinsic to the functioning of thought that pave the way for what the thinker experiences as "winds of thinking" that are at once threatening and revealing.

To begin with, the thinking ego, as distinct from the ego, goes beyond mere appearances. It becomes an "immaterial intuition" like a mind [*Geist*]: A "sheer activity," it is "ageless, sexless [that comes as no surprise!], without qualities, and without a life story."[44] We can think about the thinking ego, but we cannot have an intuition about it: "The thinking ego is indeed Kant's 'thing in itself': it does not appear to others and, unlike the self of self-awareness, it does not appear to itself, and yet it is 'not nothing.'"[45]

This thinking ego is also distinguishable from reality. Arendt criticizes Descartes's "solipsism," which she believes ignores the perceiving body as well as other people, and which withdraws into the One of the Greek nous ("faculty of thought, intelligence, mind"). Descartes wished to discover the thinking ego, or *"la chose pensante"* as he called it, whose reality went beyond the illusions of sense perception. Like Nietzsche before her, Arendt believes that the Cartesian *cogito* is a fallacy because "from the *cogito*, only the existence of *cogitationes* could be inferred." In the "I-think," the "I-am" is presupposed, and reality cannot be derived.[46] In its place, Arendt subscribes to Valéry's witticism, *"Tantôt je pense, tantôt je suis"* [At times I think, and at times I am].[47] "Common sense" is the basis of that opposition.

According to Thomas Aquinas, in fact, a sort of "sixth sense" exists that is a silent and supplementary sensation of reality preserved by a common world made up of other people who feel in the same way I do. It is also preserved by the senses, a sensation that targets the "senses in general." This sixth sense, known as *sensus communis* or "common sense," is what gives us the sensation of reality. Although it would be tempting to reduce this sixth sense to thinking because it, like thinking, is internal and invisible, "common sense" and the sensation of the real turn out to be different from the faculty of thought and from its constant state of flux: common sense stabilizes and unifies the real. Arendt objects that thinking does not destroy the real through doubt; instead, the very fact of thinking dissolves the sensation of reality. Torn in this way between the thinking activity and "common sense," the thinking ego can only affirm its own existence *momentarily* and intermittently. Its existence is innately foreign to the world of "common sense": *bios theōrētikos* is a *bios xenikos*.

This split between thought and the real is manifested quite explicitly in the experience of "de-sensing" that constitutes thought: that experience "must prepare the particulars given to the senses in such a way that the mind is able to handle them in their absence."[48] Arendt touches only briefly on the problem of thought as a sign, a notion developed by the Stoics, whom she criticizes in "Willing" for withdrawing from the world for the sake of mental representation alone.[49] It is important to keep in mind, however, that the Stoics established an important link between representation and the world of the senses. The Stoics' theory of the sign was the explicit agent of this intuition, one that Arendt passes over rather quickly. She is more concerned with reaching the outer limits of "de-sensing" by contemplating it, which is tantamount to nothing less than the experience of thinking as an anticipation of death. To "take on the color of the dead" was the formula that the Delphic oracle communicated to Zeno, the founder of Stoicism. On that front, Arendt reminds us that Heidegger, in *Being and Time*, "treated the anticipation of death as the decisive experience through which man can attain an authentic self and be liberated from the inauthenticity of the They."[50]

Still, it would be wrong to believe that Arendt's remarks are intended to dissociate her from the anticipation of death so she might structure the very act of thinking. In *The Human Condition* the philosopher went to great lengths to emphasize the awareness of mortality that culminates in the desire for immortality and that also establishes the eternity of the philosophic *nous* or the faculty of thought. Even more important, Arendt returns in "Willing" to the new place that Heidegger, following his "reversal," accorded to death as a "shrine" of being. Arendt's remark about the Delphic oracle, then, is no mere irony, and it is even less a refutation of the "professional thinkers" who conduct themselves like "the dead" because they remain helpless in the face of common-sense arguments.[51] What Arendt is doing, rather, is highlighting the conflicts inherent in the experience of thinking. In her view, thinking's withdrawal from the world is indispensable and cannot be denied; its situation is intrinsically "out of order." She leaves open the anxiety about rejoining the world, refusing to pay the price of lumping thought and reality together.[52]

The fundamental estrangement of the thinker demands to be taken seriously, so to speak, when Arendt recounts the ironic story Plato tells in *Laws*: a Thracian maid bursts out in laughter when she sees Thales fall into a well as he is watching the heavenly bodies above him. How could he know the things in the sky if he does not see what passes at his feet?[53] For a time, Arendt assumes the role of the Thracian maid, but in the end, it is not so she can mock either the peasant girl (as Plato does) or Thales (as the peasant girl does), but so she can bypass irony for the sake of comprehension, her existential passion.[54] It is essential that we grasp the particularity of the two worlds, the world of "common sense" and the world of thinking, and that we join both of them together: such is the first step in the audacity—or the utopia—of the "dismantling" of metaphysics. At the same time, we must remain on the side on which Arendt wishes to fight and which she pursues in her own personal way.

Arendt's uneasiness with the metaphysical dichotomy between the sensory and the suprasensory inspires her to develop another way of articulating these entities, one that emerges, for example, in Chinese script. In Chinese ideographs, Arendt finds Kantian "schemata,"[55] "intuition[s] drawn from the world of the senses" that enable us to grasp the general nature of an object without its being present to the senses. Through this "concrete thinking in images" that she studied in the works of Marcel Granet, Arendt reveals the primacy of vision without considering the gestural quality of Chinese calligraphy (did she perhaps consider it to be too "corporeal"?).[56] The Chinese ideograph for "friendship," the image of two united hands, preempts the Socratic question, "What is friendship?" because the answer is so clearly evident in the emblem.[57] Arendt concludes that we share the same nous as the Chinese as well as the same mental grasp of phenomena. And yet, whereas "they" think through images, "our" *logos* is the "necessity to give account of and *justify* in words."[58] In sum, although Western thought loses something by abandoning the realm of the senses to stake out a place in the world of abstraction, it also gains something in the end because this initial loss stimulates questioning concern, discursive thinking, and philosophy itself as supported by the alphabet.

Finally, the estrangement inherent in thinking is measured against its equally paradoxical temporality. Arendt asks, "where are we when we think?" By replying "nowhere," as does Plato in *The Sophist,* Arendt does not merely refer to the fact that thinking lies outside common sense, for she is also reminding us that thinking lies outside time. Extracted from linear chronology, thinking occupies an outside-time, that eternal moment that medieval philosophy approached in the *nunc stans* of the mystics.[59]

Through the diverse modalities of this divide, Arendt shows that thinking "can be understood as the actualization of the original *duality* or the *split* between me and myself which is inherent in all consciousness."[50] Deemed "subversive" by the Athenians, "corrupt" thinking does not make us wise on its own accord, nor does it serve to improve other people: the opposition between citizen and thinker remains paramount here.[61] Thinking does not even generate answers; thinking "dissolves" and "has no political relevance," and its meaning can be found only in its own activities. No one has described the dangerousness of thinking more clearly than did Socrates when he defined the essence of thought as being "two-in-one," which Plato translated into a conceptual language as the silent dialogue between me and myself [*eme amautō*].[62]

Let us pause for a moment on the duality intrinsic to the thinking ego of which Arendt is so enamored. From an anthropological or psychological point of view, the original duality ("I-am-I") endemic to the thinking human being "explains the futility of the fashionable search for identity."[63] The silent dialogue—which does not think *about* something, as cognitive reasoning does, but which continually enacts difference, the original split—acts as a "balm" for the solitude of thinking. On that front, Arendt likens the dialogism inherent in the thinking activity to the metaphor, which fills in the gap between the world and the phenomenon, while friendship is its existential realization. Under that scenario, philosophy enjoys the privilege of both imitating this dangerous activity and counteracting the destructive risks that it brings about because of the discourse and practice of friendship.

Revealed as such, the split in the thinking ego cannot help but lead us to the psychoanalytic study of psychosis, not to the pathology evoked by this term, but to an endogenous split, a sort of endemic "psychosis" that psychoanalysis, since Melanie Klein and with Lacan, locates in the psychic apparatus of the speaking subject. The term "suture" aptly describes the "split" or "duality" that Arendt discovered as she read the philosophers. "Suture" describes the relationship between the subject and his discourse as being the chain from which he is absent.[64] Without establishing an equivalence between the two systems of reasoning—the Arendtian system and the psychoanalytic system—one could argue that the "ego," as Arendt defines the term, is entirely absent from the flux of "thinking" and that it considers this absence to be a split or duality. Repression prevents us from being aware of this division. In Freud's view, on the other hand, the failure of repression lays bare the internal division of the subject, a division that can be experienced as a painful experience of rejection: a loss of the world, a loss of reality, and a loss of communication with the self and with the Other. In other words, it can be experienced as psychosis. The internal division of the subject can also be "sutured," despite any weakening in the repression, provided the repression is accompanied by an "activity" that continually questions all sorts of identities and all sorts of differences that make up both the "chain of discourse" and thinking itself (which comprises

the ego, the Other, the world, language, and each signification). In the face of the psychosis that wallows in rejection,
thinking as a means of sublimation constructs a bar, a unitary
characteristic that marks the emergence of meaning outside the
world: thinking becomes the glorious scar of the original split
that constitutes speaking and thinking beings. In sum, thinking in such a way is a poetic activity in the sense that it is articulated like a work of poetry that seeks not to produce an object
of beauty but to endlessly reveal dehiscent truths about the
experience that takes place in the condensation that makes
each word flourish and that the thinker proceeds to divide and
expose. Is that not how Heidegger thought as he broke down
the unity of Greek or German terms so he could journey into
their semantic latencies? In the light of analytic theory, this sort
of thinking appears to be a viable antidote to alienation,
though at the same time it is bound up with the risks entailed
by this so solitary and demanding human adventure. Thinking
is what reveals and uncovers the "split" or the duality of the
thinking ego, but it also provides most effective therapy for the
thinking ego when it sustains the dialogue between the parties
that constitute the split and when it can question their differences while avoiding getting stuck in any one part of the
dichotomies that gave rise to this experience.

Although Arendt, as we have seen, does not mince words
when she speaks of psychoanalysis, neither does she hesitate to
note the psychological consequences of the risks inherent in
thinking. At the end of the "Totalitarianism" section in *Origins
of Totalitarianism,* she broaches the subject of philosophical
melancholia or desolation: both the solitude of the whimsical
Hegel ("Nobody has understood me except one; and he also
misunderstood") or "the empty expectation and the yearning
waiting of the lonely" experienced by Nietzsche until he conceived *Zarathustra* and wrote, "Noon was, when One became
Two."[65] Are philosophers the precursors—or, on the contrary,
the therapists—of the desolation that drives totalitarianism?

"Thinking" gives Arendt the opportunity to poke fun one more time at the "philosophers, a notoriously melancholy tribe of men."[66]

All the same, it is at the heart of philosophical thinking itself, and not through any sort of psychoanalytic exteriority, that Arendt seeks to reveal the "fallacies" of metaphysics and eventually to come up with ways of counteracting them.

Philosophy's implicit goal of rivaling the gods is the first target of this deconstruction. Seeking immortality by putting the mortals in close proximity to the immortals, philosophic activity transforms mortals into what Cicero called "half-gods." Although Plato affirms in *Timaeus* that "there are no gods that spend their time philosophizing," Arendt has a few words to say about the Greek metamorphosis of gods into nous. In the first stage, men and gods are both spectators of the world, the divine passion to see is shared by the multitudes, and even the invisible enters into the visible. Next, by positing that it is the spectator, and not the actor, who retains the history of actions, metaphysics paves the way for the *theōria*, for the contemplation or the theory that is capable of ensuring immortality. The brilliant action, which was so highly prized during the Age of Pericles, was abandoned in favor of contemplation, which was considered from that point on to be the most dignified of activities. In that way, *bios theōrētikos* asserted its supremacy over *bios politikos*. Finally, Anaximander and Parmenides stole eternity away from the gods and turned it into a "Being" that exists forever with neither a beginning nor an end. "*Being,* birthless as well as deathless, replaced for the philosophers the mere deathlessness of the Olympian gods."[67] With Being replacing the gods, theology became ontology. Last but not least in the chronology of Arendt's tale, the eternal nous took on a central role. Because it is essential to take up one's abode with things that last forever, the Homeric term "nous," which encompasses all mental activities, is what became the new philosophic path to immortality. Being is no longer the cosmos or the universe;

rather, it is nous that now corresponds to Being. As Parmenides put it, "to be and to think . . . are the same."[68] Because Christianity grants immortality not through nous but through faith, the effort to rely on thinking to achieve immortality would later become superfluous—that is, until Hegel made history into the object of contemplation and, in reaction to the sciences, transformed the practical objective of philosophy from immortality to necessity.

This rather fantastic trajectory, which Arendt paints with a broad brush, enables her to criticize the systematization and scientific character of modern philosophy and thus the scientific ambitions of the "early" Heidegger. Is it not true that *Being and Time* promises to address the question of the meaning of Being while postulating that "'Meaning of Being' and 'Truth of Being' are the same?'"[69] Arendt sees Heidegger's view as but one example of the "fallacies" of metaphysics that systematize, unify, and eventually interpret signification according to models of truth, which amounts to the beginnings of dogmatism, if not tyranny.

Although Heidegger mooted this criticism through his "reversal" in the mid-thirties, another of Arendt's objections, one that is related to the empire of nous that she had already attacked, really hits home. In Arendt's view, Platonic duality, as well as the way Heidegger interpreted it through his reading of the *Sophist*, show that both these ways of thinking about difference (that is, Plato's and Heidegger's) project the duality of the thinking ego. When Heidegger posits that whenever there is a plurality there is difference and that this difference does not arise from the outside but is inherent in every entity in the form of duality, Arendt objects that his interpretation is "erroneous."[70] In her view, the transference here occurs between the experience of the thinking ego and things themselves: the philosopher projects the two-in-one as the essence of thought that captures the "same" and the "different." By criticizing Heidegger's line of reasoning, Arendt argues that it is not the thinking activity that constitutes the unity because nous, identified with Being, is not One merely because of its own reversal and its own grasp: "On the contrary, the two-in-one become One again when the outside world intrudes upon the thinker and cuts short the thinking process."[71] The very existence of the thinker within the plural dimension of common sense is what makes him appear as the ecstatic quality of his solitude: it is his solitude that actualizes his self-awareness and makes it into a duality. Because the mind withdraws from the world without ever being able to leave or transcend it,[72] the experience of duality is the consequence of this indispensable and constitutive tension between thinking *and* the plurality of the shared world. In Arendt's view, this explains why thinking, though solitary, is not a lonely experience. Thinking helps me "keep myself company," which means that I maintain my bond of friendship with the common sense that I share and that insinuates itself in dialogue in the form of a "self" opposed to a "thinking ego." Loneliness is experienced only when the dialogue of the two-in-one comes to an end—when, as Jaspers put it, "I am in default of myself."[73]

Arendt's remarks on the "divinity" inherent in nous and her refusal to consider the role played by the shared world as a condition of the unity at the heart of the dialogue of the two-in-one illuminate some more explicit objections that she makes about the "fallacious arguments of metaphysics." In her 1954 address to the American Political Science Association, "Concern with Politics in Recent European Philosophical Thought," for example, Arendt discussed Heidegger's concept of *Geschichtlichkeit* [historicity]. Although Heidegger intended his concept, unlike Hegel's, to leave "the arrogance of all Absolute behind us," and although he dismissed concepts and judgment laying claims to truth to get closer to the political realm, Arendt notes that the very structure of *Geschichtlichkeit* "never reaches [the center of the political realm]—man as an acting being."[74] The coincidence between thinking and the event allows Heidegger to shed new light on the basic historical tendencies of a particular era (such as the world's ceding to technology), but he appears to have forgotten more specifically philosophic questions such as "What is politics?" and "What is freedom?"[75]

Similarly, the very warm tribute that Arendt paid Heidegger on his eightieth birthday makes clear that the "scandalous" engagements of such great thinkers as Plato and Heidegger in favor of tyrants and dictators result from more than just chance occurrences or their individual character traits; they also stem from "what the French call a *déformation professionnelle*."[76] Arendt curtly reminds us (by quoting her old professor) that the thinking ego does not seek truth, but merely attempts to "'stand . . . within' the raging storm" and that the thinking self is "everything but the self of consciousness."[77] As it withdraws into listening to Being and until it reaches the "oblivion of Being," the thinking self withdraws into an "abode" far removed from worldly affairs.[78] If, however, the thinker finds himself ceding one day to the temptation of abandoning his "journey" and of "enter[ing] into human affairs" instead, it will be because he was unable to remain in his state of "wondering."[79] In Arendt's view, Heidegger was more adept than anyone else at analyzing the Will, following this distraction, as a will-to-power inherent in human action and in thought, when thinking is identified with action. But Arendt also suggests that the "penchant for tyranny" derives from the fact that few thinkers, even the greatest ones, are prepared to "accept this wondering as their abode," that is, to think about the gap between thinking and the world as much as they think about their interdependence.[80] And few thinkers are prepared to remain in their wondering and to contemplate the tension that it creates between the shared world and the world of thinking. In truth, it is all too tempting to let ourselves be carried away by the "power" of wonder and to project this "power" onto the world by using it as a way to compete with the tyrants. Arendt describes here the latent paranoid tendencies of thinking as a wondering that has been mastered and systematized, and then projected onto a world that it will master in turn, and that it will govern until the end.

Arendt has thus presented her conception of thinking as a "two-in-one" that never stops questioning the bonds it shares with the common sense of human plurality. Arendt discusses two modalities of this sort of thinking, willing and judging, so she can describe to us their respective possibilities and limitations. In Arendt's view, Kant's work on the "faculty of judgment" provides the only satisfying distinction to date between the "general" and the "particular" that allows us to probe their difference as well as their common bond. At the same time, however, in their interaction with the world of sensory appearances, the "winds of thought" emerge, under the pen of Arendt, through a metaphor that she is fond of and that must be understood beyond the banality of its expression: "the life of the mind."

Arendt, like her friend Hans Jonas, defines thinking as a "natural need of human life": "Thinking accompanies life," and it is the "de-materialized quintessence of living."[81] At the same time, human mortality, the nothingness that surrounds the interval between birth and death, "constitutes the infrastructure, as it were, of all mental activities."[82] Arendt thus maintains that death becomes the only reality of which thinking is aware once the thinking ego withdraws from appearances and loses touch with the meaning of the real. All the same, despite the deep structure that mortality represents for the faculty of thinking, it still remains that the ordeal of thinking, as well as its meaning, can be found in the very same activity. Arendt summarizes the way living thought absorbs death in one of the formulations that reveals the originality of her reflection, if not her genius: "To think and to be fully alive are the same."[83] Although Hegel develops a system, one whose "sins" Arendt could not resist criticizing and one that also claimed

that "to think is to act," he offers us an unforgettable formulation that expresses for Arendt the vibrant intensity of the experience of thinking: "The true is thus the bacchanalian revel,
where no member [i.e., no particular thought] is not
drunken."[84] Arendt resurrects the Nietzschean echoes of this
phrase and affirms, with Hegel's blessing, that no matter how
much "truth" is revealed through thinking, it presents itself to
the thinking ego as a revel and as an intoxication.

Arendt's notion of "life" undergoes a radical mutation here.
Life is no longer the process of life or the trap of reification
intrinsic to the human condition that Arendt had denounced
in her 1958 book. Beginning in 1973, life, through the interplay
between the "world of the senses" and the "winds of thinking,"
becomes an experience of life as thinking and of thinking as
life.[85] And it is not Aristotle whom she invokes here with his
"for living things, life is being" or his "the thinking activity
[*energeia* that has its end in itself] is life," that is, not the Aristotle that Arendt sometimes praises and sometimes doubts.[86]
Rather, Nietzsche is the one who gives Arendt a hand as she
deconstructs life, *zōē*, as the "life of the mind." "This ego . . .
knows only of being 'alive' in an elation that always borders on
'intoxication'—as Nietzsche once said."[87] It is incumbent
upon us to realize that this life of truth, which is nothing less
than the life of the mind, is tantamount to the thinking activity as such and that its only truth is the activity itself, which is
constantly destructive. Whether it is life-thinking or a think-
ing-life, this life of truth places us at the cusp between the questioning of significations and the intoxication that ushers in
consciousness.

More than Bergson's creative imagination, the political
activity that takes place in *amor mundi* is, in Arendt's view, the
ultimate human experience.[88] This "political activity" bears no
resemblance to the practices currently described by this term;
instead, it presents itself as an incarnation of the formerly
philosophic demands found at the heart of human affairs. Such

is Arendt's goal, and such is her saving grace. One might very well ask whether Arendt, in her later years, was not the most "post-Christian" of modern thinkers who have heeded the calls of both Nietzsche and Heidegger.

FROM THE INTERIOR MAN TO THE
VIOLENCE OF THE LIFE PROCESS

Arendt's volume on "willing" could have been entitled "On the Genius of Christianity and Its Politics." Without distancing herself from the Greek model, but by laying out a history of thinking that functions through ruptures and foundation legends, Arendt deciphers the key moments in Christian theology that construe thinking as life or as a life of the mind. She points out the fruitful discoveries as well as the mistakes and difficulties along the way. This nod toward appropriation is made possible by way of the "forgetting"—which constitutes the human condition but which secularization has turned into an object of criticism—that Arendt likes to invoke by quoting René Char: "Our inheritance was left to us by no testament."[89] Arendt is convinced that "the thread of tradition is broken and . . . we shall not be able to renew it." Although she is hostile to destruction in any form, she takes seriously the disappearance of the "Roman trinity" of religion, authority, and tradition. For Arendt the political theorist, this deconstruction is not a pure speculation but an action that touches upon—and that will always touch upon—"our political history, the history of the world."[90]

Because her thinking locates itself in a temporal scheme made up of divisions and foundation legends, Arendt is led to examine various modalities of foundation legends from before our time—and before her time. Arendt discusses two of these legends in particular: one Roman and the other Hebraic. Both tales reflect the "legendary hiatus between a no-more and a not-yet," "the abyss of nothingness," and the "love of freedom" as an "inspiring principle of action."[91] The freedom in question is either a negative freedom that frees people from oppression (slavery in Egypt, the flight from burning Troy) or a positive freedom that manifests a stable reality, a *novus ordo saeclorum* (the conquest of the Promised Land, the founding of a new city)—but freedom of this sort always keeps in mind that for the Romans, this beginning is a new beginning, a rebirth of Troy. In that sense, Arendt contrasts a renewing and reforming temporality with the cyclic temporality of the Greeks and the eternity of Being as revealed by philosophy. She suggests that this time of renewal is rooted in a Roman and biblical genealogy. As a result, it becomes necessary to return to the movement of rebirth and reform, this time based on another beginning that is constructed like a perpetually reborn thought, that is, like a living thought.

This "other beginning" is Christian thought, which, since the break in the "thread of tradition," is no longer theology, but a life of the mind. Indeed, alongside Jesus and the Apostle Paul, and by way of Saint Augustine, Thomas Aquinas, and Duns Scotus, Arendt retraces the genealogy of the concept of life as thinking action resulting from a reflection on beginning. This reflection necessitated the introduction of a previously unknown parameter: the "power to begin" that is understood as the Will and that leads to the dialectic of freedom. The Christian "beginning" thus emerges as a beginning of the Will that touches upon the problem of freedom and that results in two important consequences: it carves out a space for the interior man, who was already conceived by the Stoics, and it becomes a will-to-power, which is essentially a will to live. The goal is to overcome the various obstacles that appear along the way, and Arendt outlines her own solution by bypassing subjective psychology once again and by choosing instead to analyze the logic of the Will exclusively within the confines of the political realm—not divinity, Being, or the subject, but in the context of the political realm of a world capable of arbitrating the life of the mind as well as the life of humanity insofar as it represents a plurality of lives of the mind.

Whether it is a vision or a utopia, Arendt describes the political realm as a post-Christian—or perhaps trans-Christian— locus of new beginnings. It is a space filled with a temporality that is at once eternal and fragmented and that represents the "Eternal Recurrence" of the species and its history as well as the advent of the unique qualities of the "whos." Finding inspiration in a sort of "politics of Christianity," its successes as well as its failures, Arendt reconstructs the political realm from scratch based on two key notions—the birth of individuals and the frailty of actions—and on two psychopolitical interventions—forgiveness and the promise. Her conclusion, however, is reached only from the vantage point of an archaeology of a "life of the mind" in which the Will was a major component. Arendt tells us that "in respect to desire, on the one hand, and to reason, on the other, the Will acts like 'a kind of *coup d'état,*' as Bergson once said," which means she interprets his remarks to mean that free acts are the "immediate datum of consciousness" and that we can assign this discovery a historical date.[92]

Unknown to Greek antiquity, the Will appears to have been invented by the Apostle Paul and by Augustine. Aristotle anticipates the notion of the Will when he reflects upon the relationship between desire and reason. Because desire, or appetite (*orexis,* from *orego:* "the hand that moves toward something nearby"), is a desire for an absent object, it invites reason to intervene. For Plato, reason acts through persuasion and then culminates in truth by way of a continual release; it neither orders nor commands. Desires, which are blind and which are deprived of reason, are what command the soul, albeit without any help from the Will. When the Greeks speak about a "voluntary action," they mean an action that is not haphazard, that is essentially a bodily movement performed by an agent with his faculties fully intact: I am performing a voluntary action when I give

my money to a thief who threatens me with a gun, for I am performing this movement myself.[93] Aristotle's invention of the
notion of *proairesis,* a choice among alternatives and an intermediary between reason and desire, narrows the gap between doing
something "voluntarily" while under constraint and the modern
notion of the "voluntary act." And yet the opposite of "deliber-
ate choice or preference" is, in Aristotle's view, a pathos that
motivates or that causes us to suffer.[94] Only by deliberating
among all our choices can we experience happiness, *eudaimonia*
[living well.] *Liberum arbitrium* (the Latin translation of *proairesis*) is neither spontaneous nor autonomous.[95] Like Kant after
him, Aristotle submits the Will to the compulsion exerted on the
mind by self-evident truth or logical reasoning. Kant believed
that every "Thou-shalt" rises up in the mind itself and implies a
"Thou-canst." But freedom becomes a problem only when men
realize that the "Thou-shalt" and the "I-can" are not one and the
same.[96]

The Apostle Paul's insight played a decisive role in this discovery. Paul lent the Greek world his "worldless" Hebraic experience, an experience that centered on man himself, as subject
to the law, and that bore no relationship with the space of the
political appearance (the world and the polis) in which persuasion can be used. The Hebrews believed that immortality is
granted only to the people and not to individuals.[97] With the
propagation of the new Christian religion, the decadent
Roman world dared to promise, as a sort of consolation, eternal life for each individual.

In this context, Paul understood that the law is unattainable
because it results in a splitting of the ego and in a sort of "two-
in-one," although those two, unlike Socrates's partners, are
passionate and irreconcilable: "I-will-but-can*not.*"[98] The corollary to this sort of subjective split is that the law itself is "equiv-
ocal": it encourages obedience by presupposing disobedience
and thus implicitly provides for its own negation. Precisely
when man "wants to do right," he finds that "evil lies close at

hand."[99] What is more, "For I do not do what I want, but I do the very thing I hate" (Rom. 7:15). And on the subject of the law: "The very commandment which promised life proved to be death to me" (Rom. 7:10). This is the "curse of the law," and "if righteousness were through the law, then Christ died to no purpose" (Gal. 3:13).

Arendt invites us to see these remarks as Paul's invention of interiority. The Will, the interiority of the man-who-wills, and its ambivalence and intractable ambiguity all originate at the same time. It is impossible to satisfy the law, for our will to do so stimulates another will, the will to sin, and the one will is always accompanied by the other. Thus while the old law commands, "Thou shalt do," the new Christian law reformulates it as, "Thou shalt will." And yet this voluntary submission, which suggests that it is possible to respond either Yes or No, also leads to the discovery of "the wondrous fact of a freedom that none of the ancient peoples—Greek, Roman, or Hebrew—had been aware of."[100] It is a formidable wonder at that, for Paul draws attention to the "inner contest" that characterizes it and to the "reflexivity" that is more pronounced in the Will than in any other mental activity. If I will, then "the I-will inevitably is countered by an I-nill." In the struggle between *velle* and *nelle,* the Will transforms one into a "two-in-one" and thus creates obstacles of its own.[101] For Paul, this conflicted logical process resembles a struggle between mind and body, while Saint Augustine, for his part, will speak of "the 'monstrosity' of the Will."[102]

The Christian construction of the Will, which, as Arendt likes to point out, was influenced by Paul's insight, was just as much a product of the Stoics. For the Stoics, the omnipotence of the Will took on the well-known features of an *ataraxia*: we can be happy only through a special effort on the part of the Will to keep us from being miserable in a world that is in crisis and that is besieged with fears and death. What makes this negative will possible, however, is that the Stoics created an "inward region" that stood in contrast to a world that is no longer harmonious, as was the world of Pericles, but violently hostile.[103] If a Stoic sage such as Epictetus withdraws from the polis, it is not to sacrifice himself to the *vous,* the internal organ of truth and the invisible eye fixated on the visible. Rather, he is openly isolating himself through "impressions" [*phantasiai*] that follow a *dynamic logikē* of their own. The Stoics were logicians and semioticians who favored divination, not physics. In Arendt's view, the Stoics provided the makings of a philosophy that was aware from the start of its own weakness, which scarcely tempered Arendt's harsh evaluation of the Stoics—a highly reductive one at that. The wisdom of Epictetus determined the norms and standards of mastery, which began by avoiding pain and which culminated in insensitivity, apathy, and a complete alienation from the world. Happily, the antagonism of the two wills quelled this despair and put an end to this fundamental resignation to one's fate. Human interiority, made up of impressions, would prove to be the Stoics' primary legacy to Christianity: Saint Augustine would have a strong need for what he would call this "monstrous" faculty, for the power exerted in the domain of pure fantasy, and for the palace that separated him from external phenomena as he became "the first philosopher of the Will."[104]

Arendt is drawn to the main themes of the Augustinian Will. To begin with, Augustine understood that the Will inherited from Paul and the Stoics granted the ego "an *inward* life" that, unlike reason and desire, could respond to an idea that philosophy neither posits nor tries to reconcile: "*Quaestio mihi factus sum*" [I have become a question for myself].[105] Even more important, because there are two wills, one carnal and the other spiritual, and because the Will is an internal capacity for affirmation and negation, when the law addresses the Will (and not the mind, reason, or desires), it is addressing a faculty that functions on its own accord. Augustine was the first person to elaborate on the dialectic between the law and its transgression, a dialectic already revealed by Paul. As Augustine put it, "the greatest joy is ushered in by the greatest painfulness," a notion that prefigures, one might add, the cruelty of Sade as well as of Nietzsche and Artaud.[106] But aside from the "sadomasochism" of the Will, a notion that we know Arendt resisted quite vigorously, the power of the Will to regulate itself is what attracted Arendt's attention: every *velle* is accompanied by a *nolle*, though no created being can will against creation. Because the principal will is the Will of creation, it is impossible to refuse unequivocally to will. Accordingly, Augustine does not trust anyone who says, "I'd rather not *be*," because life always implies a desire to continue to be and thus proves to be a form of praise and thanks.[107] Based on this supremacy of the "will to live" (in the sense that life is *summum bene,* eternal life), the Will, which is inherently tragic and contradictory, is unified through love even though it exposes an interiority that is no longer a dialogue but a conflict.

Augustine relates the tripartite structure of this dynamic (two wills unified by love) to the triads that structure the life of the mind and that resonate with the Holy Trinity of the Father, the Son, and the Holy Ghost. Arendt catalogs the occurrences of being, knowing, and willing, as well as their dialectic, and she makes the Will appear to be a unifying force. As a locus for mental coherence and attention, the Will also joins the sensory organs and the real world. Turned toward action, the Will, as an agent of cohesion, can also be defined as *love* even though love, unlike the Will, is not extinguished when it reaches its goal but allows the mind "to remain *steadfast* in order to *enjoy* it."[108] In this way, the Will, as an organ of the future, describes temporality with a tone that is not one of "care" but of tension, action, and love.

Finally, the intervention of the Will is what individualizes each beginning: the *principium divinum* posed by the heavens and the earth become for man the *initium.* Man is put into the world, according to Saint Augustine (whom Arendt cites once

again), as a "new beginning" because he is conceived as a "beginning running toward an end" and because he is "endowed with
the capacity of willing and nilling."[109] Augustine's speculations
imply here a conception that he did not expressly formulate, one
that enables us to think of freedom not as *liberum arbitrium* but
as a "spontaneous beginning" along the lines of Kant's definition
of freedom. Accorded by the *principium* and prepared by the
initium of each birth, the Will, the first of the mental faculties,
reactualizes for man the possibilities of rebirth in the form of
spontaneity and freedom. Arendt believes that in light of this
articulation (between *principium, initium,* and *voluntas*), human
reason should not be ashamed to concede the freedom of a rela-
tively absolute human spontaneity: Saint Augustine posits that
the Will is the first step in causality [*initium*], if not the first in
time (because it follows the *principium*).

Put another way, the condition of life (the unique birth at
the heart of plurality) announces and prefigures the mental
faculty known as "the Will" as a major manifestation of the
life of the mind—of its spontaneity and its freedom. "The
freedom of spontaneity is part and parcel of the human condition. Its mental organ is the Will."[110] The freedom that
insinuates itself into this field is necessarily subjected to the
admonitions of consciousness and thus becomes innately negative, sinful, and even a source of suffering. That freedom can
be realized, however, in the "startling rejection of repentance,"
as observed by Meister Eckhart, who believed that the sinner
can forgive himself. And it can also be realized in the ultimate
victory of the Thinking ego over the Willing ego, as described
by Leibniz.[111]

The law implying admonition and beginning was transformed into the life of the mind as a perpetual new beginning.
The Will was to become the agent of that transfiguration and
the birth of each human body its foundation. Such is the evangelical testament, both philosophical and political, that Arendt
lays bare for modernity.

Thomas Aquinas refined and intellectualized Christian Will. He considered Being to be "good and desirable" for the Will and "true" to the Intellect, but considered Intellect the nobler faculty of the two because it precedes Will and is capable of apprehending the universal, and because it dominates and guides Will, which is free only to the extent that it deals with particulars.[112] As a result, man's ultimate happiness consists in "know[ing] God by the Intellect; it is not an act of the Will."[113] Just as Intellect relies on reasoning as its subordinate power for dealing with the particulars, "the Will has the faculty of free choice [*liberum arbitrium*] as its subservient helper in sorting out the appropriate particular means to a universal end."[114] Through this intellectualization, which deviates from Saint Augustine and which Arendt denounces, "Being" in Thomas Aquinas's system is what preoccupies Arendt and what appears to her to be "simply a conceptualization of Life and the life instinct."[115] Although this concept is already present in Saint Augustine, it is dug into by Thomas Aquinas, and it provides the first glimpse of the assimilation of the Will and the life instinct that would not be fully articulated until Schopenhauer and Nietzsche did so in the nineteenth century.

On the other hand, Arendt felt very positively toward Duns Scotus, whose original and highly personal return to Saint Augustine restored the primacy of the Will over the Intellect. By affirming the uniqueness of each birth (its *haecceity* or "thisness"), Duns Scotus does not confirm the destructive aspect of the Will, but rather the "delight" to which it is inextricably linked.[116] A mental enjoyment helps transform the Will into the love that culminates in "the full and perfect attainment of the object": love "enjoys" the thing itself.[117] The Augustinian distinction between *uti* and *grui* is comparable to Duns Scotus's beatitude: it is a way of enjoying the pure actuality that adopts its own aims. This dynamic of uniqueness and beatitude will be invaluable when we discuss Arendt's vision of "forgiveness" and the "promise." *Amo: volu ut sis* is limited to realizing "the serenity of a self-contained, self-fulfilling, everlasting movement."[118] This realization of the Will in the serenity of Duns Scotus's brand of love is admirable, particularly because it is accompanied by a reflection on the contingency of the human action. No object of derision, contingency is, for Duns Scotus, the privileged ground of human free will because it is through action that the Will takes a position "for" or "against" something, even going so far as to hate God Himself. Like Buridan's donkey that has no more trouble deciding once he begins to graze, the Will no longer exists once it begins to act in accordance with one of its own propositions. This cessation is no true extinction, however, because the Will, unlike a desire that deflates as soon as it finds its object, endures and continues to enjoy its very realization, in love and action, and not at all in a state of rest. Far removed from agitation, hatred, and rejection, affirmation is what enables Duns Scotus's Will, which is enamored of contingencies, to achieve its ultimate realization. The beatitude that extends as far as action appears to be a constant source of inspiration for Arendt, in stark contrast to the serenity of the contemplative retreat favored by the "professional thinkers."[119]

There is no doubt that Nietzsche's will-to-power inspired Arendt's return to Christian thought about the Will, a return that unearthed advances and pitfalls of which Nietzsche knew nothing, or that he at least failed to mention. With that project complete, Arendt was able to reread Nietzsche's concept of the Will without getting bogged down in Heidegger's interpretation thereof, an interpretation that reduced the Will to Being and its disclosure. In this trajectory, Christian thought about the Will made it possible to trace the space of a human action as the action of plural freedom, thereby advancing a political hypothesis that ran counter to Heidegger's dismantling the Will into nothing but the withdrawal of Being. All the same, Arendt's reading of Christian thought reveals the psychological traits and latent negativity of the Will as well. Paradoxically, but in the end very logically, Montesquieu—who bypasses Christianity and revives Greek pragmatism—gave Arendt the final keys she needed to include the Will in a humanity "of births."

The convergence of two currents of Nietzschean thought, the "will-to-power" and the "Eternal Recurrence," does not escape Arendt. She follows Nietzsche's analysis of the will-to-power as something that encompasses the battle between he who orders and he who obeys, the ambivalence between pleasure and pain, and the intensity of the sensation of liberation, which is rivaled only by the sensation of sorrow. Arendt juxtaposes two excerpts from *The Gay Science*—the first of which likens the Will to the force of a wave and the second of which heralds the benevolent acceptance of the self and of life and prefigures the "Eternal Recurrence"—in an effort to highlight the coherence between these two aspects of Nietzsche's thought.

The Will-wave is thus "roaring with overweening pleasure and malice."[120] It is only by dodging this duality that we can understand "the notion of the I, the Ego": "I am free, 'he' must obey," said Nietzsche.[121] Destructive ambivalence, however, is identified from the outset with the principle of life, because Nietzsche removed it from mental activity and conceived it instead as a joy that arises out of the abundance of the life process itself, which Nietzsche calls the Dionysian principle and which Arendt likens to Marx's "surplus value." Arendt's Nietzsche is contrasted with the Christian dolorism of Paul and with his "I-will-and-I-can*not*," and he lays claim to an ethics of total acquiescence to life. Because life proceeds through overabundance, and because a certain luxury pervades it, "we can indulge in it only after the needs of life have been satisfied."[122] Arendt detects a Nietzschean strain of Duns Scotusism in this Dionysian hymn: "Everything suits me, for everything suits you [the waves] so well, and *I am so well disposed toward you* for everything."[123] Concurrently, and after linking worldly phenomena with power and the greediness of life, Nietzsche returns to the fundamental anthropomorphism of metaphysics, in which the mechanisms of the soul enjoy their absolute primacy and exert an influence over scientific concepts.

A second Nietzschean fragment is the parable entitled "*Das grösste Schwergewicht*" [the thought that would weigh most heavily on you], a thought that desires only "the eternal hourglass of existence" and that benevolently accepts itself and life through a *Gedankenexperiment* that returns to the ancient time-concept with its cyclical motion.[124]

In both cases—in the will-to-power as well as in the "Eternal Recurrence"—the acceptance of life, in Arendt's view, "spreads a general 'feeling of strength' [*Kraftgefühl*]," the "feeling of force," and the emotion that "arises in us 'even before the deed'" and that is "occasioned by the idea of what is to be done."[125] Arendt considers these affirmations, which were subsequently interpreted as Nietzsche's prescience of the Freudian "unconscious drive," to be a reflection on time.

The Will cannot stop the passage of time, and its powerlessness creates a feeling of resentment, a desire for vengeance, and a hunger for domination and power. Only a suspension can nullify the fury against time, notably by way of the "forgetting" that Nietzsche revives and that Arendt transforms into "forgiveness"—and by way of the "Eternal Recurrence" that stems from the confrontation between the Will and the past.[126]

In the end, whether it is geared toward the past, where it realizes its own powerlessness, or toward the future where it realizes its own strength, Nietzsche's version of the Will transcends the simple "givenness" of the world—and this "gratuitous" transcendence corresponds to the superabundance of life.[127] In accord with the luxury of life, the superman is thus someone who is able to transcend himself. If an honest man is a nihilist who considers that the world as it is ought not to be, to overcome his nihilism he must muster the strength to invert his values and to deify the world.[128] To do so, however, he must do more than simply accept things as they are, as was believed by Epictetus, whom Nietzsche esteemed very highly. As Nietzsche put it, "strength of will [is great enough] to do without meaning in things . . . [who] can endure to live in a meaningless world." The "Eternal Recurrence" is the term for "the ultimate redeeming thought inasmuch as it proclaims the '*Innocence* of all Becoming' [*Die Unschuld des Werdens*] and with that its inherent aimlessness and purposelessness, its freedom from guilt and responsibility." The Will transformed itself into a force of life. Indeed, neither the "Eternal Recurrence" nor the "Innocence of Becoming" arises out of a mental faculty; they are rooted in the fact that they are "thrown" into the world (Arendt is borrowing terminology here from Heidegger's reading of Nietzsche).[129] With the elimination of cause and effect, sense and moral facts disappear from the rectilinear structure of Time (in Being "there are no moral facts," Heidegger observed while giving credit for the notion to Nietzsche). Similarly, melancholy, which the Will shelters as if it were a sort of all-devouring past, vanishes only upon accepting the cyclic recurrence.

Based on this "turmoil of aphorisms," Arendt concludes that Nietzsche comes down in favor of a "repudiation of the Will and the Willing ego" because the superman is able "to turn his own will around" solely to accomplish a negation:[130] to "look . . . away" because nothing is left but "to bless everything there is for being, 'to bless and say Amen.'"[131]

Although Arendt is satisfied here with Nietzsche's chipping away at the Will, she is hardly unaware that the political realm in which she plans to secure this "dismantled" Will poses several questions, among the most important being the question of power and authority.[132] In like manner, it is difficult to understand "who" can say Amen without recourse to the psychic "interiority" carved out by the Will, unless it is by returning to the "*theōria*" or to the reversal of Nietzschean "life" in

Being as expressed by Heidegger. What interests Arendt here is to use Nietzsche to help reject the guilt-inducing psychology and the life-centered anthropomorphism of the tradition, and then to criticize the current scientific and political trends that have internalized that tradition. Her goal does not prevent her from also relying on those who, within the tradition, leave open the possibility to break with the past as they begin again, and to affirm that thinking is coextensive with the generous superabundance that could be called a life: Saint Augustine and Duns Scotus, among others.

Arendt was obliged to conclude her questioning of the Will with a reflection on the role it played in Heidegger's work, if for no other reason than that "the Will to rule and to dominate is a kind of original sin, of which [Heidegger] found himself guilty when he tried to come to terms with his brief past in the Nazi movement." Arendt thus devoted a third and final study to Heidegger that refers to the two volumes of his *Nietzsche,* which contains lecture courses from the years 1936 to 1940, that is, from the period in which Heidegger's "reversal" occurred (she situates the reversal between the time of the two volumes, a notion she credits curiously to a single source, J. L. Mehta's *Philosophy of Martin Heidegger*).[133] At once rigorous and restrictive, Arendt's interpretation of certain aspects of Heidegger's reading of Nietzsche is notable for its ambiguity, which plays as much on caution as on endorsement.

In that sense, Arendt can only have been pleased with Heidegger's critique of the Will as a mere symptom of the life instinct, thereby uprooting Nietzsche from his biologism and sounding an accord with Arendt's own attacks against the "life process" as the very foundation, as we have seen, of the reification and alienation that lie at the core of "the human condition."[134] Without skipping a beat, however, Arendt notes that Heidegger's cleansing the Nietzschean Will of its "biological traits" is accompanied by his emphasis on the destructive effects of the Will and his underplaying what Nietzsche showed to be the Will's creativity and superabundance. And yet the Nietzschean Will was made possible only through his assimilating the Will to a Dionysian zest for life (and not to Being). All the same, Heidegger's understanding of Nietzsche strikes Arendt as "radical," as when she detects "the Will to will" in modern technology itself and when she contrasts it with calmness [*Gelassenheit*], in accordance with the practice of her Todtnauberg master.[135]

Arendt reveals some similarities between Heidegger's "Care" in *Being and Time* and Bergson's vitalism. "Care," which provides immediate evidence of consciousness and which recovers the "real and concrete self" from a "second self . . . which emerges from life in common with others," is manifested in artistic creativity.[136] Arendt points out, however, that after Heidegger's "reversal," "Care" did not disappear in the name of the Will, but was transformed into "taking care . . . of Being," of which man became the "guardian" or "shepherd," and death itself was no longer the utmost possibility that would be actualized in suicide, but was a "shrine" that "collects."[137]

All the same, Arendt describes the concept of *Seinsgeschichte* [history of Being], which Heidegger believes "determines whether men respond to Being in terms of willing or in terms of thinking" (with the ideal solution being that the thinking ego overcomes the Will and actualizes the "letting-be"), as a version of Hegel's ruse of reason that would be tantamount to his "World Spirit."[138] And yet for Heidegger, as Arendt points out, Being itself (and not the "World Spirit on horseback" in Napoleon at Jena) is what is manifested "in the thinking of the actor so that thinking and acting coincide."[139] Arendt concedes that this amalgam of acting and thinking desubjectivizes the Cartesian ego, but it is ultimately located in the province of the solitary thinker. Heidegger's "authentic self" is offered as the only way to save the city-state: the philosopher translates the hidden meaning of Being into "silent actions" that are his "thoughts" in their own soliloquy. Heidegger's "reversal" makes it clear, however, that the sage no longer acts by itself but is obedient to Being. It still remains that the personification of this concept, Hegel's ghostlike Nobody, becomes for Heidegger the "Thinker," although this *solus ipse* does not signify Heidegger's return to the world of appearances.[140] Arendt's remarks here call to mind a passage in *The Human Condition* in which she invokes the melancholy wisdom of Ecclesiastes: "Vanity of vanities; all is vanity"—a strain of melancholy that, for Arendt, is not religious per se, but is "unavoidable wherever and whenever trust in the world as a place fit for human appearance, for action and speech, is gone."[141]

Finally, Heidegger dissolves his "idea of guilt" [*Schuld*] into *Dasein*'s primordial indebtedness to Being: human existence does not "need to become guilty of something through omissions or commissions," for it is guilty "anyhow" because "it *owes* its existence to something that it is not itself." Engaged in this thought, existence invariably finds itself obliged to give thanks for this debt: what links the fate of thinking with the fate of thanking transforms guilt into grace and establishes an eternal innocence. There too, Arendt appears to endorse a logic of deliverance in the place of Judeo-Christian notions of guilt, for she considers that logic to be a more recent variant of Plato's *thaumazein*. At the same time, Arendt remarks with some irritation that "where everybody is guilty, nobody is," and she notes that Nietzsche, as well as Mandelstam and W. H. Auden, discovered this same response to wonderment and thanking, though for them it was in an "entirely secularized world."[142]

Heidegger's final reversal, which Arendt takes more seriously than its predecessors, was manifested in his reading of the Anaximander fragment: "oblivion" is forever the essence of Being, which implies that *Seinsgeschichte* exists no more, for there is no place for a history of Being enacted behind the backs of acting men.[143] Because beings are "set adrift" in errancy, errancy constitutes the "realm of error," "the space in which history unfolds."[144] At the same time, a "kind of history" emerges during the transitory moments between one epoch and the next, for example, during revolutions.[145]

Does this mean that Heidegger's solution, particularly his dissolving the Will, even beyond the "Will-not-to-will," in the "letting-be," provides a response to the difficulties inherent in the fate of the Will in Western thought? With the exception of Duns Scotus, who is the only one who "was ready to pay the price of contingency for the gift of freedom," the "professional thinkers," in Arendt's view, persist in closing themselves off inside philosophical freedom, which is limited to solitary thought and which neglects the political freedom that is demanded by human plurality.[146] Arendt's concerns about her reading of Heidegger's reversals of the Will are derived from the same principle: that the solitude of thinking and of poetic language or the enigma conceals the true abysses of freedom that are exposed, in truth, by *amor mundi*.

From that perspective, the philosopher–political theorist hypothesizes a political realm that would arise out of the impasses of the Will. Like Montesquieu, she attempts to imagine a political realm that would be founded on "power" in the sense of the "I-can," and that would stem not from an "exercise of the will" but from a multitude of relationships, such as laws, customs, and practices.[147] From Montesquieu's *Spirit of the Laws,* she highlights in particular the interplay between "liberty," "opinion," "safety," and "laws": "Philosophical liberty consists in the exercise of the Will, or at least . . . in the opinion that we exert our will. Political liberty consists in safety, or at least in the opinion of being safe." And she also adds that relationships among mortals, as opposed to the immutable realities of the divine, are unstable and "must be 'subject to all the accidents that can happen and vary in proportion as the Will of man changes.'"[148]

Unless, that is, this putative subtraction of the Will in the name of power is merely another one of Arendt's ironic gestures geared toward highlighting the "fallacies" of the "professional thinkers" and toward adding saliency to the particularities of the human condition as a political condition. In truth, once we presume the instability of these human affairs, it is not enough to say how much they depend on a plurality (on "us" rather than "me"), nor can we simply join Montesquieu in contemplating various forms of human communities and governments so that we might restore their complexity and legislate power or simply assert, as does our critic at the end of her study on the Will, that every organization made up of a free human grouping presumes an "initiation" that itself presupposes a "beginning." For by going back "to the beginning," our author calls out to the Will that actualizes, as we have seen, the logic of beginning at the very heart of human existence and that philosophy had proposed to deconstruct. Unless, that is, Arendt is thinking here of a "liberty" based on a mode of thinking other than the mode of the Will and of the beginning. But what mode would it be? Not even Montesquieu himself could protect the "private" and its liberties from legislation aimed at the "public" and at "public liberties." As for the political "I-can," it does not seem all that autonomous from the "I-will," at least not from the "I-will" of the thinking subject or of individual intimacy or the initiative of a citizen.

Arendt does not go down this path, as she seeks a nonsubjective foundation for politics. Although it deconstructs the Will and its limitations, her modest return to Saint Augustine's *initium* or to birth as a prototype of the capacity to begin suggests that the resonances of Christian and post-Christian Will will never be absent from the "frailty of human affairs" that so interests her. "Willing" is thus a version of *thinking* as Arendt understands the term: not to ascertain the truth about willing, but to retain a Socratic two-in-one. Through a dramaturgy of this sort, the various thinkers about the Will, including Arendt, each occupy the role of the "Ego" and of the "thinking Ego" in a dialogue that is continuous, demanding, and, despite everything, amicable.

Arendt, for her part, took a break from investigating the Will so she could pursue one last train of thought, a path that was more trustworthy and inherently communitarian than its predecessors and that had the potential to provide a framework for the political bond: judgment. Judgment as a choice, a moral decision, or an authority: those are only some of the weighty political questions that contributed to an elucidation of "judging" that will unfortunately remain incomplete, as it was interrupted by Hannah Arendt's death in 1975. She left on her typewriter a single page of a book that was barely begun and that was to reflect several courses she had given on the subject.

THE TASTE OF THE SPECTATOR:
TOWARD A POLITICAL PHILOSOPHY

Arendt removed the dialectic from commandment and freedom, from the law and transgression that underlie the Will: others, for their part, will claim that the dialectic is inherent in the logic of desire necessary for thinking about the human subject as well as political conflicts. Arendt hoped that her meditation on the Will would highlight the distinguishing characteristics of modern metaphysics: particularly its subjectivism, notably Marxist and existentialist, that stipulates volition as a capacity lurking inside us that allows us to claim "to make ourselves" as well as "to make History."[149] Without relying on moral categories, at least not in the beginning, Arendt sought to define the character of the political bond by isolating judgment as a distinct capacity of the mind, which, through its specificity as laid out in Kant's *Critique of Judgment,* attests to the way each person is from the outset a member of the human community.[150]

"What is man?": those are the terms of Kant's fourth question (after What can I know? What should I do? How may I hope?), a question posed not in the *Critiques* but in one of his courses. His underlying idea is no longer what matters, Arendt points out, but it evokes the plurality of human beings and could pose another question as its corollary: "How do I judge?" the question of Kant's third *Critique*.[151]

"How to organize a people into a state and how to constitute that state." That question appears to have preoccupied Kant toward the end of his life, which was punctuated with the shock of the American Revolution, not to mention the French Revolution. "[Kant's] strictly political essays . . . were written after 1790, when the *Critique of Judgment* appeared, and, more significantly, after 1789, the year of the French Revolution."[152] As the French Revolution was already underway, Kant backed away from his moralizing position and understood that "a good constitution is not to be expected from morality, but, conversely, a good moral condition of a people is to be expected under a good constitution."[153] The experience of the French revolutionaries inspired the idea that in politics the people judge as if they were a disinterested spectator and in a plural society, what he called "publicness," bad acts are generally kept secret.[154] This truly "spectacular" commentary on the French Revolution may be found in the second section of *The Contest of Faculties*, which is entitled "An Old Question Raised Again: Is the Human Race Constantly Progressing?" There, Kant explains that he is not interested in the actual acts committed by political actors, but in "the mode of thinking of the *spectators* which reveals itself publicly in this game of great revolutions, and manifests such a universal yet disinterested sympathy for the players on the one hand against those on the other, even at the risk that this partiality could be very disadvantageous for them if discovered. Owing to its universality, this mode of thinking demonstrates a characteristic of the human race in general and also (owing to its disinterestedness) a moral character of humanity, at least in its predisposition."[155]

Before Arendt discusses the articulation of judgment in

Kant, she enjoys pointing out—always with a nod to the professional philosophers—that this line of thought permanently freed Kant from his predisposition toward melancholia, a malady that is rampant among "philosophers, a notoriously melancholy tribe of men,"[156] she says, and that many of Kant's confessions continually reveal (a "burden which seems to lie on life as such, . . . even the best man 'will fret his life away'") and so forth.[157] Kant would thus be one of those rare philosophers, if not the only philosopher, to invite the thinker to delve into the life of his kind, believing as he did, unlike Plato, that every ordinary person could appreciate a pleasing or displeasing life. Rousseau, for his part, learned "to honor men," and if he wished neither to leave Plato's cave nor to participate in a philosophic sect, it is because he believed in the "equality" of men.[158] Contrary to the majority of Kant's philosophical colleagues who understood politics to be an art of governing that implies domination and obedience, and that scarcely deserves their consideration, Arendt discovered in Kant's conception of politics a commitment to life and Being: "I call out to each creature . . . : Hail us, we are! [*Heil uns, wir sind!*]." Arendt considered Kant's youthful optimism to be equally as important as his discovery of the "moral law within me" and of the impossibility of proving that God exists. "But the praise is praise of the 'whole,' i.e., of the world."[159] Kant's work, in sum, is an assent of sorts that never departs from a critical thought, a permanent questioning for which few philosophers have managed to sustain the necessary degree of vigilance: Arendt points out that since Kant, only Sartre has written a *Critique (of Dialectical Reasoning)*, although she appears to have forgotten Marx's *Critique of Political Economy*.

More than anything else, though, it is the idea of plurality, added to other aspects of Kant's thought she has underscored, that attests to the originality of the philosophy on which Arendt's approach to judgment is based. That plurality is a plurality of spectators is a notion that goes back to Pythagoras: the

actor playing a role must sustain the illusion, and the spectators alone are able to see the whole scene. The spectators, who
are theoretically impartial, have no assigned role. In the end,
the *doxa* or opinion—"how I am understood by others"—is
the actor's primary concern. The spectators make up the public domain. On the one hand, spectators are always plural in
number because the experience of a spectator must be vali-
dated by the experience of other people, which is what generates "common sense" as opposed to "private sense" (also known
as a "logical *Eigensinn* [egotism]").[160] On the other hand, without spectators, beautiful objects would never see the light of
day, for they are created by the judgment of spectators and critics. "Kant is convinced that the world without man would be
a desert, and a world without man means for him: without
spectators."[161] "Insanity consists in having lost this common
sense that enables us to judge as spectators."[162]

The spectator, who interests Kant inasmuch as he is an
authority on judgment, is distinguished not only from the
actor, in the sense that he merely looks and does not play a
role—but from the genius as well. Regardless of the ways the
genius stands out, the distinguishing feature of spectators is
taste, which is decidedly not the province of the genius. Taste
may even be the foundation of our ability to communicate as
well as to judge. Because it is at once the most particular and
the most shareable of the senses, taste prefigures our ability to
judge and to distinguish what is true from what is false. Let us
break down this enigma step by step.

Of all the senses, taste, along with smell, stimulates the most
"entirely private and incommunicable" of sensations. Even
more important, taste, which cannot be translated into words,
is impossible to memorize, and is instantaneous and irresistible; it is also different from the other senses in that taste
and smell are "quite clearly the discriminatory senses."[163] We
can refrain from judging what we see, and, less readily, what we
hear, but we cannot so refrain when it comes to taste: "it-

pleases-or-displeases-me" is endemic to taste, a discernment that is wholly idiosyncratic.

When Arendt discusses Kant, she comes close to what Freud called the "pleasure principle," but she does not force the point. She immediately brushes aside this sensory discernment based on the distinction between pleasure and displeasure and replaces it with the "approval of pleasure." Freud, for his part, had noted the immanence of an affirmation [*Bejahung*] in pleasure, and he had detected a negation [*Verneinung*] in displeasure. But his real innovation was to highlight the "primary" processes that are "primary" relative to the drive and that underlie the symbolic activity of reasoning as well as the genesis of a symbolism dependent on the negativity comprising the bond with the Other. For Arendt and Kant, on the other hand, the most important aspect of the dynamic of discernment inherent in taste is the pleasure of "approbation": what gives me pleasure is the act of approval itself. The criterion of this pleasure, a "second-degree" pleasure, we might call it because it is superimposed on Freud's instinctual pleasure, is communicability and a public character. From this perspective, we can appreciate the flavor of Kant and Arendt's example of the communicability that chooses between pleasure and unpleasure: "One is not overeager to express joy at the death of a father or feelings of hatred and envy [*author's note:* do such feelings even exist if they are not made manifest?]; one will, on the other hand, have no compunctions about announcing that one enjoys doing scientific work, and one will not hide grief at the death of an excellent husband [*author's note:* is something hidden in that particular case?]." Arendt goes on to conclude, "The criterion [of taste], then, is communicability [and not pleasure!], and the standard of deciding about it is common sense."[164]

We return here to the *sensus communis* of Thomas Aquinas, which Arendt had referred to in "Thinking" and which she defined, like Kant, as "the specifically human sense because communication, i.e., speech, depends on it."[165] Common sense is thus a "sense" as distinct from speech; it is the "effect of a reflection upon the mind" and it affects me as a sensation would.[166] It is sustained by "maxims" (to think for oneself, a maxim of the Enlightenment; to think by putting oneself in the place of all others, a maxim of an enlarged mind; to be in agreement with oneself, a maxim of consequential thought). Common sense can be communicated without the mediation of a concept: "We could even define taste as the faculty of judging of that which makes *generally communicable,* without the mediation of a concept, our feeling [like sensation] in a given representation [not perception]."[167]

We realize that this universalizing communicability—the foundation of language—operates as a form of repression and spares Kant and Arendt from having to pose the question of pleasure or displeasure in the relationship between the "subject" and the "object of satisfaction," or the Other as a pole of anguish and desire. But we also realize that this communicability, as if it were the representative of a universal form of repression, helps us think about the way we belong from the outset to a community that requires neither understanding nor moral imperatives to create itself but that nevertheless operates out of an always already socialized sensation: "*Taste* comes to be imputed to *everyone,* so to speak, as a *duty.*"[168] We might add that it is a strange taste indeed, one that effaces its extravagant singularity and submits it to the imperative of the communitarian prohibition. It is impossible to follow Arendt and Kant here without keeping in mind what they are trying to accomplish, which is to found an original political community, and not at all to distinguish the libertine or romantic excesses of a more errant taste that has successfully inspired other thinkers. Along these lines, Arendt adds, "the it-pleases-or-displeases-me, which as a feeling seems so utterly private and non-communicative, is actually rooted in this community sense and is therefore open to communication once it has been transformed by reflection, which takes all others and their feelings into account." Put another way, when we taste or judge, we judge in our role as a "member of a community."[169] Kant's reflections, which provide Arendt with the utmost satisfaction, can thus be associated with a "natural," "sensory," and "communitarian" base: "one's community sense makes it possible to enlarge one's mentality. . . . Imagination and reflection enable us to *liberate* ourselves from them and to attain that relative impartiality that is the specific virtue of judgment. . . . The Beautiful teaches us to 'love without self-interest,'" and "it 'interests only in society.'"[170] Arendt concludes that "sociability is the very essence of men insofar as they are of this world only."[171]

These words are the makings of a true political philosophy, which Kant never put to paper: this "*third* critique," the critique of judgment that follows the critique of "pure reason" and the critique of "practical reason," could be interpreted as an attempt to develop a political philosophy for which the prototype would be no more and no less than aesthetic judgment, defined as "the faculty of mysteriously combining the particular and the general."[172] Arendt could only have been inspired by this proposition as she attempted, as announced in the first two volumes of *The Life of the Mind,* to forgo the withdrawal into thought and return to the world of particulars, which is integrated with the universal through Kant's aesthetic judgment and taste, "so to speak, as a duty."[173]

The "judgment" that Arendt proposes to be the foundation of politics is not, as we have seen, a "cognitive judgment," for as an approval of taste through common sense, judgment defies understanding. Nor is it a "judgment of History" in the Hegelian sense (*Die Welgeschichte ist das Weltgericht* [The history of the world is the judgment of the world]) that would accord success the privilege of being the ultimate choice. Kant appears to have been inspired not only by the "spectacle" of the French Revolution, but by several eighteenth-century French commentaries on taste as well, commentaries with which Arendt clearly was unfamiliar, unfortunately so because it limited her ability to analyze the realm of sensation and the miming of opinion.[174] Arendt nevertheless observed that Kant's text acknowledging the sociability of man and the pleasures he feels when communicating "reads as though it had been written by one of the French moralists."[175]

And yet Kant's approach to taste, far removed from the sensualism of Montesquieu and more universalist than Voltaire's wholly European, even nationalist, perspective on the matter, is intrinsically political. The *Critique of Judgment,* in fact, links Kant's preoccupations about the human community as a whole with his aspiration toward an "eternal peace," not by eliminating conflicts but through an "enlarged mentality."[176] Governing taste as well as the judgment at the core of taste, the "enlarged mentality" gives an early glimpse of the possibility of a "cosmopolitan existence."[177] I am a member of the world community and of its potential for peace merely because I am someone who is capable of taste and/or judgment. The French moralists were better informed about the varieties—and even the excesses—underlying taste and the richness of its "structure," its complex scope ranging from simple pleasures to the Terror. Kant and Arendt, for their part, preferred a more restrained approach that favored a laudable and highly comforting communicability.

Imagination is the essential function that guarantees the enigmatic shift from the particular to the general and that represents what Kant considers to be the main problem with judgment. Returning to the *Critique of Pure Reason,* Arendt states that beyond the two strains of experience and knowledge, intuition (sensibility) and concepts (understanding), Kant recognized in the concept a "kind of image" and thus suggested that imagination is present in the intellect itself.[178] Accordingly, we are justified in thinking of imagination as "what creates a synthesis." Imagination is the "blind" function of the soul that obtains for the concept the kind of "image" that is a schema: a sort of grasping that recognizes that "this" table shares the general properties of all tables, even as it remains unique.[179] In addition, and while being a "necessary ingredient of perception itself," imagination is rooted in the community (or the communicability) that is the ability to "speak," which means that a schema can never be reduced to an image. Finally, "reflective judgments," which formulate the rule based on the particular (as opposed to "determinative judgments," which subsume the particular under the general rule), allow themselves to be "perceived" within such a schema.[180]

In the *Critique of Judgment,* the analog to the schema is the example: "The example is the particular that contains in itself, or is supposed to contain, a concept or a general rule." Achilles, Jesus, and Napoleon are each an example, in the sense of a "kind of image" or perhaps a schema, that incites a judgment worth more than the uniqueness of the event because it is an example that "is rightly chosen" by those who witnessed a particular slice of history.[181] The theme of a narrative told by observers able to determine the "greatness" of the "example," a theme already apparent in *The Human Condition,* is based here on a faculty unique to Kant, one that is itself innately political and intrinsically human.[182] The *Critique of Pure Reason* defines it as "a peculiar talent which can be practiced only, and cannot be taught" and whose "lack no school can make good."[183]

In the end, because the particular is without doubt the only mirror that is held up to the human species in general, it is hard even to imagine what this "general" would be like, although the particular acknowledges that the general exists. Thus the particular must be judged on its own terms, free from any comparison or from any desire to improve it. One of the most dire consequences of this *haecceity* or "this-ness" is that it supplants the cult of progress: "It is against human dignity to believe in progress," asserts Arendt as well as Kant.[184]

Faced with this incomplete meditation, the reader can only imagine what might have been a political community founded on this sort of "aesthetic judgment," itself founded on an immediately communicable taste that uses understanding for its own needs and that cannot be learned but merely put into practice. Would it be a realization of one of the utopias imagined by the French moralists, minus the sexual pleasure? Or would it be Nietzsche's "innocent future," without the "moral facts" and yet with the intrinsically moralizing Dionysian "taste" to transform it, through the *sensus communis,* into an "obligation"? Or would it be an aesthetic politics, though one that did not reify narrative action into "works of art"?

All these hypotheses are as appealing as they are paradoxical and unprovable. In the end, what remains is Arendt's insatiable appetite for thinking that pursues the foundations of the relationship between the general and the particular, and between the individual and plurality, in order to justify a sustainable human condition that is as free as it is fair.

As a counterpart to Gadamer's critique of Kantian aesthetics, which Gadamer accuses of "depoliticizing" the idea of *sensus communis* and of aestheticizing the faculty of taste, we might turn to Habermas's critique of Arendt.[185] Habermas takes issue with the way Arendt denies the cognitive status of judgment and dissociates practical (political) discourse and rational discourse, "opinion" and "knowledge." In Arendt's view, to accord political convictions a cognitive status would endanger opinion in its integrity, the integrity of a controversy and of a "life of the mind." Her political experience with totalitarianism made her understand how much the opinion takes shape through "crystallization." As a result, she is acting perfectly within her rights when she exposes an important gap in positive rationality, when she expands politics to include aesthetic judgment, taste, intuition, and imagination, and when she shows suspicion of "knowledge" in politics. On the other hand, after reading Gadamer and Habermas, one might hope that Arendt's vision of judgment and her political experiences do not serve to preclude but rather to deepen the "intuitive" experience that other people have mapped out with the help of an antipredicative phenomenology and, more radically, a theory of the unconscious—not outside the cognitive realm but in addition to it.

The "fourth critique," a *Critique of Political Reason* that Kant never wrote and that Arendt had no doubt planned to develop, was just getting off the ground with these reflections on judgment. Even more radically, and without leaving aside this horizon of thought, the historian–political theorist had already found a way to apply it: through the experience of "forgiveness" and the "promise" as paradoxical modalities of judgment.

JUDGMENT: BETWEEN FORGIVENESS AND PROMISE

Freed in this way from the confines of understanding, and yet made possible through the precariousness of a human community made up of spectators whose tastes, though unique, can be shared with other people, judgment is clearly vulnerable.[186] That vulnerability, however, is precisely what enables it to provide a place for the life of the mind as the revelation of a "who" and to avoid getting stuck in a "system" governed by intrinsically totalitarian values. It is therefore quite likely that although Arendt was unable to complete her work on judging, she would never have prescribed what good judgment is, nor would she have shown us the path toward obtaining it. Seduced and yet bogged down by the "frailty of human affairs," Arendt gave her attention to the two pitfalls that threaten judgment—pitfalls that appear to coexist with the linear experience of human time in the process of life and, by implication, in the modern practice of politics: irreversibility and unpredictability.

When time is experienced as being irreversible, it burdens men whose inability to turn it around causes them to succumb to resentment and revenge. Nietzsche once denounced the human "beast" who is "always resisting the great and continually increasing weight of the past"[187] and who—as the mirror image of the animal who never suffers because he forgets everything—suffers to the point of exhaustion because "he cannot learn to forget, but hangs on the past."[188] In place of a ruminative memory that fosters resentment and revenge, the human beast advocates nothing less than the "force of forgetfulness," "a power of obstruction, active and, in the strictest sense of the word, positive" that creates "a little tabula rasa of the consciousness, so as to make room again for the new."[189] Nietzsche also associates "this very animal who finds it necessary to be forgetful," an animal for which he hopes and prays, with another faculty: the ability to promise.[190] He describes the faculty of promising as "an active refusal" or a "memory of the will" before he exposes some of its formidable ambiguities:[191] the promise is a supreme sovereign in which man can "guarantee himself as a future," but it is also paired with hardness, cruelty, and pain because it inherits the debts [*Schulden*] of an invariably guilty conscience [*Schuld*] in the same way a debtor inherits the debts of his creditor.[192]

To the Nietzschean violence that rises up against the "conscience" and the "contract," however, Arendt contrasts her own serene wager on the potential rebirth of the "who," which is contingent upon a renewed relationship with time. Even so, she skirts around the unappealing picture Nietzsche paints of a contractual and indebted conscience that struggles against the throes of the will-to-power, and she considers only what Nietzsche called its "plastic power."[193] In the end, the feeling of guilt reduces to a figure of impotence—that which engenders linear time. Guilt, which appears to result from a breach of a prohibition or a moral precept, turns out to be deeply bound up with the very experience of temporality, that is, when temporality is coextensive with the life process. Breaking this chain requires an interruption, which in Arendt's view can no longer be forgetting but rather forgiveness. It is impossible to undo what has already been done, and it is impossible to imagine how one can forgive in solitude. Perhaps Arendt believes that forgiveness would be a mere inhibition if it were deprived of the space of appearance and the words of other people. But she can tolerate the idea that men, among themselves and at the heart of the frailty of their actions, free themselves from their doings and past actions whose consequences they had not foreseen or they cannot accept.

Even as she explores succinctly the complex problem of forgiveness, Arendt does not deny that some offenses are unforgivable. "Radical[ly] evil" actions exist (which she acknowledged by citing Kant in 1958, that is, long before the 1963 Eichmann trial) "about whose nature so little is known, even to us who have been exposed to one of their rare outbursts on the public scene. All we know is that we can neither punish nor forgive such offenses and that they therefore transcend the realm of human affairs and the potentialities of human power, both of which they radically destroy wherever they make their appearance."[194] In Arendt's view, however, "crime and willed evil are rare, even rarer perhaps than good deeds." What is at stake here is merely a "trespass," which turns out to be an everyday occurrence because of "the very nature of action's constant establishment of new relationships within a web of relations." Trespassing thus calls out for "forgiving [and] dismissing, in order to make it possible for life to go on by constantly releasing men from what they have done unknowingly."[195]

To this limitation on her conception of forgiveness, Hannah Arendt adds another: forgiveness is aimed at the person, and not the act. One cannot forgive the murder or the theft, but only the murderer or the thief. By being aimed at *someone* and not *something*, forgiveness becomes an act of love. With or without love, however, one always forgives by taking the person into account. Whereas justice demands that everyone is equal and weighs each act individually, mercy emphasizes inequality and evaluates each person on his own terms. In spite of that difference, however, "to judge and to forgive are but the two sides of the same coin"; "every judgment is open to forgiveness."[196]

Let us apply this framework to the "judgment" that Arendt rendered in her book on the Eichmann trial. In no way does Arendt forgive this criminal man, precisely because, "by taking into consideration the person," she discovers a nonperson, the absence of a "who" or a "someone," a robotic bureaucrat who was incapable of judging his own acts and who therefore removed himself from the realm of forgiveness. Arendt sees this argument as no less radical than the notion of an "unforgivable crime" or "radical evil" practiced by the very system Eichmann submitted to and that, by destroying the "potentialities of human power . . . dispossesses us of all power [such that] we can repeat along with Jesus: 'It were better for him that a millstone were hanged about his neck, and he cast into the sea.'"[197] Though Arendt is far from satisfied with this Christlike judgment, she wishes to create an international jurisdiction to punish crimes against humanity visited upon the Jewish people. Punishment, to the extent that it is different from vengeance, does not contradict the suspended logic of forgiveness. Like forgiveness, punishment puts an end to something that, without it, could return ad infinitum.[198]

If, on the other hand, a person is able to think and to judge, whatever the modalities and the limitation of that questioning, which itself is always tantamount to an effort to being again or to be reborn, Arendt agrees to approach him with a judgment fueled by forgiveness. Bertolt Brecht is a good example of this. Did Brecht not condemn himself before anyone else did by inflicting the worst possible self-punishment for a gifted man, which is simply the death of talent? With passion and assurance, Arendt exposes the melancholic beauty of Brecht's work, even though she still judges quite harshly the "irresponsibility" that in her view is endemic to poets, as evidenced by the words that "this poor B.B." composed in a hymn to Stalin. Based on this particular "example," Arendt draws a general conclusion: although Brecht never displayed an ounce of self-pity, he still managed to teach us "how difficult it is to be a poet in this century or at any other time."[199]

In Arendt's judgment, Heidegger deserves forgiveness more than the average person does, not only because of love, "one of the rarest occurrences in human lives" that "possesses an unequaled power of self-revelation and an unequaled clarity of vision for the disclosure of *who*," but also because the revelation of love helps awaken a respect for a thought unique among all others, which she debates and displaces without abandoning the "regard for the person from the distance."[200]

Because this insight was entirely foreign to the Greeks, Arendt credits Jesus with discovering forgiveness, which was prefigured only by the Roman principle of sparing the vanquished [*parcere subiectis*]. Although this Christlike precept of forgiveness was expressed in religious language, it was rooted, in Arendt's view, in "the experiences in the small and closely knit community of [Jesus'] followers [who were] bent on challenging the public authorities in Israel." By thereby judging Jesus' innovation to be eminently political, Arendt zealously advocates her own expansive conception of an ideal politics, and she is clearly going beyond the strict domain of religion. Arendt believes that the correctives Jesus maintains against the "scribes and Pharisees" are indispensable.[201] Not only is God not alone in His ability to forgive, but it is precisely because humans are capable of forgiveness that God will eventually forgive them. On that score, Arendt cites, among other things, the Gospel according to Saint Matthew: "For if ye forgive men their trespasses, your heavenly Father will also forgive you: But if ye forgive not men their trespasses, neither will your Father forgive your trespasses."[202] Forgiveness, which also applies to the unconscious ("for they know not what they do") owes it to itself to be consistent, even infinite: "'And if he trespass against thee seven times in a day, and seven times in a day turn again to thee, saying, I repent; thou shalt forgive him.'"[203]

Arendt's appropriation of religious practice encourages us to submit other modern acts of interpretation to ethics. Psychoanalytic listening and the analyst's speech within transference and countertransference could be considered an act of forgiveness: the donation of meaning with the effect of a scansion, beyond the madness of the illness, anguish, or symptom and beyond the disintegration of the trauma, allows the subject to be reborn and thus to be henceforth capable of reshaping his psychic map and his bonds with other people. To forgive is as infinite as it is repetitive; forgiveness rests on the desire for truth and understanding that is manifested in a subject embarking on an analysis.[204]

On the other hand, in light of the unpredictability of human actions, which underscores our uncertainty about the future, the promise is the only thing that can stabilize without suffocating and that can offer human beings a way out. The promise obviates the obscure need for security that makes us sacrifice our freedoms and that rests on self-domination and on governing other people. Whereas forgiveness is opposed to vengeance, the promise is opposed to domination. Blessed with a long heritage, as is forgiveness, the promise exists in the inviolability of the covenants and treatises of the Romans [*pacta sund servanda*] but it is moored more specifically in Abraham, "whose whole story, as the Bible tells it, shows such a passionate drive for making covenants that it is as though he departed from his country for no other reason than to try out the power of mutual promise."[205] Arendt denounced the pseudoprophetic manipulations of totalitarian propaganda, which was based on fantastic promises. Skeptical of promises guaranteeing that tomorrow would be a better day, Arendt was willing to concede only "certain islands of predictability" to the frailty of human affairs: in the end, such promises are quite limited, particularly by the mutual and contractual engagement in which "certain guideposts of reliability [such as treaties and agreements] are erected."[206] Legislation comes to the rescue here: Long live the man from Ur, and long live Montesquieu!

To the "identical will" that forges the sovereignty of a group, Arendt contrasts the way men who are connected to one another through a mutual promise "act in concert."[207] These men dispose of the future as though it were the present, and they live together in the miraculous enlargement of what Nietzsche called the "memory of the Will," which is what distinguishes human life from animal life.[208] As Arendt evokes Nietzsche's concept, she hears only the joyful touches of the superman and detects not a trace of Nietzsche's disdainful tone.

With forgiveness and the promise, Arendt believes that she has revived two "control mechanisms" of public life,[209] mechanisms that are indispensable and impenetrable to the extent that they are located at the very heart of the most characteristic and dangerous attribute of human life: the faculty of endlessly releasing new, unforeseen, and irreversible processes. Faced with the inexorable mechanization of daily life, forgiveness and the promise render "a sort of judgment" that, in the end, is tantamount to a wager on our capacity for rebirth. In the political context, the ultimate aim of such a judgment is not to return men to their mortal condition but to draw attention to men's faculty for being "beings of birth." This revelation constitutes the miracle par excellence that Christianity refers to as "glad tidings" and that it presents in the form of a narrative. The tale, moreover, is a true "reflective example" and not a "demonstrative" one in the sense that it induces, without generalizing, and that it clears the path for and announces the advent of the "who": "A child has been born unto us."[210]

Glad tidings indeed! But the good news comes at the cost of inscribing love, which by definition is apolitical and foreign to the world, in that very world—through the intermediary of the child who causes the lovers to engage the community to which their love has chased them. Arendt, who never stops questioning herself, wonders whether the glad tidings are really so welcome. The answer is unclear, because the sheer fact of belonging to the world in some ways represents "the end of love." What to think, then?

Arendt is not done thinking about the difficulties of "human affairs." Without such difficulties, however, who else would seek to understand them? In the end, the life of the mind is what it is all about for Arendt: living while thinking and understanding. Her unique passion remains: "What is important for me is to understand."[211]

Among the many "difficulties" raised by forgiveness and the promise, the difficulty of their very possibility cannot be overestimated. The radical exteriority that gave rise to Christlike forgiveness and promises as they intervened in the "political world" was known as transcendence and faith. Although Arendt invokes love for forgiveness and legislation for the promise, she does not ignore the need to think about the "Archimedean point" that is unable to establish with certainty that a "who" exists.[212] She calls this point "human plurality," thereby appropriating Kant's notion of a human communicability expanded into a peaceable cosmopolitanism. Arendt appears to discern within that notion the political version of Duns Scotus's affirmation, Nietzsche's Amen, and Heidegger's *Gelassenheit*. The certainty is tenuous at best, but it is still worth trying to attain: by exhibiting taste, by observing, and by telling a story.

In truth, insists Arendt, neither forgiveness nor the promise is a solitary act: no one can pardon himself or promise himself anything with any hope of success. On the other hand, the modalities that allow such acts to be accepted by other people culminate in the sort of forgiveness and promises that concern only the self. Not only do the two faculties "depend . . . on the presence and acting of others," but the roles they play in politics establish a set of principles that are diametrically opposed to the classical "moral" tenets that emanate from the Platonic notion of rule, a notion that is itself founded upon the relationship between me and myself.[213] In the end, then, the right and wrong of relationships depends on whatever attitudes are displayed toward one's self.[214] Accordingly, the entire public realm is seen in the image of a "man writ large." On the other hand, the moral code deduced from the faculties of forgiving and making promises "rests on experiences which nobody could ever have with himself, which, on the contrary, are entirely based on the presence of others."[215]

Even if human beings can go mad, as our century has so cruelly shown to be true, the humanity in which Arendt, despite everything, puts her faith, or at least all her confidence, cannot go mad—and must not go mad. Therein lies the transcendence—and the limits—of Arendt's thought. Because humanity, as she understands it, consists of an aptitude for the "enlargement of the mind" and for the ability to communicate common sense, it can be tantamount to language. Humanity and language are Arendt's versions of Being, and language cannot go mad. That is what Arendt believes, and when she was asked what remains for her in pre-Holocaust Germany, she replied, "What is one to do? It wasn't the German language that went crazy."[216] In the end, once I ask myself "what should I do?" I will end up believing that a language cannot go mad.

Yet is it really necessary to believe that a language cannot go mad in order to continue to "do"? Imagine that I continue "to do" while asserting that a given language can go mad and that my bond with my community, the "enlargement of the mind," the *sensus communis* of the German or of another people, even of humanity, can go mad, already have gone mad, or could start going mad once again. After all, because a language conditions the subject that inhabits it, it responds *for* the subject and it carries the possibilities of its own crises: if the discourse of subjects is mad, it is mad *since* language and *of* language.[217] What should be done, then? And how should we go about it?

It is incumbent upon us to care for the speech of each person as well as the communitarian bond itself, not so we can restore them to a fixed and sane eternal identity that would find support in our "yes" or our "amen" but so we can usher in some tentative revelations of the "who" without forgetting how tentative they really are. This goal presumes that our hopes for such a revelation are accompanied by a certain pessimism or at least by our conviction that language, humanity, all forms of identity, unicity, the mother, the father, the subject, and even Being itself are more than just "veiled," "withdrawn," "in oblivion," or "errant." The implication is that each "who" is driven by its inherent impossibility of being: it is nothingness, a crisis, or an illness. From that perspective, the bond with the Other, in the context of this undeniably fragile community, becomes a sort of care that is not an unchecked Will but that nevertheless preserves the miracle of rebirth.

Arendt was far removed from such concerns—and yet she was ever so close. As she reminds us that the "fact of natality" is the "miracle that saves the world," Arendt vaunts "the full experience of this capacity."[218] A full experience of natality would inevitably include birth, life, an affirmation of the uniqueness of each birth, and continual rebirth in the life of the mind—a mind that *is* because it begins again in the plurality of other people, and only then does it act like a living thought that surpasses all other activities. But the "miracle" also occurs, if only in a single fragment of this "full experience," which justifies the miracle through the promise it provides and the forgiveness it articulates. Arendt shared in that miracle, for she was without a doubt one of the few people of our time to attain the state of bliss in which living is thinking. Did she not write once that, although the rapture of thought is ineffable, "the only possible metaphor one may conceive of for the life of the mind is the sensation of being alive"?[219]

As for a political action that would be tantamount to a birth and that would shelter us from estrangement, Hannah Arendt—without indulging in too many illusions—invites us to think about it and to experience it in the present, while always remaining inside the realm between promise and forgiveness.

NOTES

INTRODUCTION

1. The Greek *daimōn,* and then the Latin *genius,* watched over the birth of men and their works. Women, for their part, were granted a *juno,* a profoundly protective double of the self.
2. The *Robert* dictionary traces the latter evolution to 1689.

CHAPTER I

1. Letter of March 24, 1930, *Hannah Arendt/Karl Jaspers: Correspondence,* p. 11. All future references to *Hannah Arendt/Karl Jaspers: Correspondence* will be indicated by *Jaspers Corr.*
2. Many publications, conferences, and special journal issues have been devoted to the work of Hannah Arendt. Among the most significant are the following: *Social Research* 44 (1977); *Esprit*

(June 1980); *Les Etudes phénoménologiques* 2 (1985); *Les Cahiers du GRIF* (fall 1986); *Les Cahiers de philosophie* 4 (1987); the proceedings from the conference held at the Istituto Italiano della Politica in Naples (1987); *Politique et pensée,* the proceedings from the conference held at the Collège international de philosophie (Paris: Payot and Rivages, 1996); *Hannah Arendt et la modernité,* annals of the Institut de philosophie de l'Université de Bruxelles (Brussels: Vrin, 1992); International Conference in Geneva (1997): vol. 1 (*Les Sans-Etat et le droit d'avoir des droits*); vol. 2 (*La Banalité du mal comme mal politique*) (Paris-Montreal: L'Harmattan, 1998).

3. Arendt, *The Origins of Totalitarianism,* pp. 311, 316; emphasis added. All future references to *The Origins of Totalitarianism* will be indicated by *OT.*

4. Ibid., p. 459.

5. Arendt, *The Human Condition,* p. 247. All future references to *The Human Condition* will be indicated by *HC.*

6. See Young-Bruehl, *Hannah Arendt;* and Courtine-Denamy, *Hannah Arendt.* All future references to Young-Bruehl's intellectual biography will be indicated by Y-B; all future references to the Courtine-Denamy monograph will be indicated by C-D.

7. See p. 174.

8. Arendt, *Essays in Understanding,* pp. 1–23. All future references to *Essays in Understanding* will be indicated by *EU.*

9. Ibid., p. 17.

10. See pp. 111–112, 123.

11. *EU,* p. 9.

12. Arendt, "Martin Heidegger at Eighty," pp. 51–52. Arendt wrote this text forty-five years later, and she was still identifying "life" with "thinking" as she had done since her childhood and throughout her relationship with Heidegger. See also her letter to Heidegger of April 22, 1928, *Heidegger Corr.,* doc. 42, pp. 65–66.

13. Arendt and Heidegger, *Briefe,* doc. 15, p. 30. All future references to Arendt and Heidegger, *Briefe,* will be referred to by *Heidegger Corr.*

14. Y-B, pp. 52–53.

15. Ettinger, *Hannah Arendt/Martin Heidegger,* p. 6.

16. Letter of April 22, 1928, *Heidegger Corr.*, doc. 42, pp. 65–66.

17. See Arendt, "What Is Existenz Philosophy?"

18. Letter of June 9, 1946, *Jaspers Corr.*, p. 43.

19. Ibid., pp. 47–48.

20. Letter of November 1, 1961, ibid., p. 457.

21. *Heidegger Corr.*, doc. 47, p. 74.

22. Ibid., doc. 55, pp. 89–90.

23. Ibid.

24. Ibid., doc. 57, p. 95.

25. Arendt, "Martin Heidegger at Eighty," p. 54.

26. Letter of October 28, 1960, *Heidegger Corr.*, doc. 89, pp. 149, 319.

27. "Heidegger said with great pride, 'People say that Heidegger is a true fox.' Here is the true story of Heidegger the fox:

    Once upon a time, there was a fox so wanting in slyness that he constantly got caught in traps. In fact, he could not even tell a trap when he saw one. . . . He designed a trap for himself in the form of a lair, went inside it, and acted as if it were an ordinary trap (not because he had a sudden burst of slyness but because he had always thought that other people's traps were for him). Yet he eventually decided to become sly in his own way and built the trap that he had himself and that was the right size for him alone so he could plant a trap for other foxes. Thus he let it be known once again that he truly misunderstood traps, as no other fox could ever enter his trap since he was already in there. . . . So our fox got the bright idea of decorating his trap to the hilt and of putting up signs all over it that said, "Come see this trap, which is the most wonderful trap in the world."

    If another fox wanted to pay him a visit, he would have to get inside his trap. Any other fox but him, of course, would be able to get out of the trap. Although he could never leave his trap, he said proudly, "There are so many people in my trap that I have become the greatest fox of them all." And in some ways he was right. No one is as familiar with traps as he who spends his life inside them.

August or September 1953, ibid., notebook 17, doc. A5,
Heidegger Corr., pp. 382–83.

28. See Arendt, *Rahel Varnhagen.*

29. Arendt, *The Life of the Mind,* "Thinking," p. 19. All future references to *The Life of the Mind* will be indicated by *LM.*

30. Arendt, *Men in Dark Times,* pp. 45–46. All future references to
Men in Dark Times will be indicated by *MDT.*

31. Arendt and Blücher, *Briefe.* All future references to Arendt and
Blücher, *Briefe* will be indicated by *Blücher Corr.*

32. Letter of September 18, 1937, *Blücher Corr.*, p. 83.

33. Letter of September 19, 1937, ibid., p. 84; letter of August 12,
1936, ibid., p. 44; letter of September 18, 1937, ibid., p. 83; letter
of August 4, 1941, ibid., p. 130.

34. Letter of October 31, 1939, ibid., p. 99; letter of December 4,
1939, ibid., p. 106.

35. "Stups," which means "turned-up nose," was Hannah's nick-
name for Heinrich. Letter of February 8, 1950, ibid., p. 208; letter of May 25, 1958, ibid., p. 471.

36. Letter of December 15, 1949, ibid., pp. 176–77.

37. *LM,* 'Thinking," p. 212.

38. See "The 'Who' and the Body," pp. 171–184.

39. "Weimar flapper" invokes the Weimar Republic and its emancipated and morally unencumbered women who were sus-
pected of making their sexuality into a profession.

40. C-D, p. 19.

41. In 1933, however, the young Arendt reviewed a work of social
psychology on the female question and showed she was aware
of the economic discrimination facing women. She refused to
see women simply as workers, however, and supported instead
an analysis of the family rather than of the isolated individual.
See "On the Emancipation of Women" in *EU,* pp. 66–68.
Arendt's political preoccupations are already apparent: "The
author sees the position of women in contemporary society as
doubly complicated. . . . The ambivalence of these conditions
becomes especially clear when considered from a political point
of view. Women . . . have not gone forward on political fronts,
which are still masculine fronts." Ibid., p. 67.

42. *EU,* pp. 2, 3.
43. Ibid., 17.
44. Ibid., 3.
45. During the controversy that erupted over her reporting on the Eichmann trial, Arendt complained about and attacked her detractors from the *Aufbau* group who "accused [her] of, among other things, what the Freudians call penis envy." The ensuing debate, however "ugly," remained a sore spot for her. Letter of August 12, 1964, *Jaspers Corr.,* p. 562.
46. Arendt's dissertation was first published in German by Springer Verlag in 1929. She was unsatisfied with the initial English translation by E. B. Ashton, and she completed a partial revision thereof. C-D, pp. 158–59.
47. Cited in *Jaspers Corr.,* pp. 89–90.
48. Letter of January 16, 1966, *Jaspers Corr.,* p. 622.
49. Arendt, *Love and Saint Augustine,* pp. 31, 5. All future references to *Love and Saint Augustine* will be indicated by *LSA.*
50. Ibid., p. 13.
51. *HC,* pp. 73–74.
52. *LSA,* pp. 48
53. Ibid., p. 49.
54. Ibid., p. 52.
55. Ibid., p. 58.
56. Ibid., p. 66.
57. Ibid., p. 70.
58. Ibid., p. 7.
59. *LM,* "Willing," pp. 55 ff.
60. *LSA,* p. 75.
61. See Heidegger, *Being and Time,* sec. 43, "Dasein, Worldhood, and Reality," pp. 244–56.
62. See, for example, his 1942 text on Hölderlin: "Today we know that the Anglo-Saxon world of Americanism has decided to annihilate Europe, which means the homeland, which means the beginning *(Anfang)* of the West. In the West, the hidden mind of the initial will not even show its scorn for the process of self-destruction that targets that which has no beginning; that mind shall attain its sidereal moment by succumbing to

the serene repose of the initial." Heidegger, *Gesamtausgabe,* vol. 53, p. 68.

63. *LSA,* pp. 51, 87.

64. See *LM,* "Willing."

65. *LSA,* pp. 98, 95. See also Augustine, *Homilies on the Gospel According to St. John, and His First Epistle* 8 (sec. 10), p. 1199: "Wish for him [an enemy] that he may be thy brother: when thou lovest him, thou lovest a brother. *For thou lovest in him not what he is, but what thou wishest that he may be*"; emphasis added.

66. *LSA,* pp. 96–97; letter of May 13, 1925, *Heidegger Corr.,* doc. 15, p. 31; Ettinger, *Hannah Arendt/Martin Heidegger,* p. 29.

67. *LSA,* p. 102.

68. See *OT*; see "To Be Jewish," pp. 101–112.

69. Cited in *HC,* p. 321.

70. *HC,* p. 97.

71. Ibid., 324.

72. See pp. 45–48.

73. *LM,* "Thinking," pp. 34–35.

74. See Kristeva, *The Sense and Non-Sense of Revolt.*

75. On Hannah Arendt and natality, see the pioneering work of Françoise Collin in Collin, "Du privé et du public"; and Collin, "Agir and dormir."

76. *LM,* "Willing," p. 21, citing "Also Sprach Zarathustra," in *Ecce Homo* (1889), no. 1.

77. Ibid.

78. *LM,* "Willing," pp. 217, 193.

79. Goethe, "Eins und Alles" (1921), cited in ibid., p. 194.

80. "The being that arrives is an ordinary being. In the scholastic enumeration of the transcendental values (*quolibet ens est unum, verum, bonum seu perfectum*—'the ordinary being is one, true, good, or perfect'), the term that remains unthought in each person and that alters the meaning of all the others is the adjective *quolibet*; . . . *quolibet ens* is not 'the being, no matter which one' but 'the being, in whatever way he matters.' Put another way, the ordinary being presumes a return to will *[libet]*: the ordinary being engages in an original relationship with desire." Agamben, *La Communauté qui vient,* p. 9.

81. We recall that Anne Mendelssohn introduced Arendt to Rahel Varnhagen and presented her with a rare edition of Varnhagen's complete works.

82. Arendt, *Rahel Varnhagen*, 81. All future references to *Rahel Varnhagen* will be indicated by *RV*.

83. Arendt, *Lectures on Kant's Political Philosophy*, pp. 84–85. All future references *to Lectures on Kant's Political Philosophy* will be indicated by *PP*.

84. McCarthy, "Saying Good-by to Hannah," p. 8.

85. *RV*, pp. 144–45.

86. *PP*, p. 61.

87. *HC*, p. 188.

88. *RV*, p. 81.

89. Ibid., pp. 81, 82.

90. Ibid., p. 90.

91. Lazare wrote in 1897–99, "Primitive humanity felt the need to make sacrifices. Later, as barbarianism took shape, it needed only pariahs. . . . The pariahs formed a separate class and a separate nation, and it would become possible one day to draft a history of the accursed races, which were pernicious races for those who owned that history because they were convinced that everything bad in the world could be traced to those pathetic beings. . . . In Christian civilization, [the Jews] were the pariahs *par excellence*." See Lazare, *Juifs et antisémites*, p. 127. On the other hand, "in order to assimilate, some of them were able to erase from their mind and their heart what seventeen centuries had imprinted upon them." Ibid., p. 143.

    "Who will give me freedom? . . . There are new ways of feeling, and thus greater difficulty in suffering. . . . Out of a miserable being whose misery sometimes numbs him will emerge a subtler being who will be twice as sensitive to every attack, and whose existence will thus become a thousand times more intolerable. Out of an often unconscious pariah will emerge a conscious pariah." Ibid., p. 151.

92. Ibid., p. 93.

93. See Arendt, "From the Dreyfus Affair to France Today," pp. 195–240.

94. Lazare, *Job's Dungheap*, p. 87. "Schlemiel" is a Yiddish term commonly used in colloquial German and English to describe "someone with rotten luck." See Chamisso, *Peter Schlemiel.*

95. Letter of August 23, 1952, *Jaspers Corr.*, pp. 192–96.

96. *RV,* p. 15.

97. The book was first published in 1978.

98. *RV,* pp. 92, 96, 97.

99. Ibid., p. 109.

100. Ibid., pp. 124–25, 128.

101. Ibid., p. 138–39.

102. Joan Riviere, analyzing the "negative therapeutic reaction," wrote the following in 1936: "Where narcissistic resistances are very pronounced, resulting in the characteristic lack of *insight* and absence of therapeutic results under discussion, these resistances are in fact part of a highly organized system of defence against a more or less unconscious depressive condition in the patient and are operating as a *mask* and *disguise* to conceal the latter." Riviere, "A Contribution to the Analysis of Negative Therapeutic Response," p. 307; emphasis added. Riviere relates this *mask* and this *disguise* to the defense of mania, to the feeling of omnipotence, and to intellectual rationalization, and she explains that people deny reaching psychic truth because they are afraid of discovering "something worse." In the end, dissimulation, like illness or the impossible analysis of these patients, is a compromise that hides the patient's "love for his internal objects" (for his internalized parents): "It is *the love for his internal objects,* which lies behind and produces the unbearable guilt and pain, the need to sacrifice his life for theirs, and so the prospect of death, that makes this resistance so stubborn." Ibid., p. 319.

The emotional troubles of these personalities recall the splitting of the schizophrenic, although the two phenomena are distinct. They are most prominent in political types and in hysterics, particularly female ones. Deutsch notes judiciously, and directly in line with Arendt (who does not appear familiar with Deutsch's work), that "as-if personalities" might have avoided (or hidden) their psychopathology had they been able to invest in the "favorable circumstances" of political action. This work prefigures the subsequent studies of D. W. Winnicott on the "false self." See Winnicott, "Ego Distortion in Terms of True and False Self."

103. *RV,* pp. 121, 120.

104. Ibid., pp. 149–50.

105 Ibid., p. 150.

106. Ettinger, *Hannah Arendt/Martin Heidegger,* p. 39; *Heidegger Corr.,* doc. 42, p. 66.

107. See p. 243, n. 77.

108. Y-B, p. 302; letter of October 28, 1960, *Heidegger Corr.,* doc. 89, p. 149.

109. Y-B, p. 307.

110. *RV,* pp. 150, 149.

111. Ibid., pp. 152, 155; letter of January 25, 1952, *Jaspers Corr.,* pp. 175–76.

112. *RV,* pp. 207, 209, 217.

113. Ibid., pp. 156, 158, 157, 163.

114. Ibid., pp. 196, 198, 199, 203, 201.

115. Ibid., p. 175.

116. Ibid., pp. 223, 220.

117. Ibid., p. 234.

118. Ibid., pp. 166, 171; Leibovici, *Hannah Arendt, une juive,* pp. 59–60.

119. *RV,* pp. 243, 247–48.

120. Ibid., p. 193.

121. Ibid., p. 187. Hannah wrote in her poems: "When I regard my hand / Strange thing accompanying me / Then I stand in no land" ("Lost in Self-Contemplation"); "Why do you give me your hand / Shyly, as if it were a secret" ("The Shadows"). Cited in Y-B, pp. 50, 54. And from Rahel herself: "It pressed my hands with its paws . . . it took me by the hand . . . its paws down to the second joint sinking through the floorboards . . . it seemed to be concealing a profound, highly significant secret." *RV,* p. 187.

122. Ibid., p. 189.

123. Ibid., p. 190.

124. Ibid., pp. 248, 249.

125. Ibid., pp. 252, 253.

126. Arendt, *The Jew as Pariah,* p. 246. For Arendt, in fact, "everything that our birth mysteriously grants us" has no "legal" or "political" status even though in the "exceptional circumstances" of the Jewish people the fact of birth can also lead to "political consequences," if only negative ones. Ibid. All future references to *The Jew as Pariah* will be indicated by *JP*.

127. *RV,* pp. 253–54; emphasis added.

128. Ibid., pp. 254, 259; letter of August 23, 1942, *Jaspers Corr.,* p. 195; letter of September 7, 1952, *Jaspers Corr.,* p. 197.

129. *RV,* pp. 164, 167.

130. In particular, see Villa, *Arendt and Heidegger,* which brilliantly encapsulates Arendt's debt to Heidegger while demonstrating that Arendt appropriated Heidegger's work in her own way and in the context of her particular political era.

131. *HC,* pp. 207, 245, 206.

132. Ibid., p. 198.

133. Ibid., p. 169.

134. *Translator's note:* See *HC,* p. 183. Arendt defines the "'web' of human relationships" as the "subjective in-between [that] is not tangible." But for all its intangibility, she adds, "this in-between is no less real than the world of things we visibly have in common."

135. *HC,* p. 178.

136. See Ricoeur, *Time and Narrative.*

137. *HC,* pp. 186, 180.

138. Ibid., p. 205 n. 1, citing Aristotle, *Poetics,* 1450b, 25.

139. Ibid., p. 206.

140. See Arendt, *Between Past and Future,* p. 6. All future references to *Between Past and Future* will be indicated by *BPF*.

141. *HC,* p. 205 n. 1, citing Aristotle, *Poetics,* 1450b, 34.

142. See the insightful analysis of these points in Stevens, "Action et narrativité chez Paul Ricoeur et Hannah Arendt," p. 103.

143. *HC,* p. 192, citing Heraclitus, frag. 93.

144. In that sense, Arendt interprets the function of "god" in Plato:

God symbolizes the fact that true stories, in contrast to those that are invented, have no author.

145. Arendt's notion of disclosure should be read in the context of Heidegger's [*Erschlossenheit, Unverborgenheit*]

146. *HC,* p. 187.

147. Aristotle, *Nicomachean Ethics,* 1177b, 31.

148. *HC,* p. 56.

149. Ibid., pp. 176–78, 187.

150. "Each of them appears to me to tell us a sort of myth, as if we were children." Plato, *The Sophist,* 242c.

151. Aristotle, *Poetics,* 1450a, 15; *HC,* p. 187; Heidegger, "The Anaximander Fragment," p. 583.

152. *HC,* p. 194.

153. Ibid., p. 197, citing *Nicomachean Ethics,* 1126 b12.

154. Ibid., pp. 197–98.

155. See Taminiaux, *The Thracian Maid,* pp. 39 ff.

156. Aristotle, *Nicomachean Ethics,* 1177b, 27 ff.; 1141b, 10.

157. Ibid., 1142a, 27 ff. Arendt specifies that the perception in question here is "not the perception of the special senses, but the sort of intuition whereby we perceive that the ultimate figure in mathematics is a triangle." Ibid.

158. See *PP.*

159. Aubenque, *La Prudence chez Aristote,* p. 162.

160. As a parallel to Aristotle's limiting *phronēsis,* it is useful to examine Arendt's definition of *truth,* which she considers to be respectful of political borders: "Since philosophical truth concerns man in his singularity, it is unpolitical by nature. . . . However, . . . this whole sphere [politics], its greatness notwithstanding, is *limited . . .* by those things which men cannot change at will. And it is only by respecting its own *borders* that this realm, where we are free to act and to change, can remain intact, preserving its integrity and keeping its promises." *BPF,* pp. 263–64; emphasis added.

161. See Nussbaum, *The Fragility of Goodness.*

162. *LM,* "Thinking," pp. 190–91.

163. Arendt, "Philosophy and Politics," p. 90.

164. Arendt, *On Revolution,* p. 285; all future references to *On Rev-*

olution will be indicated by *OR.* See also *HC,* p. 199, citing *Nicomachean Ethics,* book 10, 1172b, 36ff.

165. *HC,* pp. 199 ff.
166. On the continuity between the solipsist thought of *Dasein* and Heidegger's political involvement in the controversy surrounding his appointment as rector of Freiburg University, see Taminiaux, *The Thracian Maid,* pp. 44–45: "But [Heidegger] radically removes himself from Aristotle's views, or if one prefers he metamorphoses Aristotle *in toto,* when to this thought of Being he assigns the role not of being dissociated from *praxis* and *phronēsis* but of compounding these very notions, which is to say, of compounding the finite movement of a mortal resolute existence in his effort to found it ontologically. To think Being, henceforth, means to think the finite time of *praxis.* From which there results the fact that the thinker on Being is in the end the true judge on human affairs."
167. *HC,* p. 199.
168. *BPF,* pp. 116–17.
169. Ibid., p. 224. We are reminded here of Arendt's description of Lessing: "Lessing's thought is not the (Platonic) silent dialogue between me and myself, but an anticipated dialogue with others, and this is the reason that it is essentially polemical." *MDT,* p. 10.
170. *HC,* pp. 193–94.
171. *LM,* "Thinking," pp. 98–125.
172. Ibid., pp. 103, 110, 100.
173. Ibid., p. 123, citing Aristotle, *Metaphysics,* 1072b27.
174. *HC,* pp. 176–77.
175. *BPF,* p. 61.
176. Heidegger, *Being and Time,* p. 242.
177. Ibid., p. 63. Heidegger returns to the "complacent negligence of hasty opinion" that suffices to read Thucydides and Sophocles in Heidegger, "The Anaximander Fragment," p. 588.
178. *LM,* "Willing," p. 192.
179. *HC,* p. 197; Thucydides, *The Peloponnesian War 2,* 41
180. *HC,* pp. 197–98; emphasis added.

181. See p. 252, n. 169.

182. Proust, *In Search of Lost Time*, 4:487; *OT*, p. 84; Kristeva, *Time and Sense*, pp. 155–63.

183. *OT*, pp. 81–83.

184. *LM*, "Thinking," pp. 202–4.

185. Arendt, "Franz Kafka," in *La Tradition Caché*, p. 97. *Translator's note:* The version of the "earlier study" to which the author refers has not been translated into English.

186. *EU*, pp. 72, 75–77.

187. *JP*, pp. 113, 121.

188. See Arendt, "Isak Dinesen: 1885–1963," "Hermann Broch: 1886–1951," and "Walter Benjamin: 1882–1940," in *MDT*.

189. *MDT*, pp. 95, 97, 101.

190. Ibid., p. 105.

191. Ibid., pp. 101–9, 231.

192. Céline's correspondence with the American professor Milton Hindus took place in July and August 1948, at which point Arendt had already begun preparing the work that in 1951 would become *The Origins of Totalitarianism*.

193. *OT*, pp. 49, 335. Céline returned to France on July 1, 1951, and Gallimard reprinted his collected works—except for his notorious pamphlets—in 1952.

194. Ibid., pp. 325–28.

195. Ibid., pp. 208–9, 219, 226; *EU*, p. 74.

196. Arendt, "Natalie Sarraute," p. 6.

197. See pp. 223–226.

198. *MDT*, p. 219.

199. *LM*, "Thinking," p. 206.

200. *La Tradition cachée*, p. 98.

201. *EU*, pp. 79, 80.

202. Arendt, "Philosophy and Politics," p. 75.

203. *LM*, "Thinking," pp. 171 ff.

204. Ibid., p. 178; emphasis added.

205. See Philippe Lacoue-Labarthe's argument that the work of art is the culmination of politics. Lacoue-Labarthe, *Heidegger, Art, and Politics*.

206. Significantly, Arendt's only collaborative work was a study

coauthored with her first husband, Günther Stern Anders, on Rilke's *Duino Elegies*. Their analysis focuses on divine perdition, the destruction of the self by the beloved, and the essential futility of elegiac poetry.

207. See pp. 8–30.

208. Adorno, "Cultural Criticism and Society," p. 34. Adorno later revised this comment, most notably in his *Negative Dialectics,* p. 362: "Perennial suffering has as much right to expression as a tortured man has to scream; hence it may have been wrong to say that after Auschwitz you could no longer write poems."

209. Arendt was never sympathetic to Frankfurt School Marxists, and she was especially quick to reject Adorno, the reader who had deemed "unsatisfactory" her first husband Günther Stern's thesis on music—and the suspicious, if not openly hostile, "friend" of Walter Benjamin, who was believed to be a bad Marxist. See Y-B, pp. 80, 167. In 1964, long after Arendt had articulated her views on narrative in *The Origins of Totalitarianism* (1951) and *The Human Condition* (1958), she discovered in a Frankfurt student newspaper a debate with Adorno—which revealed that the same man who had declared poetry impossible after Nazism had in 1934 praised songs whose words came from a collection dedicated to Hitler. In voicing his "regret," Adorno defended himself by accusing Heidegger, making it clear that when he declared poetry to be henceforth impossible, he was thinking of Heidegger's own defense of poetry. Arendt was outraged by Adorno and by his "unsuccessful attempt at cooperation in 1933": "He had hoped that being Italian on his mother's side (Adorno versus Wiesengrund) would help him through." Letter of July 4, 1966, *Jaspers Corr.,* p. 644. Arendt's subsequent defense of Heidegger implicated Adorno by commenting that "Heidegger himself corrected his own 'error' more quickly and more radically than many of those who later sat in judgment over him he [s*ic*] took considerably greater risks than were usual in German literary and university life during that period. We are still surrounded by intellectuals and so-called scholars . . . who . . . prefer to dress up

the horrible gutter-born phenomenon with the language of the humanities and the history of ideas." "Martin Heidegger at Eighty," p. 54; and C-D, p. 83.

210. "In 1945–46 it seemed to me that poetry would be better suited than prose to explain what was weighing inside me. . . . After Auschwitz, there can be no more poetry, except about Auschwitz." Levi, October 28, 1984, interview in *Corriere della Sera,* cited in Anissimov, *Primo Levi,* pp. 368–69.

211. As a voice issuing forth from hell or emerging from "an animalistic sadness," poetry could also be, for Arendt, an elegy for the world and a means of accepting (or denying) despair: "O Happy Grief!" See Arendt, "Remember Wynstan H. Auden," pp. 39–40, 45–46.

212. See pp. 134–135, 139.

213. Kazin, *New York Jew,* p. 199.

214. *LM,* "Thinking," p. 137. We might add to Arendt's elliptical remark Aristotle's own concept of God, which is distinct from those of Plato and the Stoics. Aristotle intuits a fundamental *separation* or incommensurable distance between God and man. Moreover, if the Aristotelian sage is autarkic, he is not alone in this view: while God "is himself his own well-being . . . for us well-being has reference to something other than ourselves." Aristotle, *Eudemian Ethics,* 7, 12, 1245, 618–19. See also Aubenque, *La Prudence chez Aristote,* p. 81. Arendt herself recalls the famous formulation of Saint Augustine: "*Socialis vita sanctorum,* even the life of the saints is a life together with other men." *BPF,* p. 73.

215. "*Wagen wir das unmittelbare Wort: Das Seyn ist die Erzitterung des Götterns des Vorklangs der Götterentscheidung über ihren Gott.*" Cited in Safranski, *Martin Heidegger,* pp. 307–8.

216. *LM,* "Thinking," p. 86.

217. *HC,* p. 211.

CHAPTER 2

1. "The Nature of Totalitarianism," lecture at the New School for Social Research, 1954, Library of Congress, cited in Y-B, p. 203.

2. Arendt, "Rejoinder," p. 78.

3. See pp. 223–230; C-D, p. 137.

4. Raymond Aron, who summarized Arendt's book in the January 1954 issue of the journal *Critique,* criticized her for "replacing a true story with a story that, at every instance, is ironic or tragic," which does not seem to have prevented the two authors from finding common ground. Aron, *Democracy and Totalitarianism,* p. 87.

5. *EU,* p. 6.

6. "Let me tell you of a conversation I had in Israel with a prominent political personality [it was Golda Meir, whose name was left out of the published version at Scholem's request] who was defending the—*in my opinion disastrous—nonseparation of religion and the state in Israel.* . . . 'You will understand that, as a Socialist, I, of course, do not believe in God; I believe in the Jewish people.' I found this a shocking statement. . . . *The greatness of this people was once that it believed in God,* and believed in Him in such a way that its trust and love towards him was greater than its fear. And now this people believes only in itself? What good can come out of that?" See Y-B, pp. 332–33; emphasis added.

7. "I have always consciously refused to lose my mother tongue. . . . There is no substitution for the mother tongue." *EU,* pp. 12–13. "I looked Jewish, . . . different from the other children, . . . a bit different from the usual." *EU,* p. 7.

8. Letter of December 17, 1946, *Jaspers Corr.,* p. 70; *EU,* p. 12.

9. Letter of October 31, 1948, *Jaspers Corr.,* p. 117.
   Arendt understood Yiddish and learned Hebrew, but her writings rarely cite the Bible. The Hebraic tradition is thus contrasted with antiquity in the sense that it does not discredit work but makes it "as intimately bound up with life as giving birth." *HC,* p. 106. David and Goliath as well as Ecclesiastes are placed in the context of power and the space of appearance. Ibid., pp. 199–204. And, with respect to "Hebrew truth, which was *heard,* . . . Greek truth is *seen.*" *LM,* "Thinking," p. 111, and the Jewish idea of the "foundation" owed to the Creator-God, Jehovah ("I am who I am"). *LM,* "Willing," pp. 208 ff.

10. *Heidegger Corr.,* doc. 48, p. 76.

11. "When spring awoke one day they'd find her, / From whence she came no one could tell. / The stranger left no trace behind her / And vanished when she said farewell. / Exalted by her blessed presence, / All hearts were gladdened, spirits rose. / Yet sensing there some lofty essence / No mortal dared to come too close."

12. See *Heidegger Corr.*, doc. 50, pp. 79–80.

13. Courtine-Denamy, "To be or not to be: Hannah Arendt etait-elle boiteuse?" p. 41.

14. *HC,* p. 194.

15. *LM,* "Thinking," p. 94.

16. Letter of June 30, 1947, *Jaspers Corr.*, p. 91.

17. *JP,* p. 246

18. Ibid.

19. *HC,* p. 242.

20. *JP,* p. 247.

21. Arendt's letter has not been preserved; for Heidegger's response, see *Heidegger Corr.,* doc. 45, pp. 68–69.

22. Ettinger, *Hannah Arendt/Martin Heidegger,* p. 44.

23. Y-B, pp. 119, 139.

24. Ibid., p. 153.

25. Ibid., p. 183.

26. Ibid.

27. Arendt, "To Save the Jewish Homeland: There Is Still Time," p. 401.

28. Halpern, "The Partisan in Israel," pp. 6–7.

29. *JP,* pp. 237–38, 250.

30. See the chronology put together by Sylvie Courtine-Denamy, in *Le Magazine Littéraire,* no. 337, special issue on Hannah Arendt (November 1995):20. See also Arendt's rejection of "Jewish politics" beginning in 1946: "And so I have no other choice but to content myself with a modest cultural-political opportunity" (letter of November 11, 1946, *Jaspers Corr.*, p. 65) even though Arendt, after the Arabs declared war following the creation of the State of Israel, retracted her position: "Because of the war in Palestine I've started to be politically active again" (letter of July 16, 1948, *Jaspers Corr.*, p. 175).

31. Y-B, 391; letter of June 10, 1967, *Jaspers Corr.*, p. 672. ("I came home from Chicago quite tired a week and a half ago, and since then we've spent most of our time glued to the radio. The Israelis did a wonderful job [in the Six-Day War], even though Nasser was a paper tiger. I like Dayan's proclamations a lot, and I read yesterday—hidden away somewhere—a report from Jerusalem that said he had suggested to Hordan a federation or confederation. That would solve a lot of problems at one stroke.")

32. See Mary McCarthy, "America the Beautiful: The Humanist in the Bathtub" and "Mlle Gulliver en Amérique," both in *Humanist in the Bathtub.*

33. See Furet, *The Passing of an Illusion.* See also the 1940 American Philosophical Society colloquium "The Totalitarian State," which generated papers, particularly one by J. H. Carlton Hayes, that anticipated the ideas generally attributed to Neumann, *Behemoth: The Structure and Practice of National Socialism, 1933–1944*; and to Borkenau, *The Totalitarian Enemy.*

34. Arendt, "Reflections on Little Rock." Arendt's article and its proposed publication in *Commentary* proved controversial. See Y-B, pp. 308–18.

35. See Y-B, p. 312, citing Arendt, "A Reply to Critics," p. 179.

36. Y-B, p. 386, citing Arendt, "Kennedy and After," p. 10.

37. See Lotte Köhler, preface to *Blücher Corr.*, p. 11.

38. Arendt, "What Is Existenz Philosophy?" p. 46.

39. C-D, p. 86.

40. Letter of August 17, 1946, *Jaspers Corr.*, pp. 52, 53.

41. Letter of December 17, 1946, ibid., p. 70.

42. *Translator's note:* The phrase "potent wizard" comes from the title of the chapter on Disraeli in *OT,* pp. 68–79, and it is derived "from a sketch of Disraeli by Sir John Skelton in 1867," ibid., p. 68.

43. *OT,* p. 79.

44. Ibid., pp. 47, 100–106.

45. Ibid., p. 46.

46. Ibid., pp. 162–64, 170–75, 107, 107 n. 62.

47. Ibid., p. 113.

48. Ibid., p. 23.
49. *HC,* pp. 202–3.
50. *OR,* p. 148.
51. Arendt, "Rejoinder," p. 84.
52. *LM,* "Thinking," p. 140.
53. *OT,* pp. 290 ff., 302.
54. Ibid., 302.
55. *LM,* "Willing," p. 257.
56. See pp. 202–204, 210–212, 214–215, 219.
57. *HC,* p. 52.
58. *OR,* p. 8.
59. *OT,* pp. xv, xvi. On Arendt's political thought, see Canovan, *The Political Thought of Hannah Arendt;* Enégren, *La Pensée politique de Hannah Arendt;* Leibovici, *Hannah Arendt, une Juive;* Roviello, *Sens commun et modernité chez Hannah Arendt;* Witfield, *Into the Dark.*
60. *OT,* p. 7.
61. Ibid., p. 8.
62. Ibid., p. 27.
63. Ibid., p. 4.
64. Ibid., pp. 70–71.
65. Ibid., p. 21.
66. Ibid., pp. 29–30, 33.
67. Ibid., p. 36.
68. Ibid., p. 39.
69. Ibid., p. 41.
70. Ibid., pp. 45–57.
71. Ibid., p. 54.
72. Ibid.
73. Ibid., p. 56.
74. Ibid., p. 87.
75. Ibid.
76. Ibid., p. 120.
77. Ibid., p. 261.
78. Ibid., pp. 230 ff.
79. Ibid., p. 231.
80. Ibid., p. 156.

81. Ibid., p. 161.

82. Ibid., pp. 158 ff.

83. Ibid., p. 245.

84. Ibid., p. 232.

85. Ibid., p. 243.

86. Ibid., pp. 250, 175.

87. Ibid., p. 176.

88. *OR*, pp. 153–95.

89. *OT*, p. 263 ("There was not a single party in Europe that did not produce collaborators").

90. Ibid., p. 264.

91. Ibid., p. 261.

92. Ibid., pp. 389 ff.

93. Ibid., p. 268.

94. Ibid., p. 289.

95. Ibid., p. 290.

96. Ibid., pp. 315, 348.

97. Ibid., p. 345.

98. Ibid., pp. 457–58. An example of this ideological "consistency" that Arendt does not define as paranoia but that displays all its characteristics is the following: Without the Communist system, we could not build a subway; the Parisian subway is therefore suspect; we must destroy the Parisian subway. Ibid., p. 458.

99. Ibid., pp. 469–73.

100. Ibid., p. 375.

101. Ibid., p. 363.

102. Ibid., p. 375. See Koyré, "The Political Function of the Modern Lie." His analysis likens totalitarian parties to secret societies in their cult of the secret, their internal hierarchies, rituals, chosen elites, and so forth, and he concludes that the anthropology of totalitarianism has paradoxically made parties into "the pseudo-aristocratic totalitarians [that] represent the lower category, that of the gullible who cannot think" (p. 300); see also *OT*, p. 376.

103. *OT*, pp. 382, 380.

104. Ibid., pp. 354 ff.

105. Ibid., pp. 356–58.

106. Ibid., p. 411.

107. Ibid., p. xvii.

108. Ibid., p. 310.

109. Only in her 1966 study of Rosa Luxembourg did Arendt distance herself from Leninism and from the dogmatism endemic to Communist parties. See *MDT,* pp. 345–46.

110. *OT,* p. xxi.

111. Ibid., p. 441.

112. Ibid., p. 458.

113. Ibid., pp. 444–45.

114. Ibid., p. 445.

115. Ibid., p. 451.

116. Ibid., p. 442; the quotations are on p. 452.

117. Ibid., pp. 454–55.

118. Ibid., p. 466.

119. Ibid., p. 455.

120. Ibid., p. 466.

121. Ibid., p. 473.

122. Ibid., p. 477.

123. Ibid., p. 474.

124. Ibid., p. 476.

125. Ibid.

126. Ibid., p. 477.

127. Ibid., p. 478.

128. Y-B, pp. 328 ff.

129. *JP,* p. 236.

130. *OT,* p. 459.

131. See "Social Science Techniques and the Study of the Concentration Camps," in *EU,* pp. 232–47; Arendt's preface to Naumann, *Auschwitz; OT,* pp. 437–59; C-D, pp. 180–81.

132. *OT,* p. 441.

133. January 2, 1961, letter to Vassar College, cited in Y-B, p. 329.

134. Arendt and McCarthy, *Between Friends,* p. 168.

135. Y-B, p. 349.

136. C-D, p. 106.

137. See the analyses of Annette Wieviorka in *Le Procès Eichmann; Déportation et génocide;* and *L'Ere du témoin.*

138. Arendt, "Eichmann in Jerusalem," p. 11. All future references to "Eichmann in Jerusalem" will be indicated by "EJ."

139. Y-B, p. 344, citing "EJ."

140. "EJ," p. 125. See also Hilberg, *The Destruction of the European Jews.*

141. "EJ," p. 26.

142. Ibid., p. 48.

143. Ibid., p. 49.

144. Ibid., pp. 55, 95.

145. See ibid., p. 278: "And even if eighty million Germans had done as you did, this would not have been an excuse for you." On this point, see Goldhagen, *Hitler's Willing Executioners,* which invokes the collective responsibility of the Germans, as opposed to Arendt's position, which judges in the first instance the guilt or innocence of individuals.

146. "EJ," pp. 269, 252.

147. Ibid., pp. 287, 279, 289.

148. *OT,* p. 453.

149. "EJ," p. 114.

150. Ibid., pp. 136, 247.

151. See Goldhagen, *Hitler's Willing Executioners.*

152. Y-B, pp. 369 ff.

153. *LM,* "Thinking," p. 150.

154. Arendt, *Crises of the Republic,* p. 155. All future references to *Crises of the Republic* will be indicated by *CR.*

155. Y-B, p. 374, citing notes prepared for *Look* magazine interview.

156. *LM,* "Thinking," p. 149.

157. Ibid., p. 150.

158. Ibid., p. 79.

159. *LM,* "Willing," p. 21, citing *Thus Spoke Zarathustra.*

160. Y-B, p. 377, citing letter to William O'Grady.

161. Y-B, p. 377, citing Arendt, "Isak Dinesen: 1885–1963," in *MDT.*

162. *JP,* pp. 250–51.

163. *LM,* "Willing," p. 191–94.

164. Ibid., p. 194.

165. Ibid., p. 193.

166. Gurian was a highly cultivated man with a warm spirit; a Russ-

ian Jew who had early in his life converted to Catholicism, he invited Arendt to deliver a lecture, "Ideology and Terror," at the University of Notre Dame in November 1950. See C-D, p. 228. Gurian was later the subject of a glowing essay by Arendt. See "Waldemar Gurian: 1930–1954," in *MDT,* pp. 251–62.

167. Voegelin, "The Origins of Totalitarianism," pp. 73–75

168. Arendt, "Rejoinder," p. 81.

169. Ibid., p. 82.

170. See p. 19.

171. Arendt, "Rejoinder," p. 81.

172. *HC,* p. 179.

173. *BPF,* pp. 74–75.

174. Ibid., p. 90.

175. Ibid., p. 73.

176. See my remarks on Arendt's reading of *Nicomachean Ethics,* 1177b, 31, pp. 70–74.

177. *HC,* p. 184.

178. Ibid., p. 38.

179. Ibid., pp. 37 ("Politics is never for the sake of life"), 40.

180. Ibid., pp. 40–41.

181. Ibid., p. 60.

182. Ibid., p. 85 n. 13.

183. Ibid., pp. 77–78.

184. See ibid. In another text, Arendt sees in Machiavelli "what the Romans themselves had to say about foundation" and about virtue, which is neither a moral code nor a path toward excellence, but a harmony between man and his world that justifies all means toward a supreme end. It is as if Arendt made the Italian prince into a predecessor to Robespierre. See *BPF,* p. 139.

185. See Mondzain, *Image, icône, économie;* Kristeva, *Visions capitales,* pp. 57–69.

186. *HC,* p. 98.

187. Ibid., pp. 108, 116.

188. Ibid.

189. Ibid., p. 118.

190. Ibid., p. 117.

191. *OR*, pp. 27–28.

192. Preface to *BPF*, p. 8.

193. *OR*, p. 251.

194. Ibid., p. 284.

195. Ibid., pp. 234, 280.

196. Ibid., pp. 281–82.

197. Y-B, p. 412.

198. *CR*, p. 170.

199. Ibid., p. 231.

200. *LM*, "Willing," p. 192

201. Ibid., p. 191.

202. Ibid., p. 192.

203. Ibid. The passage Arendt quotes comes from the following passage from Heidegger: "The *epoche* of Being belongs to Being itself; we are thinking it in terms of the experience of the oblivion of Being. From the *epoche* of Being comes the epochal essence of its destining, in which world history properly consists. . . . Every epoch of world history is an epoch of errancy. The epochal nature of Being belongs to the concealed temporal character of Being and designates the essence of time as thought in Being. . . . For us, however, the most readily experienced correspondence to the epochal character of Being is the ecstatic character of *Da-sein*. The epochal essence of Being lays claim to the ecstatic nature of *Da-sein*. The *eksistence* of man sustains what is ecstatic and so preserves what is epochal in Being, to whose essence the *Da,* and thereby *Da-sein,* belongs." Heidegger, "The Anaximander Fragment," pp. 591–92.

204. *LM*, "Willing," p. 192.

205. *OR*, p. 283.

206. *BPF*, p. 140

207. *LM*, "Willing," pp. 195 ff.

208. Ibid., p. 204.

209. *MDT*, pp. 4–5.

210. Arendt, "Angelo Giuseppe Roncalli: A Christian on St. Peter's Chair from 1958 to 1963," in *MDT*, pp. 57–69.

211. Letter of March 4, 1951, *Jaspers Corr.*, pp. 165—66.

CHAPTER 3

1. See Lyotard, "Le survivant," p. 275; and Lyotard, *"Sensus communis,"* which both offer a reading of Kant's notion of aesthetic judgment that is in marked contrast to Arendt's.

2. *HC,* p. 179.

3. Taminiaux, *The Thracian Maid,* pp. 56, 75.

4. Ibid., pp. 64, 67, 76.

5. *HC,* pp. 179–80, 211.

6. See pp. 154–55; *EU,* pp. 401–8.

7. *HC,* pp. 193–94.

8. Dante, *Monarchia* I, 13.

9. See pp. 73–78.

10. *LM,* "Willing," pp. 120–21.

11. Ibid., p. 144.

12. *LM,* "Thinking," pp. 73–74.

13. Y-B, p. 233, citing October 3, 1948, letter from Arendt to Magnes.

14. *LM,* "Thinking," pp. 98 ff.

15. Ibid., pp. 23, 33.

16. *HC,* pp. 112–13.

17. *LM,* "Thinking," pp. 34–35.

18. Ibid., p. 35.

19. See *CR,* p. 107 ("The chief reason warfare is still with us is neither a secret death wish of the human species, nor an irrepressible instinct of aggression").

20. *BPF,* p. 133.

21. *PP,* p. 69

22. Ibid., pp. 68–69; see p. 107.

23. *JP,* p. 246.

24. *LM,* "Thinking," p. 191.

25. *HC,* p. 8 n. 1.

26. See Linda M. G. Zerilli, "The Arendtian Body," in Honig, *Feminist Interpretations of Hannah Arendt,* pp. 167–93.

27. *HC,* p. 8.

28. See *Les Cahiers du GRIF* 7 (June 1975):22–27; and *Anthologie des "Cahiers du GRIF": Le langage des femmes* (Brussels: Ed. Complexe, 1990).

29. Letter of March 4, 1951, *Jaspers Corr.,* p. 166.

30. *EU,* p. 13
31. Ibid., pp. 12–14.
32. Ibid., p. 13.
33. Ibid.
34. "To remain in authority requires respect for the person or the office. The greatest enemy of authority, therefore, is contempt, and the surest way to undermine it is laughter." *CR,* p. 144
35. "Original repression" presides over the inscription of unconscious representations. It is different from repression itself and from impression after the fact, which seek to defend themselves from representations (thoughts, images, or memories) by repressing them in the unconscious.
36. *LM,* "Thinking," p. 7.
37. Ibid., p. 9.
38. Ibid., p. 44.
39. Ibid., pp. 12–14.
40. Ibid., pp. 55, 57.
41. Ibid., p. 55.
42. Ibid., p. 62.
43. Ibid., p. 64.
44. Ibid., p. 43.
45. Ibid., pp. 42–43.
46. Ibid., pp. 48–49.
47. Ibid., p. 198.
48. Ibid., p. 77.
49. See pp. 26–27.
50. *LM,* "Thinking," pp. 79–80.
51. Ibid., p. 82.
52. Ibid., p. 78.
53. Ibid., p. 82.
54. *EU,* p. 3
55. *LM,* "Thinking," p. 101.
56. Ibid., pp. 103, 101.
57. Ibid., p. 101.
58. Ibid., p. 102.
59. Ibid., pp. 197 ff.
60. Ibid., p. 75; emphasis added.
61. Ibid., p. 178.

62. Ibid., pp. 192, 185.

63. Ibid., p. 187.

64. Miller, "La suture," pp. 39, 49.

65. *OT,* p. 477.

66. *LM,* "Willing," p. 179.

67. *LM,* "Thinking," p. 135.

68. Ibid., p. 136.

69. Ibid., p. 115.

70. Ibid., p. 184.

71. Ibid., p. 185.

72. Ibid., p. 45.

73. Ibid., p. 185.

74. Cited in Y-B, p. 303.

75. Ibid., pp. 303–4.

76. Arendt, "Martin Heidegger at Eighty," p. 54.

77. Ibid., p. 52.

78. Ibid., pp. 53, 52.

79. Ibid., 52.

80. Ibid., p. 54.

81.. *LM,* "Thinking," p. 191. See Jonas, *The Phenomenon of Life,* p. 1 ("The organic even in its lowest forms prefigures mind, and that mind even on its highest reaches remains part of the organic") and p. 3 ("But if mind is prefigured in the organic from the beginning, then freedom is too").

82. *LM,* "Thinking," p. 201.

83. Ibid., p. 178.

84. Cited in ibid., p. 91.

85. In the spring of 1973 Arendt delivered the Gifford Lectures at Aberdeen University in Scotland. Her remarks were the germ of the "Thinking" section of *The Life of the Mind.*

86. Aristotle, *De Anima,* 415b13, cited in *HC,* p. 19; Aristotle, *Metaphysics,* 1072b27, cited in *LM,* "Thinking," p. 123. Arendt's view toward Aristotle depends on whether he sees in the life cycle the circular image of the movement of thought (see *LM,* "Thinking," p. 123) or whether he guides the "good life" of the polis toward the vital but restrictive necessities of the private realm (see *HC,* pp. 36–37).

87. *LM,* "Thinking," p. 91.

88. Ibid., p. 123; and *LM*, "Willing," pp. 183–84.

89. Preface to *BPF*, p. 3.

90. *LM*, "Thinking," p. 212.

91. *LM*, "Willing," p. 207.

92. *LM*, "Thinking," pp. 213–14.

93. *LM*, "Willing," p. 16.

94. Ibid., p. 60.

95. Ibid., p. 61.

96. Ibid., p. 63.

97. See *HC*, p. 315 ("The Hebrew legal code . . . made the preservation of life the cornerstone of the legal system of the Jewish people," which is an intermediary position between the "pagan immortality of the world on one side and the Christian immortality of individual life on the other [and] the Hebrew creed which stresses the immortality of the people").

98. *LM*, "Willing," p. 67.

99. Letter to the Romans 7:21, drafted between 54 and 58 a.d., cited in ibid., p. 64.

100. *LM*, "Willing," 68.

101. Ibid., p. 69.

102. Ibid., p. 71.

103. Ibid., p. 75.

104. Ibid., p. 84.

105. Ibid., p. 85.

106. Ibid., p. 90.

107. Ibid., p. 91.

108. Ibid., p. 102.

109. Ibid., p. 109.

110. Ibid., p. 110.

111. Ibid., p. 39.

112. Ibid., p. 120.

113. Ibid., p. 122.

114. Ibid., p. 120.

115. Ibid., p. 119.

116. Ibid., p. 143.

117. Ibid., p. 144.

118. Ibid., p. 145.

119. Ibid., pp. 125–46.
120. Ibid., pp. 164–65, citing "Also Sprach Zarathustra," in *Ecce Homo* (1889), no. 1.
121. Ibid., p. 161.
122. Ibid., p. 163.
123. Ibid., p. 165, citing Nietzsche, *The Gay Science*, no. 310.
124. *LM,* "Willing," p. 166.
125. Ibid., p. 167.
126. Concerning the "forgetting" that Nietzsche revives see p. 237; and Paul Ricoeur, paper presented at the Hannah Arendt Conference at the Grande Bibliothèque de France, December 6, 1997.
127. *LM,* "Willing," p. 169.
128. Ibid., pp. 169–70, citing Nietzsche, *The Will to Power*, no. 585 A, pp. 316–19.
129. *LM,* "Willing," p. 170, citing *Der Wille zur Macht.*
130. Ibid., p. 172.
131. *LM,* "Willing," p. 172, citing Nietzsche, *Thus Spoke Zarathustra,* pt. 3, "Before Sunrise."
132. See Arendt, "On Violence," in *CR*, pp. 142 ff.
133. After writing "What Is Existenz Philosophy?" and "Martin Heidegger at Eighty," Arendt returned to Heidegger for a third time in *LM,* "Willing," pp. 172–94.
134. *HC,* p. 132 (the "reckless dynamism of a wholly motorized life process").
135. *LM,* "Willing," p. 178.
136. Ibid., p. 183.
137. See ibid., p. 182.
138. Ibid., pp. 179, 188.
139. Ibid., p. 180.
140. Ibid., p. 187.
141. *HC,* p. 204.
142. *LM,* "Willing," pp. 184–85.
143. Ibid., p. 192.
144. Cited in ibid., pp. 191–92.
145. Ibid., p. 192; see pp. 165–68.
146. *LM,* "Willing," p. 195.

147. Ibid., p. 162

148. Ibid., pp. 199, 200, citing Montesquieu, *L'Esprit des lois.*

149. *LM,* "Thinking," p. 115.

150. See "Imagination," seminar on Kant's *Critique of Judgment,* New School of Social Research, fall 1970, in *PP.*

151. *PP,* p. 20.

152. Ibid., p. 15.

153. Cited in ibid., p. 17.

154. Ibid., p. 19.

155. Ibid., p. 124; emphasis added.

156. *LM,* "Willing," p. 179.

157. Ibid., p. 25

158. Ibid., p. 29.

159. *PP,* p. 30.

160. Ibid., pp. 63, 64.

161. Ibid., p. 62.

162. Ibid., p. 64.

163. Ibid.

164. Ibid., p. 69.

165. *LM,* "Thinking," pp. 50, 70.

166. Ibid., p. 71.

167. Ibid., p. 72; emphasis added.

168. Ibid; emphasis added.

169. Ibid.

170. Ibid., p. 73.

171. Ibid., p. 74.

172. Ibid., p. 76.

173. Ibid., p. 72.

174. Voltaire, for example, emphasized the importance of society and its cohesiveness in forming our perception of "taste" ("Where there is little sociability, the mind shrinks and grows dull because there is little to educate its taste"). Voltaire even goes so far as to assert that taste may be found only among Europeans because other peoples have not yet refined their societies. Voltaire, "Taste," p. 340. Voltaire's essay, "Taste," appears in Diderot, *Encyclopedia: Selections.* More subtly than Voltaire, Montesquieu clearly subordinates taste to pleasure,

which he links to the body and the soul: "These different pleasures of the mind constitute the proper objects of *taste*, . . . which is nothing more than the faculty of discovering, with quickness and delicacy, *the degree of pleasure* we should receive from each object that comes within the sphere of our perceptions." Montesquieu, "An Essay on Taste," in Gerard, *An Essay on Taste*, pp. 249, 252; emphasis added. Montesquieu distinguishes between *natural* pleasures and tastes and *acquired* pleasures and tastes. Pleasures essentially depend on the body, on an "organ" in "the constitution of our nature," even "another contexture of the organs we possess," ibid., p. 254, and they operate through "the quick and exquisite application of rules which, in speculation, may be really unknown to the mind," ibid., p. 256. Even more subtly, the soul receives pleasures through ideas and feelings because "there are no subjects so abstrusely intellectual, which it does not perceive in reality or in fancy, and which, of consequence, it does not feel." Ibid., p. 257.

175. *PP,* p. 11.
176. Ibid., p. 74.
177. Ibid., p. 75.
178. Ibid., p. 81.
179. Ibid., p. 82.
180. Ibid., p. 83.
181. Ibid., p. 84.
182. *HC,* pp. 193 ff.
183. *PP,* p. 84.
184. Ibid., p. 77.
185. See Habermas, "Hannah Arendt's Communications Concept of Power."
186. *LM,* "Thinking," p. 215 ("Judgments are not arrived at by either deduction or induction. . . . We shall be in search of the 'silent sense,' which . . . has always, even in Kant, been thought of as 'taste' and therefore belonging to the realm of aesthetics").
187. Ibid., citing Nietzsche, "The Use and Abuse of History," pp. 6, 7.
188. Ibid., p. 6.

189. Ibid., citing Nietzsche, *The Genealogy of Morals,* p. 61.
190. Ibid., p. 62.
191. Ibid., pp. 63, 62.
192. Ibid., pp. 63, 72–73 ("even in old Kant: the categorical imperative reeks of cruelty").
193. Ibid., citing Nietzsche, "The Use and Abuse of History," p. 9.
194. *HC,* p. 241.
195. Ibid., p. 240.
196. *MDT,* p. 248.
197. Ibid., p. 241, citing Luke 17:2.
198. *MDT,* p. 241.
199. Ibid., p. 249.
200. *HC,* pp. 242, 243.
201. Ibid., p. 239.
202. Ibid., p. 239 n. 2, citing Matt. 6:14–15.
203. Ibid., pp. 239–40, citing Luke 17:4.
204. See Kristeva, "Dostoyevsky, the Writing of Suffering and Forgiveness," in *Black Sun,* pp. 173 ff.
205. *HC,* p. 243.
206. Ibid., p. 244.
207. Ibid., pp. 245, 244.
208. Ibid., p. 245.
209. Ibid., p. 246.
210. Ibid., p. 247.
211. *EU,* p. 3
212. Ibid., p. 248.
213. Ibid., p. 237.
214. Ibid., pp. 237–38.
215. Ibid. p. 238.
216. Ibid., p. 13.
217. See Derrida, *Monolinguism of the Other,* pp. 84–90, which attributes Arendt's cult of a language incapable of going mad to the bond with the mother, itself cultivated from and defended against "the energy of madness." A true imaginary matricide is a precondition for creating an abyss out of the mother tongue—which can sometimes be accomplished with serenity (Heidegger) and even joy (Joyce), and which

women (Virginia Woolf, Marguerite Duras), approach by subsuming female homosexuality or the loss of the self into melancholia.

218. *HC,* p. 247.
219. *LM,* "Thinking," p. 123.

BIBLIOGRAPHY

WORKS BY HANNAH ARENDT

Between Friends: The Correspondence of Hannah Arendt and Mary McCarthy. Ed. and intro. Carol Brightman. New York: Harcourt Brace, 1995.

Between Past and Future: Eight Exercises in Political Thought. Enlarged edition. New York: Penguin Books, 1968.

Crises of the Republic. New York: Harcourt Brace Jovanovich, 1972.

"Eichmann in Jerusalem." *Encounter* (January 1964):51–56. (An exchange of letters between Arendt and Scholem.)

Essays in Understanding, 1930–1954. Ed. Jerome Kohn. New York: Harcourt Brace, 1994.

"From the Dreyfus Affair to France Today." *Jewish Social Studies* 4 (July 1942):195–240.

Hannah Arendt and Heinrich Blücher, Briefe, 1936–1968. Munich: Piper GmbH, 1996.

Hannah Arendt and Martin Heidegger, Briefe, 1925–1975. Frankfurt: Vittorio Klostermann, 1998–99.

Hannah Arendt/Karl Jaspers: Correspondence, 1926–1969. Ed. Lotte Kohler and Hans Saner. Trans. Robert and Rita Kimber. New York: Harcourt Brace Jovanovich, 1985.

"Herzl and Lazare." *Jewish Social Studies* 4 (July 1942):235–40.

The Human Condition. Chicago: University of Chicago Press, 1958.

The Jew as Pariah: Jewish Identity and Politics in the Modern Age. Ed. Ron H. Feldman. New York: Grove Press, 1978.

"Kennedy and After." *New York Review of Books,* December 26, 1963, p. 10.

Lectures on Kant's Political Philosophy. Ed. Ronald Beiner. Chicago: University of Chicago Press, 1982.

The Life of the Mind. New York and London: Harcourt Brace Jovanovich, 1978.

Love and Saint Augustine. Ed. and trans. Joanna Vecchiarelli Scott and Judith Chelius Stark. Chicago: University of Chicago Press, 1996.

"Martin Heidegger at Eighty." *New York Review of Books,* October 21, 1971, pp. 51–55.

Men in Dark Times. New York: Harcourt, 1971.

"Natalie Sarraute." Review of *The Golden Fruits.* Trans. Maria Jolas. *New York Review of Books,* March 5, 1964, pp. 5–6.

On Revolution. Westport, Conn.: Greenwood, 1982.

The Origins of Totalitarianism. New York: Harcourt, Brace, 1966.

"Philosophy and Politics." *Social Research* 57 (1990).

Rahel Varnhagen: The Life of a Jewess. Ed. Liliane Weissberg. Trans. Richard and Clara Winston. Baltimore and London: Johns Hopkins University Press, 1997.

"Reflections on Little Rock." *Dissent* 6:1 (winter 1959):45–56.

"Rejoinder to Eric Voegelin's Review of *The Origins of Totalitarianism.*" *Review of Politics* 15 (January 1953):76–85. Reprinted in *Essays in Understanding, 1930–1954,* pp. 401–8. Ed. Jerome Kohn. New York: Harcourt Brace, 1994.

"Remember Wynstan H. Auden." *New Yorker,* January 20, 1975, pp. 39–40.

"A Reply to Critics." *Dissent* (spring 1959):179–81.

"To Save the Jewish Homeland: There Is Still Time." *Commentary* (May 1948):398–406.

La Tradition cachée: Le Juif comme pariah. Trans. Sylvie Courtine-Denamy. Paris: Christian Bourgois, 1987.

"What Is Existenz Philosophy?" *Partisan Review* 8:1 (winter 1946): 34–56.

WORKS ABOUT HANNAH ARENDT

Canovan, Margaret. *The Political Thought of Hannah Arendt.* New York: Harcourt Brace Jovanovich, 1974.

Collin, Françoise. "Agir and dormir." In *Hannah Arendt et la modernité.* Paris: Vrin, 1992, pp. 27–46.

———. "Du privé et du public." *Les Cahiers du Grif* 33 (1985):47–67.

Courtine-Denamy, Sylvie. *Hannah Arendt.* Paris: Hachette Littérature, 1997.

———. "To Be or Not to Be: Hannah Arendt était-elle boiteuse?" *L'Infini* 62 (1998).

Enégren, André. *La Pensée politique de Hannah Arendt.* Paris: PUF, 1984.

Ettinger, Elzbieta. *Hannah Arendt/Martin Heidegger.* New Haven, Conn.: Yale University Press, 1995.

Habermas, Jürgen. "Hannah Arendt's Communications Concept of Power." *Social Research* 44 (1977).

Halpern, Ben. "The Partisan in Israel." *Jewish Frontier* (August 1948).

Honig, B., ed. *Feminist Interpretations of Hannah Arendt.* University Park: Pennsylvania State University Press, 1995.

Leibovici, Martine. *Hannah Arendt, une juive: Experiénce politique et histoire.* Paris: Desclée de Brouwer, 1998.

McCarthy, Mary. "Saying Good-by to Hannah." *New York Review of Books,* January 22, 1967.

Roviello, Anne-Marie. *Sens commun et modernité chez Hannah Arendt.* Paris: Anthropos, 1990.

Stevens, Bernard. "Action et narrativité chez Paul Ricoeur et Hannah Arendt." *Etudes phénoménologiques* 2 (1985).

Taminiaux, Jacques. *The Thracian Maid and the Professional Thinker:*

Arendt and Heidegger. Trans. and ed. Michael Gendre. Albany: State University of New York Press, 1997.

Villa, Dana R. *Arendt and Heidegger: The Fate of the Political*. Princeton, N.J.: Princeton University Press, 1995.

Voegelin, Eric. "The Origins of Totalitarianism." *Review of Politics* 15 (1953).

Witfield, Stephen J. *Into the Dark: Hannah Arendt and Totalitarianism*. Philadelphia: Temple University Press, 1980.

Young-Bruehl, Elisabeth. *Hannah Arendt: For Love of the World*. New Haven: Yale University Press, 1982.

OTHER WORKS

Adorno, Theodor W. "Cultural Criticism and Society." In *Prisms*. Trans. Samuel and Sherry Weber. London: Neville Spearman, 1967.

———. *Negative Dialectics*. Trans. E. B. Ashton. New York: Continuum, 1992.

Agamben, Giorgio. *La Communauté qui vient: Théorie de la singularité quelconque*. Paris: Editions du Seuil, 1990.

Anissimov, Myriam. *Primo Levi: Tragedy of an Optimist*. Trans. Steve Cox. London: Aurum Press, 1998.

Aron, Raymond. *Democracy and Totalitarianism*. Trans. Valence Ionescu. London: Widenfeld and Nicolson, 1968.

Aubenque, Pierre. *La Prudence chez Aristote*. Paris: PUF, 1963.

Augustine, Saint. *Homilies on the Gospel According to St. John, and His First Epistle*. Oxford, 1849.

Borkenau, Franz. *The Totalitarian Enemy*. London: Faber and Faber, 1940.

Chamisso, Adelbert von. *Peter Schlemiel: The Man Who Sold His Shadow*. Trans. Peter Wortsman. New York: Fromm International, 1993.

Colloque des Hautes Etudes en Sciences Sociales. *L'Allemagne nazie et le génocide juif*. Paris: Hautes Etudes-Gallimard-Seuil, 1985.

Diderot, Denis, et al. *Encyclopedia: Selections*. Trans. Nelly S. Hoyt and Thomas Cassirer. Indianapolis, New York, and Kansas City: Bobbs-Merrill, 1965.

Furet, François. *The Passing of an Illusion: The Idea of Communism in the Twentieth Century*. Trans. Deborah Furet. Chicago: University of Chicago Press, 1999.

Gerard, Alexander. *An Essay on Taste*. Edinburgh, 1764.

Goldhagen, Daniel. *Hitler's Willing Executioners: Ordinary Germans and the Holocaust*. New York: Alfred A. Knopf, 1996.

Heidegger, Martin. "The Anaximander Fragment." Trans. David Ferrell Krell. *Arion* 1:4 (1973–74):576–626.

———. *Being and Time*. Trans. John Macquarrie and Edward Robinson. New York and Evanston: Harper, 1962.

———. *Gesamtausgabe*. Frankfurt: Vittorio Klostermann, 1989.

Hilberg, Raul. *La Destruction des Juifs d'Europe*. Paris: Fayard, 1988.

Jonas, Hans. *The Phenomenon of Life: Toward a Philosophical Biology*. New York: Harper and Row, 1966.

Kazin, Alfred. *New York Jew*. New York: Alfred A. Knopf, 1978.

Koyré, Alexander. "The Political Function of the Modern Lie." *Contemporary Jewish Record* (June 1945):290–300.

Kristeva, Julia. *Black Sun: Depression and Melancholy*. Trans. Leon S. Roudiez. New York: Columbia University Press, 1989.

———. *The Sense and Non-Sense of Revolt: The Powers and Limits of Psychoanalysis*. Trans. Jeanine Herman. New York: Columbia University Press, 2000.

———. *Time and Sense: Proust and the Experience of Literature*. Trans. Ross Guberman. New York: Columbia University Press, 1996.

———. *Visions capitales*. Paris: Réunion des musées nationaux, 1998.

Lacoue-Labarthe, Philippe. *Heidegger, Art, and Politics: The Fiction of the Political*. Trans. Chris Turner. Oxford: Basil Blackwell, 1990.

Lazare, Bernard. *Job's Dungheap: Essays on Jewish Nationalism and Social Revolution*. New York: Schocken Books, 1948.

———. *Juifs et antisémites*. Paris: Allia, 1992.

McCarthy, Mary. *Humanist in the Bathtub*. New York: Farrar, Straus, 1951.

Miller, Jacques-Alain. "La suture." *Cahiers pour l'analyse* 1 (1966): 39–49.

Mondzain, Marie-Josée. *Image, icône, économie: Les sources byzantines de l'imaginaire contemporain*. Paris: Seuil, 1996.

Neumann, Franz L. *Behemoth: The Structure and Practice of National Socialism, 1933–1944.* Oxford: Oxford University Press, 1942.

Nussbaum, Martha. *The Fragility of Goodness.* Cambridge: Cambridge University Press, 1986.

Proust, Marcel. *In Search of Lost Time.* Trans. C. K. Scott Moncrieff and Terence Kilmartin. Revised D. J. Enright. London: Chatto and Windus, 1992.

Ricoeur, Paul. *Time and Narrative.* Trans. Kathleen McLaughlin and David Pellauer. Chicago: University of Chicago Press, 1984.

Riviere, Joan. "A Contribution to the Analysis of Negative Therapeutic Response." *International Journal of Psycho-Analysis* 18 (1936).

Safranski, Rüdiger. *Martin Heidegger: Between Good and Evil.* Trans. Ewald Osers. Cambridge: Harvard University Press, 1998.

Winnicott, D. W. "Ego Distortion in Terms of True and False Self." In *The Maturational Processes and the Facilitating Environment: Studies in the Theory of Emotional Development.* New York: International Universities Press, 1965.

EUROPEAN PERSPECTIVES

A Series in Social Thought and Cultural Criticism

LAWRENCE D. KRITZMAN, Editor

JULIA KRISTEVA	*Strangers to Ourselves*
THEODOR W. ADORNO	*Notes to Literature*, vols. 1 and 2
RICHARD WOLIN, Editor	*The Heidegger Controversy*
ANTONIO GRAMSCI	*Prison Notebooks*, vols. 1 and 2
JACQUES LEGOFF	*History and Memory*
ALAIN FINKIELKRAUT	*Remembering in Vain: The Klaus Barbie Trial and Crimes Against Humanity*
JULIA KRISTEVA	*Nations Without Nationalism*
PIERRE BOURDIEU	*The Field of Cultural Production*
PIERRE VIDAL-NAQUET	*Assassins of Memory: Essays on the Denial of the Holocaust*
HUGO BALL	*Critique of the German Intelligentsia*
GILLES DELEUZE and FÉLIX GUATTARI	*What Is Philosophy?*

KARL HEINZ BOHRER — *Suddenness: On the Moment of Aesthetic Appearance*

JULIA KRISTEVA — *Time and Sense*

ALAIN FINKIELKRAUT — *The Defeat of the Mind*

JULIA KRISTEVA — *New Maladies of the Soul*

ELISABETH BADINTER — *XY: On Masculine Identity*

KARL LÖWITH — *Martin Heidegger and European Nihilism*

GILLES DELEUZE — *Negotiations, 1972–1990*

PIERRE VIDAL-NAQUET — *The Jews: History, Memory, and the Present*

NORBERT ELIAS — *The Germans*

LOUIS ALTHUSSER — *Writings on Psychoanalysis: Freud and Lacan*

ELISABETH ROUDINESCO — *Jacques Lacan: His Life and Work*

ROSS GUBERMAN — *Julia Kristeva Interviews*

KELLY OLIVER — *The Portable Kristeva*

PIERRA NORA — *Realms of Memory: The Construction of the French Past*
    vol. 1: *Conflicts and Divisions*
    vol. 2: *Traditions*
    vol. 3: *Symbols*

CLAUDINE FABRE-VASSAS — *The Singular Beast: Jews, Christians, and the Pig*

PAUL RICOEUR — *Critique and Conviction: Conversations with François Azouvi and Marc de Launay*

THEODOR W. ADORNO — *Critical Models: Interventions and Catchwords*

ALAIN CORBIN — *Village Bells: Sound and Meaning in the Nineteenth-Century French Countryside*

ZYGMUNT BAUMAN — *Globalization: The Human Consequences*

EMMANUEL LEVINAS — *Entre Nous*

JEAN-LOUIS FLANDRIN and MASSIMO MONTANARI — *Food: A Culinary History*

ALAIN FINKIELKRAUT — *In the Name of Humanity: Reflections on the Twentieth Century*

JULIA KRISTEVA — *The Sense and Non-Sense of Revolt: The Powers and Limits of Psychoanalysis*

RÉGIS DEBRAY — *Transmitting Culture*

SYLVIANE AGACINSKI — *The Politics of the Sexes*

ALAIN CORBIN — *The Life of an Unknown: The Rediscovered World of a Clog Maker in Nineteenth-Century France*

MICHEL PASTOUREAU — *The Devil's Cloth: A History of Stripes and Striped Fabric*

ELISABETH ROUDINESCO — *Why Psychoanalysis?*

CARLO GINZBURG — *Wooden Eyes: Nine Reflections on Distance*